Food Lovers' London

Jenny Linford

Photography by Chris Windsor

Food Lovers' London

Written by Jenny Linford
Photography by Chris Windsor
Edited by Abigail Willis
Design by Susi Koch & Lesley Gilmour
Maps by Lesley Gilmour

First published in Great Britain 1991 by Macmillan, updated editions published in 1995, 1999 and 2003 by Metro Publications.

Published 2005 by
Metro Publications
PO Box 6336
London
N1 6PY

Reprinted 2007

Printed and bound in India by Replika Press Pvt. Ltd.

© 2005 Jenny Linford

Photography©Chris Windsor
chris@chriswindsor.com
www.chriswindsor.com

British Library Cataloguing in Publication Data.
A catalogue record for this book is available from the British Library.

ISBN 1 902910 22 2

*for Mummy, Daddy, Chris and Ben
and in memory of Harry Greenwald
who believed in me.*

ACKNOWLEDGMENTS

Firirst of all, my thanks to Andrew and Susi at Metro for their enthusiasm, interest and support for the book and Rosie Kindersley for suggesting Metro. Thanks also go to Richard Ehrlich for much good advice and Chris for putting so much time and energy into taking such great photographs. Many people spared time to talk to me and my grateful thanks go to the following: everyone I spoke to at the BBC World Service; and especially Nina Dekhan, Jon Cannon, Antonio Carluccio, Anna del Conte, Alan Dein, Fuchsia Dunlop, Sarah Edington, Clare Ferguson, Anna Giacon, Wendy Godfrey, Roopa Gulati, Pat Howard, Shehzad Husain, the Jewish Chronicle, Sav Kyriacou, Michael Michaud, Sri Owen, Laki Pattelis, Sudi Pigott, Mary Pininska, Claudia Roden, Evelyn Rose, Polly Russell, Margaret Shaida, Siyu magazine, Imogen Smith, the late Yan-Kit So, Marlena Spieler, Jan and Dinah Wieliczko of the Centaur Gallery, Kate Whiteman and, finally, the shopkeepers themselves who patiently answered my many questions and from whom I learned so much.

Price Key
These are approximate, average prices, per head, for a meal without wine

£	£5-£10
££	£10-£20
£££	£20-£30
££££	£30-£50
£££££	£50-£70

CONTENTS

About the Author

Jenny Linford lived in Ghana, Trinidad, Singapore and Italy before settling in London, where she now works as a freelance food writer and restaurant reviewer. Her work has included journalism for magazines and newspapers including The Guardian, The Evening Standard, The Illustrated London News, Time Out and The Times. Her books include 'Writing About Food', 'Tastes of the Orient' and 'A Taste of London'. An inveterate food shopper, Jenny also founded the highly successful 'Gastro-Soho Tours', which have been running since 1994 (see page 305 for further details).

INTRODUCTION

When I was a child my family moved to Florence and English food took on an especial importance. Visitors were entreated to bring packets of 'ordinary' tea, cheese and onion crisps and Walls' sausages. One small shop near the Duomo, Ye Olde English Store, sold a quaint mixture of English food: tinned asparagus, lemon puffs and Gentleman's Relish. Small jars of Marmite cost a few thousand lire more than they should have but were savoured nevertheless. Now that I am back in London, I buy fresh pasta, basil and Parmesan and try to recreate the sunny tastes of Tuscany.

This book started out of personal nostalgia but turned into an enjoyable and fascinating journey of discovery. London, where I have lived for so many years, suddenly revealed glimpses into new and varied worlds: the aesthetic delight of a Japanese fish counter, dainty, pistachio-dusted, baklava from a Turkish patisserie, the hustle and bustle of Brixton Market, freshly baked bagels in a busy Jewish bakery in Golders Green, being offered a free soft drink in Southall to commemorate a Sikh martyr who had preached tolerance to all. Encounters have been, on the whole, enjoyable (although one Iranian shop-owner accused me, only half-jokingly, of being a tax inspector!). Waiting in a Polish bakery while three old ladies brought their rye bread and sausages chatting away in Polish, I gathered, from their sideways glances to me standing notebook in hand, that they were wondering what I was doing there. As one opened her purse to pay the baker, she suddenly broke into English "Daylight robbery!" she exclaimed, and shot a wicked, amused glance in my direction.

We are so much creatures of habit that new things are avoided almost automatically and this is certainly true with food. One of the great pleasures for me in writing this book has been the discovery of new ingredients and dishes. I had, for example, walked down Drummond Street many times to buy some fudge-like barfi from the Ambala Sweet Centre, but had never stopped to look at the unusual Asian vegetables on sale outside the grocers on the same street. Now I know a little more about them and have tried and enjoyed many.

Since I first wrote Food Lovers' London in 1991, food shopping in Britain has changed enormously. In those days, if I wanted mascarpone cheese or lemon grass, I had to visit an Italian delicatessen or a shop in Chinatown. Today, my nearest supermarket stocks these and many other foodstuffs alongside them. Supermarkets, however, cannot offer everything or keep it in the best conditions, especially 'exotic' fruits and vegetables.

Tired-looking rambutans or rock-hard mangoes in a supermarket compare badly with the excellent quality and good value fruit on offer in Gerrard Street, Asian greengrocers or West Indian markets.

One of the pleasures of shopping for food is to visit a shop where the staff know what they're doing and take pride in it. My local weekly fruit and veg market has a fish stall, run with cheery friendliness by Rita and her husband Alan, which sells a small selection of wonderfully fresh fish. Visiting this stall has become a satisfying weekly ritual. There's always a queue, predominantly made up of old age pensioners who obviously care about the freshness of the fish they eat, waiting patiently while Rita and Alan skillfully gut, fillet or skin the fish as requested. I get a similar pleasure from visiting I Camisa, an Italian delicatessen in Soho, where the Parma ham or mortadella is expertly sliced to the right thickness and they'll know how much pasta I need when I ask for "fresh white tagliatelle, to serve two for a main course".

Food is an important part of culture and a primary means of identification, especially for ex-patriot communities for whom it takes on a new significance. Fourteen years ago, I wrote about the tragedy of witnessing small food shops being forced to close down, hit hard by steeply rising rents and competition from supermarkets able to offer cheaper food and round-the-clock opening hours. Today, the outlook remains bleak. Of the six or so Italian delicatessens that used to be in Soho, only two remain. As this book goes to press, Soho's Chinatown community is seeing two food shops and Chinatown's only fishmonger being forced to move out of their current premises by developers. Given that Chinatown is home to only seven food shops, this is a great loss to the community.

Short-sighted 'development' by councils continues to adversely affect communities across London. The poet Benjamin Zephaniah, writing in defence of his beloved, vibrant local market, Queen's Market in Newham, which Newham Council wants to 'regenerate' by putting an Asda supermarket on the site, summed up how important food and food shops are to a community's sense of identity: "For some it is a space where they can earn a living, for some it is a place to get good food at good prices, and for others it is an important place of interaction. Saving the market is not just about money, it's also about culture, and our culture is priceless."

London has so many gastronomic riches to offer, but they are under threat on many fronts. If you've bought this book, I'm guessing that you too love food and I do urge you to support your local food shops and markets and enjoy the pleasure of shopping in this way.

General Food Shops

Bakers & Patisseries

Poilâne

Pioneered by chef Sally Clarke, London's bread scene has undergone something of a renaissance with a number of fine quality bakeries opening in the capital and wholesale bakers such as Flour Power finding a receptive audience at farmers' markets and Borough Market. While there are now bakeries offering decent ciabattas, sourdoughs, baguettes and focaccia, however, the traditional English high-street bakery, selling something as simple as a good quality fresh tin loaf, is frustratingly elusive. For further patisseries, look in the French chapter of this book.

CENTRAL

Baker & Spice

⌂ *54-56 Elizabeth Street, SW1*
☎ *020 7730 3033*
🚇 *Sloane Square LU, Victoria LU/Rail*
🕐 *Mon-Sat 8am-7pm*

This attractive shop offers not only an appetising range of Baker & Spice's own-baked cakes, pastries and breads, but also features a meat counter stocked with free-range, organic or rare-breed meat and poultry. A salad bar and café area complete the picture.

De Gustibus

⌂ *4 Suffolk Street, SE1*
☎ *020 7407 3625*
🚇 *London Bridge LU/Rail*
🕐 *Mon-Sat 7am-5pm*

In a prime position backing onto Borough Market, this corner shop is a London outlet for Oxfordshire-based baker Dan Schickentanz, offering a range of his breads such as Six Day Sour (made with a sourdough starter) and Milwaukee Rye. The lunchtime trade is catered for with superior sandwiches.

Branch: 53 Blandford Street, W1 (020 7486 6608)

Konditor & Cook

⌨ *27 Cornwall Road, SE1*
☎ *020 7261 0456*
🚌 *Waterloo LU/Rail*
🕐 *Mon-Fri 7.30am-6.30pm, Sat 8.30am-2pm*

Gerhard Jenne's bakery is noted for its creative cakes and pastries, from wildly colourful iced gingerbread skeletons at Halloween to imaginatively personalised birthday cakes (much in demand with celebrity clients). One reason for Gerhard's success is that he firmly believes everything should taste as good as it looks.

Branches: 10 Stoney Street, SE1 (020 7407 5100)
46 Gray's Inn Road, WC1 (020 7404 6300)

Paul

⌨ *29 Bedford Street, WC2*
☎ *020 7836 3304*
🚌 *Covent Garden LU*
🕐 *Mon-Fri 7.30am-9pm, Sat and Sun 9am-9pm*

This first London branch of the well-established French chain is an impressive operation. While the pastries and cakes are alluring, the extensive range of French-style breads on offer, all baked on the premises, is a particular draw. When the shop first opened English customers asked for 'normal bread', now this thoroughly Gallic enterprise attracts patient queues both for the bakery and the back-room salon du thé, (see also French London, pages140 &144)

Branches: 115 Marylebone High Street, W1 (020 7836 3304)
147 Fleet Street, EC4 (020 7353 5874)

Le Pain Quotidien

⌨ *72-75 Marylebone High Street, W1*
☎ *020 7486 6154*
🚌 *Baker Street LU*
🕐 *Mon-Fri 7am-7pm, Sat 8am-6pm, Sun 9am-6pm*

London's first branch of this bakery-cum-café (founded in Brussels in 1990), is a spacious, stylishly rustic affair, complete with a signature large communal table. A range of sourdough breads, made from organic stone-ground flour, is on offer here, either to take away or to sample in the café area with organic jams or moreish hazelnut paste and a cup of tea or coffee.

Poilâne

⌂ *46 Elizabeth Street, SW1*

☎ *020 7808 4910*

🚌 *Sloane Square LU, Victoria LU/Rail*

🕑 *Mon-Fri 7am-7.30pm; Sat 7.30am-6pm*

This dainty shop is a lovingly recreated replica of a famous Parisian bakery, complete with a wood-fired oven in the basement. Regulars return for Poilâne's huge, round sourdough loaves, with their distinctive, addictive tang, which are here sold whole, halved, quartered or simply by the slice, (see also French London, p.140).

St John

⌂ *26 St John Street, EC1*

☎ *020 7251 0848*

🚌 *Farringdon LU/Rail*

🕑 *Bread sold from 7am Mon-Sat*

This much-applauded Clerkenwell restaurant, noted for chef Fergus Henderson's appreciative approach towards offal, also does a side-line trade in bread baked on the premises, with the St John sourdough being particularly popular.

NORTH

Baker & Spice

75 Salisbury Road, NW6

020 7604 3636

Queen's Park LU/Rail

Mon-Fri 7am-8pm, Sat 7am-7pm, Sun 8.30am-5pm

A tempting range of breads, including sourdough and focaccia and sweet treats such as muffins, cookies and pastries.

Victoria Bakery

83 High Street, Barnet, EN5

020 8449 0790

High Barnet LU

Mon-Sat 7.30am- 5pm

This small, traditional English bakery offers freshly baked white, brown and soda breads, scones and currant buns, with the iced ring doughnuts going down a storm with local schoolchildren.

WEST

Baker & Spice

47 Denyer Street, SW3

020 7589 4734

Knightsbridge LU, South Kensington LU

Mon-Sat 7am-7pm, Sun 8.30am-5pm

The full range of Baker & Spice's breads are carried at this smart branch of an established bakery.

& Clarke's

122 Kensington Church Street, W8

020 7229 2190

High Street Kensington LU, Notting Hill LU

Mon-Fri 8am-8pm, Sat 9am-4pm

An elegantly rustic shop next door to Sally Clarke's restaurant, that sells her famous breads, such as rosemary, raisin and sea-salt plus own-baked treats ranging from savoury pizzas to sweet tarts, including fresh fruit, chocolate and (at Thanksgiving) pumpkin. The discerningly selected stock features own-made treats such as delectable chocolate truffles, puff pastry made with French unsalted butter, and chutneys.

The Lighthouse Bakery

Exeter Street Bakery

⌑ *18 Argyll Road, W8*

☎ *020 7937 8484*

🚌 *High Street Kensington LU*

🕑 *Mon-Sat 8am-7pm, Sun 9am-7pm*

This smart shop offers Londoners a chance to sample excellent traditionally-made Italian breads, such as ciabatta or pane Pugliese.

South-West

The Lighthouse Bakery

⌑ *64 Northcote Road, SW11*

☎ *020 7228 4537*

🚌 *Clapham Junction Rail*

🕑 *Tue-Sat 8.30am-5pm*

Lovingly-made bread, freshly baked on the premises, is the raison d'être of this friendly, unpretentious artisan bakery, set up by Rachel Duffield, who is often in the shop serving, and Elizabeth Weisberg, who does the baking behind-the-scenes. Elizabeth's and Rachel's commitment to quality is evident in both the flour used (organic stone-ground flour from Shipton Mill and Cann Mill) and the long fermentation and rising to add flavour; as Rachel explains "There's no substitute for time". The 'humble British loaf' is a star attraction here, but the bakery carries a large range of breads (15 basics plus 3-5 daily specials on weekdays, rising to 30 breads on Saturday) plus treats such as doughnuts and seasonal goodies including hot cross buns at Easter and mince pies at Christmas. A stream of regulars, all on first name terms, ensure this is very much as a community shop.

Newens: the Original Maids of Honour

⌑ *288 Kew Road, TW9*

☎ *020 8940 2752*

🚌 *Kew Gardens LU*

🕑 *Mon 9.30am-1pm, Tue-Sat 9.30am-6pm*

The Newens family have been baking Maids of Honour cakes, (traditional almond tarts) in the Richmond area since 1850 and the recipe continues to be a closely guarded family secret. Their pretty, Tudor-style old-fashioned bakery-cum-tea room, just by Kew Gardens, serves up classic British treats including custard tarts, scones, tea cakes and Maids of Honour, plus truly splendid steak and salmon pies.

William Curley

⌨ *10 Paved Court, TW9*

☎ *020 8332 3002*

🚌 *Richmond LU/Rail*

🕐 *Tue-Sat 10am-5.30pm, Sun 11am-4pm*

William Curley's minimalist shop, discreetly located on a historic Richmond side-street, showcases William's own exquisite patisserie, freshly baked on the premises. Signature treats include his chocolate mille-feuille and exotic fruit tarts.

South-East

East Dulwich Deli

⌨ *15-17 Lordship Lane, SE22*

☎ *020 8693 2525*

🚌 *East Dulwich Rail*

🕐 *Mon-Sat 9am-6pm, Sun 10am-4pm*

This large, smart delicatessen showcases freshly baked breads from Born & Bread, their own wholesale bakery which produces organic breads made from stone-ground flour and baked in a splendid wood-fired oven. Born & Bread's crunchy baguette is a popular choice here. For their deli review see p.36.

East

De Gustibus

⌨ *53-55 Carter Lane, EC4*

☎ *020 7236 0056*

🚌 *St Paul's LU*

🕐 *Mon-Fri 7.30am-6pm*

A City-based café outlet for De Gustibus breads, with diners being able to mix and match breads and fillings.

Butchers

The Ginger Pig

E ven the most basic high-street butcher's is a fast-vanishing breed, while a really decent one is extremely hard to find. One encouraging thing to emerge from the aftermath of the BSE crisis is that those butchers who put the emphasis on providing quality, plant-fed, free-range or organic meat have seen sales improve, as customers realise the value of buying meat from a trustworthy, traceable source.

CENTRAL LONDON

Allen & Co.
▢ *117 Mount Street, W1*
☎ *020 7499 5831*
🚌 *Bond Street LU*
🕐 *Mon-Fri 3.30am-4pm, Sat 3.30am-12noon*
With its beautiful tiles and huge wooden chopping blocks, this venerable butcher's is a Mayfair institution with customers ranging from film stars to famous restaurants. Allen & Co. is particularly noted for the quality and range of its game and also for its Scotch beef.

Biggles
▢ *66 Marylebone Lane, W1*
☎ *020 7224 5937*
🚌 *Bond Street LU*
🕐 *Mon-Sat 9.30am-4.30pm, Tue-Fri 9.30am-6pm*
Tucked away down a charming side-street, Biggles is a sausage specialist selling made-on-the-premises, high-meat sausages in a huge range of varieties, from Toulouse to Greek.

The Ginger Pig
▢ *8-10 Moxon Street, W1*
☎ *020 7935 7788*
🚌 *Bond Street LU*
🕐 *Mon-Sat 8.30am-6.30pm, Sun 9am-3pm*
This spacious shop showcases Tim and Anne Wilson's own-reared meat from their farm in the Yorkshire Dales, including flavourful, well-hung beef from long horn cattle, prime pork from rare breed pigs, and lamb and mutton from the Swaledale sheep that graze on the hills behind their farm. The Ginger Pig also has a splendid charcuterie counter laden with their own-made pork pies, sausage rolls, terrines and pâtés.

Simply Sausages

⌨ *Harts Corner, 341 Central Markets,*
  Farringdon Street, EC1

☎ *020 7329 3227*

🚍 *Farringdon LU/Rail*

🕐 *Mon-Fri 8am-6pm*

Appropriately situated next to Smithfield meat market, this corner shop sells over 40 different seasonal own-made bangers at any time of the year. In addition to truly meaty sausages – such as venison or pork – seafood and vegetarian sausages are also stocked.

Wyndham House Poultry

⌨ *2-3 Stoney Street, SE1*

☎ *020 7403 4788*

🚍 *London Bridge LU/Rail*

🕐 *Mon-Fri 8.30am-6pm, Sat 8.30am-4.30pm*

Right by Borough Market, Wyndham House specialises in poultry and game, offering Lee Mullet's excellent own-reared, free-range Label Anglaise chickens, plus organic Welsh chickens, French ducks and game birds. As one might expect, the shop stocks a range of turkeys at Christmas time, including rare Bourbon Red, plus geese and three-bird roasts. Usefully, Wyndham House also sells chicken carcasses for stock as well as tubs of own-made stock.

NORTH

B & M Seafoods

⌨ *258 Kentish Town Road, NW5*

☎ *020 7485 0346*

🚍 *Kentish Town LU/Rail*

🕐 *Mon-Sat 7.30am-5.30pm*

'Say no to factory farming' declares a sign outside Harry Dasht's, friendly, down-to-earth shop which, despite its name, offers not only fish but an excellent range of organic meat and poultry, carefully sourced from small-scale, organic suppliers. B & M has a committed local following, with regulars returning for the prime meat, including well-hung beef, helpful, knowledgeable service and Harry's cooking tips and recipe suggestions.

Baldwins

⌨ *469 Green Lanes, N4*
☎ *020 8340 5934*
🚌 *Manor House LU, then bus 29, 141, 341*
🕐 *Mon-Sat 8.30am-6.30pm*

Attractively spick and span, this smart corner shop with friendly staff, offers an excellent selection of meat and poultry, including more unusual meats such as rabbit and venison. At Christmas they do a roaring trade with their free-range bronze turkeys.

James Elliott

⌨ *96 Essex Road, N1*
☎ *020 7226 3658*
🚌 *Angel LU*
🕐 *Mon-Thurs 8am-5pm, Fri 8am-7pm, Sat 7am-4pm*

A splendidly old-fashioned shop, with marble counters and wood fittings, which sells excellent, well-hung, free-range meat and poultry, plus a discerningly chosen selection of cheeses. Elliot's is particularly known for its prime Scotch beef and its own-cooked hams and attracts a steady steam of regulars, who enjoy the butcher's banter as he expertly cuts their meat to order.

Frank Godfrey Ltd

⌨ *7 Highbury Park, N5*
☎ *020 7226 2425*
🚌 *Arsenal LU*
🕐 *Mon-Fri 8am-6pm, Sat 9am-5pm*

This down-to-earth family butcher's – now run by fourth generation brothers Chris and Jeremy Godfrey – has a loyal and devoted following who know good meat when they see it. All the meat sold here is free-range and very good quality, from the English corn-fed chickens to the plant-fed pork and Orkney Island beef. The brothers work closely with their suppliers to ensure high feed and welfare standards, and the results are reflected in the meat that they sell.

Highland Organics

⌕ *14 Bittacy Hill, NW7*
☎ *020 8346 1055*
🚌 *Mill Hill LU*
🕐 *Mon-Sat 8am-6pm*

As the name suggests, organic meats are the thing here, from Welsh Black beef steaks to huge plump home-made sausages. Customers can also stock up on basic organic groceries, from fresh bread to baked beans.

Midhurst

⌕ *2 Midhurst Parade, N10*
☎ *020 8883 5303*
🚌 *East Finchley LU, then the 102 bus*
🕐 *Mon-Thur 8am-5.15pm, Fri 7am-5.15pm, Sat 7am-4.30pm*

Tucked away in a little parade of shops between Muswell Hill and East Finchley, this small shop offers decent meat (some organic) with fresh fruit and veg outside.

Moore & Sons

⌕ *25 Greenhill Parade,*
  Great North Road, EN5
☎ *020 8449 9649*
🚌 *High Barnet LU*
🕐 *Mon-Thur 8am-530pm, Fri 7am-5.30pm, Sat 7am-4pm*

A small, traditional, well-established butcher with friendly staff. Specialities include Scotch beef, own-made sausages and game.

WEST

Kingsland Edwardian Butchers

⌕ *140 Portobello Road, W11*
☎ *020 7727 6067*
🚌 *Notting Hill Gate LU*
🕐 *Mon-Sat 7.30am-6pm*

A bright red frontage marks out this attractive, old-fashioned butcher's shop. There is a good range of meat, from their own dry-cured bacon to Orkney Aberdeen Angus beef. Their speciality, however, is rare breeds meat, from Gloucester Old Spot pork to extremely rare, seaweed-fed North Ronaldsay lamb from Orkney. Staff are jocular and helpful.

C. Lidgate

⌷   *110 Holland Park Avenue, W11*
☎   *020 7727 8243*
🚋   *Holland Park LU*
🕐   *Mon-Thur 7.30am-6pm, Fri 7am-6pm, Sat 7am-5pm*

A grand old butcher's established in 1850, which specialises in high-quality, naturally-grown and fed meat and poultry. Run with great expertise and commitment by David Lidgate, the shop's stock includes organic meat from Highgrove (The Prince of Wales' estate), free-range bronze turkeys and geese. In addition, this family-run business sells award-winning home-made pies such as steak and kidney, and own-cooked hams.

Macken Bros

⌷   *44 Turnham Green Terrace, W4*
☎   *020 8994 2646*
🚋   *Turnham Green LU*
🕐   *Mon-Fri 7am-6pm, Sat 7am-5.30pm*

A seemingly perpetual queue testifies to this well-established shop's popularity. Staff are helpful and friendly and the range of meat and poultry is extensive while the quality is excellent.

Meat Like It Used To Be

⌷   *50 Cannon Lane, HA5*
☎   *020 8866 4611*
🚋   *Pinner LU*
🕐   *Mon-Fri 7am-6pm, Sat 7am-5pm, Sun 8am-1pm*

The name says it all, with this friendly, well-run butcher's stocking an impressive range of fully-traceable free-range meat and poultry, including certified Aberdeen Angus beef, Kelly Bronze turkeys and a good selection of game.

Randalls

⌷   *113 Wandsworth Bridge Road, SW6*
☎   *020 7736 3426*
🚋   *Fulham Broadway LU*
🕐   *Mon-Fri 8.30am-5.30pm, Sat 7am-4pm*

This upmarket butcher offers top-notch, free-range or organic meat. Attractively presented, the meat looks as good as it tastes, with the marinaded meats and own-made sausages being particularly popular.

Richardsons

⌧ *88 Northfield Avenue, W13*

☎ *020 8567 1064*

🚌 *Northfield LU*

🕐 *Mon-Thur 8am-5.30pm, Fri 8am-6pm, Sat 8am-4.30pm*

A member of the Q Guild of Butchers, this down-to-earth, busy butcher's attracts a loyal clientele, drawn back by the quality of the meat on offer, which includes well-hung beef and award-winning sausages.

Wyndham House

⌧ *339 Fulham Road, SW10*

☎ *020 7352 7888*

🚌 *Fulham Broadway LU*

🕐 *Mon-Fri 7am-6.30pm, Sat 7am-5pm*

This small, smart shop offers a cracking range of attractively presented, free-range meat and poultry, including Label Anglaise chickens, Welsh organic chickens, lamb, pork and Welsh Black beef. Rabbits and game are also stocked.

SOUTH-WEST

A. Dove & Son

⌧ *71 Northcote Road, SW11*

☎ *020 7223 5191*

🚌 *Clapham Junction Rail*

🕐 *Mon 8am-1pm, Tue-Sat 8am-6pm*

This characterful butcher's shop, run with passion by Bob Dove, has a loyal clientele. Highlights include the well-hung beef, Linda Dove's frozen meat pies and excellent bronze turkeys.

M. Moen & Sons

⌧ *24 The Pavement, SW4*

☎ *020 7622 1624*

🚌 *Clapham Common LU*

🕐 *Mon-Fri 8am-6.30pm, Sat 7.30am-5pm*

This well-established butcher's offers a distinctly upmarket stock. The meat is good quality, from home-made sausages to a range of in-season game. Additional delights include wild mushrooms and seasonal produce like sea-kale.

M. Moen & Sons

Pether

⬚ *16 Station Parade, Kew Gardens, TW9*

☎ *020 8940 0163*

🚌 *Kew Gardens LU*

🕐 *Mon-Fri 7.30am-6.30pm, Sat 7.30am-5pm*

An appetising smell of spit-roasted chicken wafts out from this old-fashioned butcher's. All the meat here is free-range and the shop does a roaring trade in home-made pies.

South-East London

P. & J. Baker

⬚ *147 Evelina Road, SE15*

☎ *020 7732 2820*

🚌 *Nunhead Rail*

🕐 *Tue-Sat 6am-4pm*

A cheerful family-run butcher where popular items include excellent home-made pork bangers (made to a 100 year old recipe), well-hung beef and free-range chickens.

Cheese Shops

Hamish Johnston

Cheese Shops

CENTRAL

La Fromagerie

- 2-4 Moxon Street, W1
- 020 7935 0341
- Baker Street LU
- Mon 10.30am-7.30pm, Tue-Fri 8am-7.30pm, Sat 9am-7pm, Sun 10am-6pm

Just off Marylebone High Street, Patricia Michelson's spacious, attractive shop is a mecca for cheese-lovers, with its temperature-controlled cheese room very much at the heart of the shop. Owner Patricia Michelson, whose passionate enthusiasm for cheese is genuine and infectious, makes a point of sourcing cheeses direct from small farms and suppliers. The shop stocks between 150-200 seasonal farmhouse cheeses, with the focus on French and Italian artisanal cheeses.

Neal's Yard Dairy

- 17 Shorts Gardens, WC2
- 020 7379 7646
- Covent Garden LU
- Mon-Sat 9am-7pm, Sun 11am-5pm

A pioneering champion of British farmhouse cheeses, this small dairy shop has an impressive range of traditionally-made farmhouse cheeses including classics such as Appleby's Cheshire, Keen's Cheddar and Kirkham's Lancaster. Other produce includes a carefully sourced range of good quality breads, cream, yogurt and farmhouse butter. Staff are friendly and knowledgeable and customers are encouraged to taste before buying – one of the joys of artisanal-made cheese being that they vary in flavour from batch to batch.
Branch: 6 Park Street, SE1 (020 7407 1800)

Paxton & Whitfield

- 93 Jermyn Street, SW1
- 020 7930 0259
- Piccadilly Circus LU
- Mon-Sat 9am-5.30pm

This picturesque, vintage shop, established in 1797, is a well-known name in cheese-selling. Staff are helpful and there is a range of over 200 classic cheeses from Stilton to chestnut leaf-wrapped Banon goat's cheese, plus an assortment of wafers, biscuits and relishes.

La Fromagerie

www.lafromagerie.co.uk

Selected farmhouse cheeses matured on site available for both Retail & Wholesale, along with carefully sourced produce from France, Italy, Spain and the UK.

Open everyday.

2 – 4 Moxon St W1
Tel: 0207 935 0341
Shop & Tasting Café with a daily changing seasonal kitchen menu / Freshly prepared dishes to take away / Farmhouse cheeses / Homemade cakes & pastries / Wines / Fresh bread & store cupboard essentials / Tutored cheese & wine tastings / Monthly dinner events.

30 Highbury Park, N5
Tel: 0207 359 7440
Farmhouse cheeses / Homemade cakes & pastries / Wines / Fresh bread & store cupboard essentials.

Rippon Cheese Stores

⌨ *26 Upper Tachbrook Street, SW1*

☎ *020 7931 0628*

🚌 *Pimlico LU, Victoria LU/Rail*

🕐 *Mon-Sat 8am-6.30pm*

In this cool, neat shop Karen and Philip Rippon stock an astonishing assortment of around 550 European cheeses. Here, one can find seven different Cheddars, six different Bries and a range of differently aged Crottin. Stock is clearly priced and labelled and Karen and Philip are very happy to offer advice.

NORTH

Cheeses

⌨ *11 Fortis Green Road, N10*

☎ *020 8444 9141*

🚌 *East Finchley LU, Bus 134*

🕐 *Tue-Fri 10am-6pm, Sat 9.30am-6pm*

Tucked away in an old-fashioned parade of shops just off Muswell Hill Broadway, this tiny shop offers an excellent array of European cheeses, served by friendly and helpful staff.

La Fromagerie

- 🖃 *30 Highbury Park, N5*
- ☏ *020 7937 8004*
- 🚌 *Highbury & Islington LU/Rail*
- 🕐 *Mon 10.30am-7.30pm, Tue-Fri 9.30am-7.30pm, Sat 9.30am-7pm Sun 10am-5pm*

Patricia Michelson's first shop features a cool backroom, filled with a carefully sourced range of between 200-250 seasonal farmhouse cheeses from France, Italy and Great Britain.

SOUTH-WEST LONDON

Hamish Johnston

- 🖃 *48 Northcote Road, SW11*
- ☏ *020 7738 0741*
- 🚌 *Clapham Junction Rail*
- 🕐 *Mon-Sat 9am-6pm*

This dapper shop now approaching its eleventh year has a loyal following, drawn by the carefully chosen selection of cheeses, numbering from 100-150 depending on the time of year. Preference is given to small-scale cheese producers, with delights on offer including Vintage Lincolnshire Poacher, Cotherstone and Llanboidy. The shop also sells a good range of biscuits to accompany cheese, plus chutneys, jams and olives. Knowledgeable and helpful staff are undoubtedly part of the shop's appeal.

SOUTH-EAST LONDON

The Cheese Block

- 🖃 *69 Lordship Lane, SE22*
- ☏ *020 8299 3636*
- 🚌 *East Dulwich Rail*
- 🕐 *Mon-Fri 9.30am-6.30pm, Sat 9am-6pm*

This small, down-to-earth shop stocks around 260 cheeses from Britain and Europe, ranging from classics to less well-known ones.

Chocolates

Rococo

CENTRAL

L'Artisan du Chocolat

⌁ *89 Lower Sloane Street, SW1*
☎ *020 7824 8365*
🚌 *Sloane Square LU*
🕐 *Mon-Sat 10am-7pm*

This austerely smart shop showcases the considerable talents of chocolatier Gerard Coleman and his partner Anne Weyns. Here one can buy Gerard's elegant ganache-filled chocolates, with their distinctive sophisticated flavourings such as sea-salted caramel, lemon and thyme, chestnut honey or green cardamom. Easter and Christmas see the shop filled with stylish Easter eggs and moulded figures, all lovingly made from the finest chocolate.

Charbonnel et Walker

⌁ *1 The Royal Arcade, 28 Old Bond Street, W1*
☎ *020 7491 0939*
🚌 *Piccadilly Circus LU*
🕐 *Mon-Fri 9am-6pm, Sat 10am-5pm*

An elegant chocolatiers, established in 1875, which sells high quality chocolates, including classic rose and violet creams, charming novelties and smartly-packaged chocolate gifts.

Chocolates

The Chocolate Society

- 36 Elizabeth Street, SW1
- ☎ 020 7259 9222
- Sloane Square LU or Victoria LU/Rail
- ◷ Mon-Fri 9.30am-5.30pm, Sat 9.30am-4pm

This small, cosy shop-cum-café offers a wide range of fine French Valrhona chocolates. Bestsellers include handmade fresh truffles and chocolate-coated honey-pokey (honeycomb) while their hot chocolate, made from flaked chocolate, goes down well with chocoholics.

Branch at:
- 32-24 Shepherd Market, W1
- ☎ 020 7495 0302
- Green Park LU, Hyde Park Corner LU
- ◷ Mon-Fri 9am-5.30pm, Sat 9.30am-4pm

Valrhona chocolates are the attraction at this smart shop, which also has a few tables at which to enjoy chocolate-flavoured treats, such as seriously rich hot chocolate and brownies.

La Maison du Chocolat

- 45-46 Piccadilly, W1
- ☎ 020 7287 8500
- Piccadilly LU
- ◷ Mon-Sat 10am-7pm

Seriously elegant, La Maison du Chocolat, with its marble and wood fittings and phalanx of suited staff, brings chocolate-shopping à la Parisienne to London. On offer are hand-made French chocolates, created by Robert Linxe, a famous chocolatier who opened his first chocolate 'boutique' in Paris in 1977. With an emphasis on the finest ingredients, the flavours, which include fresh raspberry and lemon, are subtle but profound.

Rococo

- 45 Marylebone High Street, W1
- ☎ 020 7935 7780
- Baker Street LU
- ◷ Mon-Sat 10am-6.30pm, Sun 12noon-5pm

Chantal Coady's second distinctly chic shop offers the same delicious blend of frivolous chocolate treats and sweets as her first, including praline quail's eggs, Venus lips and nipples, and lime-flavoured wafers.

WEST

Pierre Marcolini

- 6 Lancers Square, W8
- 020 7795 6611
- High Street Kensington LU
- Mon-Sat 10am-7pm, Sun 12noon-5pm

This discreetly smart shop, complete with a café area in which to sip hot chocolate, offers a chance to sample acclaimed Belgian chocolatier Pierre Marcolini's distinctive, refined handmade chocolates. Marcolini sources his own cocoa beans directly from suppliers, ensuring the quality of his chocolate creations. This is very much haute couture chocolate, with the emphasis on seasonal creations and understated yet stylish packaging.

Rococo

- 321 King's Road, SW3
- 020 7352 5857
- Sloane Square LU, then the 11, 19 or 22 bus
- Mon-Sat 10am-6.30pm, Sun 12noon-5pm

Chocolate lover Chantal Coady (a founder of the Chocolate Society) set up this pretty shop which offers an imaginative range of goodies (including in-house handmade chocolate bars flavoured with spices and flowers) and an enticing range of chocolate novelties.

Theobroma Cacao

- 43 Turnham Green Terrace, W4
- 020 8996 0431
- Turnham Green LU
- Mon-Sat 9.30am-6pm

This pretty little shop, complete with a cocoa bar, is filled to brimming with own-made chocolate treats, ranging from chilli chocolate shards to chocolate incense sticks.

SOUTH-WEST

William Curley

🖃　*10 Paved Court, Richmond, TW9*
☎　*020 8332 3002*
🚌　*Richmond LU/Rail*
🕐　*Tue-Sat 10am-6pm, Sun 11am-4pm*

William Curley's elegant shop showcases not only William's eye-catching patisserie but his own carefully-made, distinctly contemporary chocolates, made on the premises, with flavourings such as salt and pepper ganache, chilli and ginger and Sichuan pepper.

SOUTH EAST

Hope and Greenwood

🖃　*20 North Cross Road, SE22*
☎　*020 8613 1777*
🚌　*East Dulwich Rail*
🕐　*Mon-Sat 10am-6pm, Sun 10am-5pm*

Hidden down a side-street, this dainty little shop offers 160 jars of old-fashioned sweets, including classics like strawberry bonbons and aniseed twists, plus posh choc by makers such as Valrhona and Prestat. Needless to say, customers range from sweet-toothed children to adults enjoying a nostalgic trip down memory lane.

Delicatessens

East Dulwich Deli

Delicatessens

CENTRAL

Flaneur Food Hall

⌧ *41 Farringdon Road, EC1*
☎ *020 7404 4422*
🚌 *Farringdon LU/Rail*
🕐 *Mon-Fri 8am-10pm, Sat 9am-10pm, Sun 9am-6pm*

Housed in attractive high-ceilinged premises this spacious deli-cum-diner has a convivial, buzzy feel to it. Eye-catching elements include tall shelves filled with oils, vinegars, condiments and confectionery and a central counter complete with a pastry chef busy at work producing savoury and sweet baked goods. Stock, ranging from wine and cheese to confectionery and dairy produce, is extensive and upmarket, with French goods particularly well represented.

The Grocer on Warwick

⌧ *21 Warwick Street, W1*
☎ *020 7437 7776*
🚌 *Piccadilly Circus LU*
🕐 *Mon-Sat 8am-11pm*

This smart central London establishment, sister to The Grocer on Elgin, offers elegantly packaged, own-made 'ready meals' to take home and microwave, plus breads, pastries and treats. The back houses a spacious dining area offering a globe-trotting, grazing menu taking in dishes such as harissa-spiced chicken, oxtail soup and soba noodle salad en-route.

Villandry

⌧ *170 Great Portland Street, W1*
☎ *020 7631 3131*
🚌 *Great Portland Street LU*
🕐 *Mon-Sat 8.30am-10pm, Sun 11am-4pm*

This upmarket deli-cum-diner is housed in large, airy premises on Great Portland Street. The attractively presented stock ranges from breads and own-baked patisserie and baskets of fresh produce to an enticing selection of sophisticated chocolates. Ample space allows shoppers to wander round and browse in a leisurely fashion, with particular highlights being the superior cheeses and charcuterie. Diners can sample produce in the refectory-style dining room.

NORTH

Melrose & Morgan

⌂ *42 Gloucester Avenue, NW1*
☎ *020 7722 0011*
🚌 *Chalk Farm LU*
🕐 *Tue-Sat 9am-8pm, Sun 10am-6pm*

Strikingly housed in a large, high-ceilinged, modern space, Ian James's and Nick Selby's contemporary take on a grocer's includes an open-plan kitchen, with chefs busy cooking up predominantly British fare, including Beef Wellington, game soup and homity pie, served up on a magnificent long table which stretches down the center of the shop. The stock is chosen on the basis that less is more, with James and Nick selecting the limited range of fine quality foodstuffs, including Chegworth apple juice, Emmett's baked ham, unsalted Sussex farm butter, cut from a block, Madame Oiseau's hand-made chocolates and Martin Pitt eggs.

Myddletons

⌂ *25A Lloyd Baker Street, WC1*
☎ *020 7278 9192*
🚌 *Angel LU*
🕐 *Mon-Fri 7am-6.30pm, Sat 7am-5pm*

Tucked away on a peaceful Islington back-street Myddletons evokes the feel of a corner shop while stocking a good range of delicatessen basics.

Rosslyn Delicatessen

⌂ *56 Rosslyn Hill, NW3*
☎ *020 7794 9210*
🚌 *Hampstead LU*
🕐 *Mon-Sat 8.30an-9.30pm, Sun 8.30am-8pm*

Very much a Hampstead institution, this spacious, well-established delicatessen offers upmarket foodstuffs, including traiteur dishes, cheeses, charcuterie and store cupboard staples. Hampstead Heath picnickers are catered for by a hamper service.

WEST

Del' Aziz

☏ *020 7386 0086*

🚇 *Fulham Broadway LU*

See full review on page 222.

Felicitous

🖂 *19 Kensington Park Road, W11*

☏ *020 7243 4050*

🚇 *Notting Hill Gate LU/Rail*

🕘 *Mon-Fri 8am-9pm, Sat 8am-7pm, Sun 9am-6pm*

This pretty, friendly shop, decorated in blue and yellow, is crammed with tasty things to eat, ranging from the sweet (confectionery, jams, pastries and cakes) to the savoury (olive oils, vinegars, cheeses and charcuterie). Own-cooked traiteur dishes, such as fishcakes and quiches, are a popular draw.

The Grocer on Elgin

🖂 *6 Elgin Crescent, W11*

☏ *020 7221 3844*

🚇 *Ladbroke Grove LU, Notting Hill Gate LU*

🕘 *Mon-Fri 9am-8pm, Sat-Sun 9am-6pm*

This large, sophisticated shop, with a café area at the back, specialises in traiteur meals, vacuum-packed in stylish microwavable bags. On offer are dishes such as cassoulet, braised beef and upmarket mashed potato, flavoured with ingredients such as mustard, black truffle or chestnuts. Deli goods include New Zealand jams, Belgian chocolates and caviar.

Indigo

🖂 *98 Turnham Green Terrace, W4*

☏ *020 8995 9000*

🚇 *Turnham Green LU*

🕘 *Tue-Fri 10am-7pm, Sat 9am-6pm*

Joseph Viner's friendly deli-cum-café offers both own-made traiteur dishes (ranging from lasagne to pan-fried salmon), plus a range of deli basics, including around 40 cheeses, dried pasta, olive oils and Italian wines. Popular items include tiramisu, pesto and, in the run up to Christmas, home-made award-winning mince pies.

Delicatessens

Elizabeth King

⌨ *34 New King's Road, SW6*
☎ *020 7736 2826*
🚇 *Parsons Green LU*
🕐 *Mon-Fri 9am-8.30pm, Sat 9am-6pm, Sun 10am-3.30pm*

In a residential part of Fulham, this well-stocked, upmarket food shop offers a one-stop shop, carrying an extensive range of groceries, from basics to indulgences. Stock includes meat and fish, fresh fruit and vegetables, cheeses and charcuterie.

Mortimer & Bennett

⌨ *33 Turnham Green Terrace, W4*
☎ *020 8995 4145*
🚇 *Turnham Green LU*
🕐 *Mon-Fri 8.30am-6.30pm, Sat 8.30am-5.30pm*

This small, well-established shop is crammed with goodies, from cheeses, salamis and pâtés to a range of up to 30 different olive oils. Sweet treats are a particular forte, including upmarket French chocolates, tempting biscuits and beautifully packaged confectionery.

Mr Christians

⌨ *11 Elgin Crescent*
☎ *020 7229 0501*
🚇 *Notting Hill Gate LU*
🕐 *Mon-Fri 6am-7pm, Sat 5.30am-6.30pm., Sun 7am-5pm*

Now owned by Jeroboam's, who have a smart wine shop next door, this well-established delicatessen does a roaring business in traiteur dishes, such as soups and quiches, plus breads, cheeses, cold meats and a host of treats.

Tavola

⌨ *155 Westbourne Grove, W11*
☎ *020 7229 0571*
🚇 *Notting Hill Gate LU*
🕐 *Mon-Fri 10.30am-7.30pm, Sat 9.30am-5pm*

Chef Alistair Little and his wife Sharon have created a delicious food shop, showcasing Alistair's own cooking. Home-made dishes, such as coq au vin, roast vegetables or poached pears in wine are brought out from the kitchen to cool off on a large wooden table in the center of the store, offering an appetising glimpse of what's on offer that day. Deli goods are carefully chosen; "We only stock foods that we think taste good and we cook with the ingredients we stock," explains Sharon. Stock ranges from fresh vegetables, such as cavalo nero or chanterelles, through bread and cheese to a charcuterie counter which offers delicious own-cooked ham, Brindisa chorizo and truffle salami. Handmade Spanish chocolates, tarts and pastries and Hill Station ice cream cater for those with a sweet tooth.

Troubadour Delicatessen
- 267 Old Brompton Road, SW5
- 020 7341 6341
- Earl's Court LU, West Brompton LU/Rail
- Mon-Sat 7am-9pm, Sun 10am-3pm

Attractively decked out in dark green and burgundy, this smart new deli, linked to the Troubadours café next door, has been greeted with enthusiasm by locals pleased to find a proper food shop opening up in their midst. Stock includes cheese, chacuterie, wine and assorted breads – while the traiteur counter hits the spot with weary, homeward bound commuters.

SOUTH-WEST

MacFarlane's
- 48 Abbeville Road, SW4
- 020 8673 5373
- Clapham Common LU, Clapham South LU
- Mon-Fri 10am-7pm, Sat 9am-6pm, Sun 10am-5pm

Tucked away as it is on a residential Clapham side-street MacFarlane's has been described as "South London's best-kept secret." Despite its discreet location, the shop has built up a loyal local following. Run with friendliness and enthusiasm by Angus MacFarlane Wood and Angie Laycock, MacFarlane's is a textbook example of what a neighbourhood deli should be. Pride of place goes to the cheese counter, which carries up to 110 farmhouse cheeses from Britain, Ireland, France and Italy. Unique to the shop is the olive oil, sourced from a Pescara co-operative through a family connection. The deli counter stocks freshly made salads, dips and olives, while frozen treats include butter puff pastry and upmarket ice cream. Angus's Scottish roots proudly manifest themselves in the presence of Macsween's haggis, Scottish smoked fish and black and white pudding.

Delicatessens

Mise-en-Place

⌖ *21 Battersea Rise, SW11*

☎ *020 7228 4392*

🚌 *Clapham Junction Rail*

🕐 *Mon-Fri 8.30am-8pm, Sat & Sun 9am-8pm*

A stylish delicatessen with upmarket stock, including an extensive choice of olives, French farmhouse cheeses, pastas and traiteur dishes.

The North Street Deli

⌖ *26 North Street, SW4*

☎ *020 7978 1555*

🚌 *Clapham Common LU*

🕐 *Mon-Sat 10am-5pm*

Relaxed and welcoming, the North Street deli, run by Maddalena Bonino and her partner Nathan Middlemiss, does a roaring trade in home-made sandwiches, salads and coffees. Maddalena cooks a daily-changing range of dishes in the small kitchen downstairs, including soups and salads, which are consumed as soon as she brings them up to the shop. Foodstuffs include top-notch breads, a carefully chosen range of charcuterie and cheeses, groceries including dried pasta, olives and vinegars and fresh fruit and vegetables, bought daily for Maddalena's use but on sale until they are used up.

Rosie's Deli Café

⌖ *14e Market Row, SW9*

☎ *020 7733 0054*

🚌 *Brixton Rail*

🕐 *Mon-Tue & Thur-Sat 9.30am-5.30pm, Wed 9am-3pm*

In the middle of Brixton Market, this friendly shop-cum-café offers a carefully chosen range of deli fare, including fresh breads, farmhouse cheeses and store cupboard staples, plus treats like pastries and Tunnocks tea cakes. Customers can also sit and enjoy a coffee and a snack such as cinnamon toast or scrambled egg on toast.

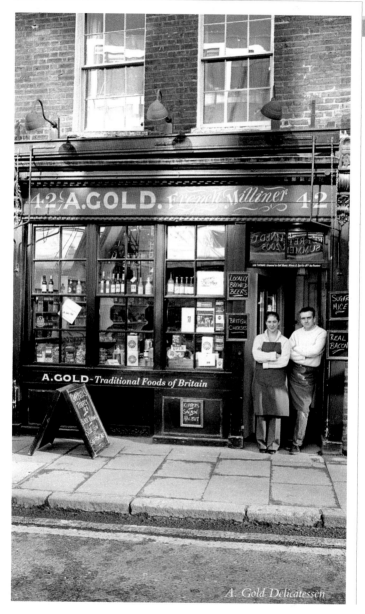

A. Gold Delicatessen

Delicatessens

Vivian's

⊡ *2 Worple Way, TW10*
☎ *020 8940 3600*
🚌 *Richmond LU/Rail*
🕐 *Mon-Fri 9am-7pm, Sat 9am-6pm, Sun 9am-2pm*

Behind an elegant art nouveau shop façade, Vivian's offers Richmond residents a carefully chosen range of edibles. Pride of place goes to the English, French and Italian cheeses, but other good things include coffee (ground to order), fresh baguettes, upmarket ice cream, olives and excellent British fruit vinegars.

South-East

East Dulwich Deli

⊡ *15-17 Lordship Lane, SE22*
☎ *020 8693 2525*
🚌 *East Dulwich Rail*
🕐 *Mon-Sat 9am-6pm, Sun 10am-4pm*

Tracey Woodward's and Tony Zuccola's splendidly light and airy delicatessen stylishly showcases an impressive selection of food, from basics to luxurious treats. Pride of place goes to an excellent range of breads, including handmade organic breads, baked in wood-fired ovens, from Born and Bread, the wholesale bakery set up by Tracey and Tony. The deli counter offers charcuterie (including own-baked hams, Brindisa chorizo and Italian salami), around 50 English, French and Italian farmhouse cheeses and own-made dishes, such as quiches, lasagne and roasted vegetables, while a separate wine room specialises in Italian wines. Sweet treats are abundant, including Rococo chocolates, popular own-baked brownies and Wendy Brandon jams. This is very much a family-friendly shop (complete with a children's cookery school upstairs) and tasting tables at weekends are a popular draw with local customers, many of whom are on first name terms with the staff.

Mimosa

⊡ *16 Half Moon Lane, SE24*
☎ *020 7733 8838*
🚌 *Herne Hill Rail*
🕐 *Mon-Fri 9am-7pm, Sat 9am-5.30pm, Sun 10am-3pm*

This pretty delicatessen-cum-traiteur, complete with a small café area in which to enjoy a coffee and snack, has built up a loyal local following.

The emphasis is on French food, with a Moroccan twist, so French charcuterie and cheeses sit in the counter alongside own-made Moroccan dishes such as humous, tchachouka and baba ghanoush.

EAST

L'Eau à la Bouche
- 🏠 *49 Broadway Market, E8*
- ☎ *020 7923 0600*
- 🚇 *London Fields Rail*
- 🕐 *Mon-Fri 9am-7pm, Sat 9am-5pm, Sun 10am-4pm*

In a prime position on a picturesque, old-fashioned street, this cosy delicatessen offers a good range of carefully chosen deli goods, including chacuterie and cheeses, plus a café corner where locals can enjoy a coffee and a snack.

Extravaganza
- 🏠 *4 Warner Place, E2*
- ☎ *020 7613 0303*
- 🚇 *Bethnal Green LU*
- 🕐 *Mon-Tue and Thur-Sun 8am-8pm*

Patrick's small, friendly café-cum-deli offers a small range of foodstuffs from France, Italy, Spain and reflecting Patrick's roots, Martinique. Locals pop in for a freshly made coffee, sandwiches or a tipple of Patrick's fine rum.

Food Hall
- 🏠 *374-378 Old Street, EC1*
- ☎ *020 7729 6005*
- 🚇 *Old Street LU*
- 🕐 *Tue-Sat 9am-6pm, Sun 11am-5pm*

An impressive enterprise, housed in a handsome, tiled former dairy, Food Hall stocks a huge range of top-notch foods, including organic meats from Daylesford Farm, Ginger Pig bacon, excellent breads, L'Artisan du Chocolate chocolates and wines from the Languedoc. One part of the shop has been turned into a separate, glassed-off cheeseroom, offering around 100 British, French and Italian artisan cheeses and charcuterie. A café area serves up a short, daily-changing menu of dishes, showcasing the shop's stock.

Delicatessens

A.Gold

⌂ *42 Brushfield Street, E1*

☏ *020 7247 2487*

🚌 *Liverpool Street LU/Rail*

🕐 *Mon-Fri 11am-8pm, Sat-Sun 11am-6pm*

Housed in atmospheric 18th-century premises, with the shop retaining the name of its 18th-century French milliner owner, this delightful shop evokes an old-fashioned grocer's or village shop. Unusually, British produce, rather than the more usual French or Italian, takes pride of place here – hence, an eye-catching array of jars of old-fashioned sweets, tins of Campbell's 'perfect Tea', Rosebud preserves and traditional tipples including fine cider and perry. Basics include bread, English farmhouse cheeses, Richard Woodall's bacon and quality sausages. With space definitely at a premium, owners Safia and Ian choose their stock with discrimination and also with an eye for vintage packaging.

Leila's

⌂ *17 Calvert Avenue, E2*

☏ *020 7729 9789*

🚌 *Old Street LU/Rail*

🕐 *Tue-Sat 9am-6pm, Sun 11am-5pm*

Pavement boxes of fresh produce, such as flavourful Italian tomatoes, unwaxed lemons and apples, mark this quirky shop. Basics include bread from St John's, apple juice, excellent eggs, pulses, Comte cheese and good olive oil, but Leila aims also to showcase different cuisines throughout the year, moving, for example, from Persian to Polish.

Verde & Co.

⌂ *40 Brushfield Street, E1*

☏ *020 7247 1924*

🚌 *Liverpool Street LU/Rail*

🕐 *Mon-Fri 8am-8pm, Sat 11am-6pm, Sun 11am-4pm*

Just by Spitalfields Market, housed in a beautifully restored late 18th century building owned by novelist Jeanette Winterson, Verde's evokes a different era, with boxes of lovingly arranged fruit and vegetables on display outside and a solid fuel-burning stove inside its atmospheric interior. Good things on offer here include Pierre Marcolini's subtly rich, handmade chocolates, superior Italian sweets, pasta and sausages and dried fruits and spices.

Fishmongers

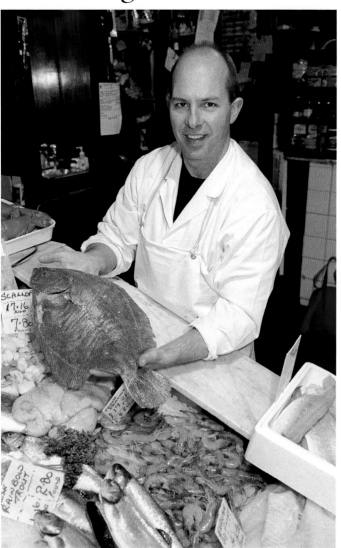

H.S. Linwood & Son

Fishmongers

CENTRAL

Fishworks

- 89 Marylebone High Street, W1
- 020-7935 9796
- Baker Street LU
- Tue-Sun 10am-10.30pm

This attractive recent addition to Marylebone High Street offers a small fishmonger's at the front of a contemporary fish restaurant. Stock is nicely displayed and offers a choice selection of upmarket fish and seafood, including excellent own-made taramasalata

NORTH

B & M Seafoods

- 258 Kentish Town Road, NW5
- 020 7485 0346
- Kentish Town LU/Rail
- Tue-Sat 9am-6pm

This friendly, well-established shop, unusually combining a fishmonger's with a butcher's, has an excellent range of carefully sourced, choice fish. Stock ranges from basics like herring and mackerel to upmarket fish such as turbot, wild sea bass and prime smoked salmon.

France Fresh Fish

⌕ *99 Stroud Green Road, N4*
☎ *020 7263 9767*
🚇 *Finsbury Park LU/Rail*
🕐 *Mon-Sat 9am-7pm, Sun 11am-5pm*

An eye-catching window display of brightly coloured tropical fish is an attractive feature of this long-established fish-shop, owned by the same Mauritian family who run the Chez Liline restaurant next door. Staff are friendly and happy to offer advice on the exotic stock.

Hampstead Seafoods

⌕ *78 Hampstead High Street, NW3*
☎ *020 7435 3966*
🚇 Hampstead LU
🕐 *Tue-Fri 7.30am-5pm, Sat 7.30am-4.30pm*

Tucked away off the High Street, this small shop offers a good range of quality seafood.

Steve Hatt

⌕ *88-90 Essex Road, N1*
☎ *020 7226 3963*
🚇 *Angel LU*
🕐 *Tue-Sat 7am-5pm*

An Islington institution, this down-to-earth fishmonger has a good range of fish, stocking everything from herring to swordfish. The own-smoked fish is very popular.

Poisson

⌕ *7 Station Parade, Cockfosters Road, EN4*
☎ *020 8449 0335*
🚇 *Cockfosters LU*
🕐 *Tue-Fri 8am-6pm, Sat 8am-5.30pm*

A smart fishmonger's with an excellent assortment of fish and seafood, including luxuries such as monkfish, raw clams and scallops. Staff are friendly and helpful, and are happy to take orders in advance.

Fishmongers

Walter Purkis & Sons

▭ *17 The Broadway, N8*

☎ *020 8340 6281*

🚌 *Finsbury Park LU/Rail, then the W7 bus*

🕐 *Tue-Sat 8am-5pm*

Right in the middle of Crouch End's bustling Broadway, this friendly shop sells a good range of fish, from herring to salmon.

A. Scott & Son

▭ *94 High Road, N2*

☎ *020 8444 7606*

🚌 *East Finchley LU*

🕐 *Tue-Thur 8.30am-5.30pm, Fri 8.30am-6pm, Sat 8.30am-5pm*

This small, friendly fishmonger's has an excellent range of fresh fish and seafood, with luxury items including clams, raw tiger prawns and frozen crabmeat.

SOUTH-WEST

Moxon's

▭ *Westbury Parade, Nightingale Lane, SW4*

🚌 *Clapham South LU*

☎ *020 8675 2468*

🕐 *Tue-Fri 9am-8pm, Sat 9am-6pm*

Right by Clapham South tube, Robin Moxon's immaculate, white-tiled fishmonger, much appreciated by locals, sells an excellent range of carefully sourced fish. Stock ranges from sardines and mackerel to rod-and-line-caught sea bass, 'unsoaked scallops', razor clams and oysters, plus additional treats such as sea salt, crevettes gris and Elvas plums.

Sandys

▭ *56 King Street, TW1*

☎ *020 8892 5788*

🚌 *Twickenham Rail*

🕐 *Mon-Sat 8am-6pm*

This large fishmonger impresses with its range of stock. The shop's ethos is summed up by a tiled sign on the walls which reads, 'Welcome to Sandys where only the best is good enough'. Halibut, sea bass and raw langoustines sit alongside jellied eels and cod roes. As used to be traditional with fishmongers, Sandys also offers a range of poultry.

SOUTH-EAST

Soper's
- 141 Evelina Road, SE15
- ☎ 020 7639 9729
- Nunhead Rail
- ⏰ Tue-Fri 9am-5.30pm, Sat 8.30am-5.30pm, Sun 9am-2pm

The appropriately-named Whiting family run this classic 'wet fish shop', which has been in the family since 1897. Customers come from a large catchment area to purchase prime, professionally-prepared fish.

EAST

H.S. Linwood & Son
- ☎ 6-7 Grand Avenue, Leadenhall Market, EC3
- ☎ 020 7929 0554
- Monument LU
- ⏰ Mon-Fri 6am-3pm

Today, alas, the sole remnant of Leadenhall's glory days is Linwood's, with its eye-catching display of fish and seafood and expert fishmongers in attendance.

WEST

Copes Seafood Company
- 700 Fulham Road, SW6
- ☎ 020 7371 7300
- Fulham Broadway LU
- ⏰ Mon-Fri 10am-8pm, Sat 9am-6pm

The sheer quality of the fresh, Cornish-caught fish on offer here has gained this fishmonger a notable reputation and loyal local following.

Covent Garden Fishmonger's
- 37 Turnham Green Terrace, W4
- ☎ 020 8995 9273
- Turnham Green LU
- ⏰ Tue, Wed & Fri 8am-5.30pm, Thur & Sat 8am-5pm

Despite small premises, veteran fishmonger Phil Diamond's shop stocks an impressive range of seafood, from fresh wild Scotch salmon to Pallourde clams and langoustines.

The Fish Shop

☐ *201 Kensington Church Street, W8*
☎ *020 7243 6626*
🚌 *Notting Hill LU*
🕐 *Tue-Fri 9am-7pm, Sat 9am-5pm*

This small, sleek annexe to the Kensington Place restaurant sells a select range of predominantly English fish, plus tuna and swordfish. The majority of the fish on sale is delivered from Cornwall fresh and whole, before being filleted on the premises.

Fishworks

☐ *8 Turnham Green Terrace, W4*
☎ *020 8994 0086*
🚌 *Turnham Green LU*
🕐 *Tue-Sat 8.30am-10.30pm, Sun 11am-3pm*

This first London branch of Mitch Tonks's Fishworks combines a small fishmonger's at the front of a contemporary fish restaurant. Stock is select, with the emphasis very much on prime, spanking fresh fish and seafood, such as Fine du Claire oysters, reel-caught langoustines and Megrim sole. The restaurant connection is apparent in the own-made fishcakes and classy taramasalata, made to an Elizabeth David recipe.

Golborne Fisheries

☐ *75 Golborne Road, W10*
☎ *020 8960 3100*
🚌 *Ladbroke Grove LU*
🕐 *Mon 9.30am-4pm, Tue-Sat 8am-6pm*

George's bustling fish shop is a local institution, always busy with customers. The range of stock is enormous, from live eels and octopuses to tropical fish such as barracuda and parrot fish, and an excellent range of shellfish.

La Maree

☐ *76 Sloane Avenue, SW3*
☎ *020 7589 8067*
🚌 *South Kensington LU*
🕐 *Mon-Sat 8am-6pm*

This tiny annexe of the Poisonnerie restaurant sells a small but select range of seafood, including scallops in their shells and wild salmon. Prices are high but so is the quality and the staff are knowledgeable and helpful.

Food Halls

CENTRAL

Fortnum & Mason
- 181 Piccadilly, W1
- 020 7734 8040
- Piccadilly Circus LU
- Mon-Sat 9.30am-6pm

With its carpeted floors, pastel-coloured walls and chandeliers, this famous high-class grocer's, established in 1707, retains an appealing degree of pomp – and certainly pulls in the tourists. Traditional and regional British foodstuffs are very much to the fore. Luxuries include smoked wild salmon, vintage whiskies and champagnes and pheasant's, partridge's and pullet's eggs.

Harrods
- 87 Brompton Road, SW1
- 020 7730 1234
- Knightsbridge LU
- Mon, Tue & Sat 10am-6pm; Wed-Fri 10am-7pm

The beautiful food halls – some complete with vintage tiling – recall Harrods' roots as a tea merchant's. As one would expect, the range of foodstuffs stocked is enormous: from the eye-catching fresh fish display to exotic fruits and vegetables. Highlights include the extensive charcuterie and cheese counters.

Food Halls

Harvey Nichols Food Hall

Knightsbridge, SW1

020 7235 5000

Knightsbridge LU

Mon-Fri 10am-8pm; Sat 10am-6pm

This stylish food hall, with its high-tech marketplace feel, adjoining restaurant and smartly-dressed customers, offers an upmarket range of products. The bakery section and butcher's and fishmonger's counters are all impressive.

Selfridges

400 Oxford Street, W1

020 7629 1234

Bond Street LU Marble Arch LU

Mon-Wed, Fri & Sat 9.30am-7pm; Thur 9.30am-8pm

Immaculate and gleaming, the food hall at Selfridges reflects its cosmopolitan clientele with an impressively international range of ingredients and ready-made foods, including Middle Eastern, Japanese and Italian. Particularly eye-catching is the long fresh fish counter, with its attractive display of fresh fish and shellfish.

Health Food Shops

CENTRAL

Fresh & Wild
⌂ *69-75 Brewer Street, W1*
☎ *020 7434 3179*
🚇 *Piccadilly Circus LU*
🕐 *Mon-Fri 7.30am-9pm, Sat 9am-9pm, Sun 11.30am-8.30pm*

Where there was once a vintage butcher's shop, there's now this thriving funky health food shop – a sign of the times. Housed over two storeys and manned by friendly, helpful staff, it carries an impressive range of organic foodstuffs, plus a fresh salad bar and juice bar, popular with local workers.

Planet Organic
⌂ *22 Torrington Place, WC1*
☎ *020 7436 1929*
🚇 *Goodge Street LU*
🕐 *Mon-Fri 8.15am-8pm, Sat 11am-6pm, Sun 12noon-6pm*

An attractive branch of the West London store, complete with a juice-bar and café area offering organic, vegan and vegetarian food, busy at lunchtime.

" Vibrant produce, great breads, organic takeaway and juicebar and a huge selection of organic foods and natural remedies. *"*

Soho
69-75 Brewer Street
London W1F
020 7434 3179

Camden
49 Parkway
London NW1
020 7428 7575

Notting Hill
210 Westbourne Grove
London W11
020 7229 1063

Clapham Junction
305-311 Lavender Hill
London SW11
020 7585 1488

City
194 Old Street
London EC1V
020 7250 1708

Stoke Newington
32-40 Church Street
London N16
020 7254 2332

Clifton
85 Queens Road
Bristol
0117 9105930

FRESH
& WILD
THE REAL FOOD STORE

Total Organics

⌨ *6 Moxon Street, W1*

☎ *020 7935 8626*

🚇 *Baker Street LU*

🕐 *Mon-Fri 10am-6.30pm, Sat 10am-6pm, Sun 10am-3pm*

A sister shop to the popular Borough Market stall, this bright, neat shop combines an organic juice bar and deli counter with a selection of vegetarian and organic foodstuffs and household essentials.

NORTH

Bumblebee

⌨ *30, 32 & 33 Brecknock Road, N7*

☎ *020 7607 1936*

🚇 *Kentish Town LU/Rail, then the 29 bus*

🕐 *Mon-Wed, Fri & Sat 9.30am-6.30pm; Thur 9.30am-7.30pm*

Colonising their particular stretch of Brecknock Road, this trio of busy shops offers an excellent range of health foods, from fresh organic produce to vegetarian cheeses. Staff are very friendly and helpful.

Fresh & Wild

⌨ *49 Parkway, NW1*

☎ *020 7428 7575*

🚇 *Camden Town LU*

🕐 *Mon-Fri 8am-9pm, Sat 9,30am-9pm, Sun 11am-8pm*

This large, funky shop is very much a new-wave health food shop, complete with juice bar, breakfast bar and Latino music playing in the background. Highlights include an eye-catching display of fresh organic produce and a huge array of self-serve pulses, nuts and dried fruits. The extensive general stock includes a small organic meat section and freezers filled with organic Rocombe Farm and Green & Black ice creams.

Fresh & Wild

⌨ *32-40 Stoke Newington Church Street, N16*

☎ *020 7254 2332*

🚇 *Bus: 73*

🕐 *Mon-Fri 9am-9pm, Sat 9am-8.30pm, Sun 10am-8pm*

Attractive airy branch of the organic food shop chain, offering the hallmark extensive range and friendly service. The in-house organic café and juice bar is a popular meeting place for mums with toddlers.

Gill Wing Foods

🖃 *304 St Paul's Road, N1*
☎ *020 7226 7272*
🚌 *Highbury & Islington LU/Rail*
🕐 *Mon-Fri 8am-6pm, Sat 8am-5pm, Sun 10am-5pm*

Just off Highbury Corner, this small, neat shop offers a select range of predominantly organic foodstuffs, plus a deli counter selling own-made ready-meals such as pies and salads.

Haelan Centre

🖃 *41 The Broadway, N8*
☎ *020 8340 4258*
🚌 *Finsbury Park LU, then W7 bus*
🕐 *Mon-Thur 9am-6pm, Fri 9am-6.30pm,*
   Sat 9am-6pm, Sun 12noon-4pm

Just by Crouch End's Clock Tower, this corner shop is a local institution. The groundfloor shop sells fresh organic produce and health-food groceries ranging from goat's milk to honey, while upstairs there is a health clinic.

Just Natural

🖃 *304 Park Road, N8*
☎ *020 8340 1720*
🚌 *Finsbury Park LU, then the W7 bus*
🕐 *Mon-Sat 9am-7pm, Sun 11am-3pm*

Housed in an old, tiled butcher's shop in a pretty parade of shops at the foot of Muswell Hill, this health-food shop's stock is both vegetarian and 100% organic, from the wheat grass juices and babyfood to the spices and Rocombe Farm ice cream. Staff are friendly and helpful. Mums with buggies are particularly well catered for.

Paradise Stores

🖃 *164 Kentish Town Road, NW4*
☎ *020 7284 3402*
🚌 *Kentish Town LU/Rail*
🕐 *Mon-Sat 10am-6pm*

This well-established shop, run with chatty friendliness by Charlie and Maria, specialises in organic foodstuffs, from fresh fruit and vegetables to pulses, tofu and sprouts. The stock is eclectically global, including Indian mangoes, fufu flour and coconut milk.

WEST

Fresh & Wild
⊞ *210 Westbourne Grove, W11*
☎ *020 7229 1063*
🚇 *Notting Hill LU, Bayswater LU*
🕐 *Mon-Sat 8am-9pm, Sun 10am-7pm*
This huge health food shop offers Notting Hill residents a superb range of organic foods and natural remedies. The organic deli and juice bar, serving a range of truly fresh juices, is particularly popular.

Here
⊞ *Chelsea Farmers Market, 125 Sydney Street, SW3*
☎ *020 7351 4321*
🚇 *Sloane Square LU*
🕐 *Mon-Sat 9.30am-8pm, Sun 10am-6.30pm*
A distinctly stylish health food shop, with an attractively displayed, top end range of organic foods, plus helpful staff.

Planet Organic
⊞ *42 Westbourne Grove, W2*
☎ *020 7221 7171*
🚇 *Bayswater LU, Queensway LU*
🕐 *Mon-Sat 9.30am-8pm, Sun 11am-5pm*
This stylish superstore sells everything for the healthy lifestyle, from freshly-pressed juices at the juice bar to organic muesli. There is a large grocery section, a seafood counter, and a particularly extensive fresh produce section and butcher's counter.

SOUTH-WEST

Brixton Wholefoods Transatlantic
⊞ *59 Atlantic Road, SW9*
☎ *020 7737 2210*
🚇 *Brixton LU*
🕐 *Mon 9.30am-7pm, Tue-Thur & Sat 9.30am-5.30pm,*
    Fri 9.30am-6pm
This is a friendly, laid-back wholefood shop, so-named because its former premises were on the other side of Atlantic Road. Organic fruit and veg are delivered three times a week. The self-serve selection of

around 300 herbs and spices (organic and non-organic) and the range of 20 breads (such as three-seed wholemeal and organic sunflower and sesame) are particularly popular.

Fresh & Wild

⌖ *305-311 Lavender Hill, SW11*
☎ *020 7585 1488*
🚌 *Clapham Junction Rail*
🕐 *Mon-Fri 9am-9pm, Sat 8.30am-7.30pm, Sun 12noon-6pm*

This large branch of the new wave organic food specialists features an impressive display of fresh produce, plus a juice bar where Claphamites can enjoy a reviving classic shot of wheatgrass.

Kelly's Organic Foods

⌖ *46 Northcote Road, SW11*
☎ *020 7207 3967*
🚌 *Clapham Junction Rail*
🕐 *Mon-Thur 9am-8pm, Fri-Sat 9am-6pm*

Attractively housed in a corner site, Daniel Kelly's fresh-looking shop offers a good choice of organic stock, from baby foods (jarred and frozen) to bacon and wheat-free bread. Particular highlights include the fresh fruit and vegetables and the deli counter, stocked with home-cooked quiches and cakes. An added draw for customers is an arrange-ment whereby Cope's sell their upmarket seafood in an annexe on Tuesdays, Thursdays, Fridays and Saturdays.

Oliver's Wholefood Store

⌖ *5 Station Approach, TW9*
☎ *020 8948 3990*
🚌 *Kew Gardens LU*
🕐 *Mon-Sat 9am-7pm, Sun 10am-7pm*

This attractive airy shop boasts an impressive overall stock. Its good selection of fresh organic produce (including blood oranges, sweet pota-toes and young garlic) is delivered daily and is complemented by neatly arranged shelves of groceries, laden with basics such as organic grains and pulses as well as treats such as organic chocolate. On offer in the chill counter are Sheepdrove's organic meat, organic fresh yeast and a range of dairy products. Staff are friendly and helpful.

Health Food Shops

SOUTH-EAST

Baldwin's Health Food Centre
⌗ 171-73 Walworth Road, SE17
☎ 020 7703 5550
🚌 Elephant & Castle LU
🕐 Mon-Sat 9am-5.30pm

A South London institution this established business carries a truly impressive range of herbals remedies plus a good general organic and health food stock.

SMBS Foods
⌗ 75 Lordship Lane, SE22
☎ 020 8693 7792
🚌 East Dulwich Rail
🕐 Mon-Fri 9am-6.30pm, Sat 9am-5.30pm, Sun 10am-4.30pm

Kash Rao's splendidly eclectic shop has been selling organic foods since 1985, with stock ranging from fresh fruit and vegetables to grains and pulses, spices, ice cream, dairy products, meat and poultry. Despite space constraints, the stock is impressively wide-ranging and globe-trotting.

EAST

Fresh & Wild
⌗ 194 Old Street, EC1
☎ 020 7250 1708
🚌 Old Street LU
🕐 Mon-Fri 9.30am-7.30pm, Sat 10.30am-5.30pm

A small, friendly branch of the well-established organic chain, offering organic foodstuffs, take-away snacks and natural remedies.

Markets

London Farmers' Markets

We grow it
We sell it

Where is my nearest market?

Swiss Cottage
Wednesdays 10am–3pm
02 Centre Car Park
(near Homebase)
Finchley Rd, NW6

Pimlico Road
Saturdays 9am–1pm
Orange Square corner of
Pimlico Road & Ebury St, SW1

Peckham
Sundays 9.30am–1.30pm
Peckham Square
Peckham High Street, SE15

Wimbledon Park
Saturdays 9am–1pm
Wimbledon Park First School
Havana Road, SW19

Blackheath
Sundays 10am–2pm
Blackheath Rail Station Car Park
Blackheath, SE3

Islington
Sundays 10am–2pm
Essex Road
Opposite Islington Green, N1

Twickenham
Saturdays 9am–1pm
Holly Road Car Park
Off King St, TW1

Marylebone
Sundays 10am–2pm
Cramer St Car Park
off Marylebone High St, W1

Ealing
Saturdays 9am–1pm
Leeland Road
West Ealing, W13

Twickenham
Saturdays 9am–1pm
Holly Road Car Park
Off King St, TW1

Notting Hill
Saturdays 9am–1pm
Car park behind Waterstones
access via Kensington Place, W8

For more information
See our website www.lfm.org.uk
E-mail us info@lfm.org.uk

Send us an SAE for a list of markets to
PO Box 37363, London N1 7WB

Markets

O ne of the most exciting recent developments on London's food shopping scene has been the growing number of new, specialist food markets. The success of markets such as Borough demonstrates that there is a real appetite for fresh, good food.

Sillfield Farm at Borough Food Market

Markets

Borough Food Market

⊞ *Southwark Street, SE1*

🚌 *London Bridge LU/Rail*

🕐 *Fri 12noon-3pm, Sat 9am-4pm*

Shops

1) De Gustibus,
2) Konditor & Cook
3) Neal's Yard Dairy
4) Wyndham House Poultry

Eateries

a) Monmouth Coffee Company
b) Brindisa

Housed in Borough's wholesale market (atmospherically situated under the railway arches next to Southwark Cathedral) Borough food market continues to grow and grow, attracting food-loving Londoners and tourists alike. Fundamental to its success is the range and quality of the goods on offer, excellent meat (including farmed wild boar), diver-picked scallops, myrtle-flavoured ham from Sardinian Organics, delicious cheese from Borough Cheese Co., biodynamic produce from Fern Verrow and Moroccan argan oil. A wide range of take-away foods is also available, from fiery chorizo sandwiches and free-range chicken wraps to proper pork pies and falafel.

Borough Market also acts as a showcase for retailers such as Brindisa (who sell superb Spanish foodstuffs), L'Artisan du Chocolat, and Clarke's (purveyors of exquisite tarts and elegant breads). Standout wholesalers here include Booths, with their picturesque display of fresh fruit and vegetables.

The nearby side-streets are also home to a clutch of food specialists such as Neal's Yard Dairy, Monmouth Coffee House, poultry specialists Wyndham House, cake makers Konditor & Cooke, with bakers De Gustibus backing onto the market.

Food Lover's Fair

Henrietta Green's annual London-based Food Lover's Fair, usually held in November, features producers from around Britain offering a range of edibles. For details of dates and times check *www.foodloversbritain.com*

Organic Market

- *Spitalfields Market,*
  Old Spitalfields Market, Brushfield Street, E1
- *Liverpool Street LU/Rail*
- *Sun 9.30am-5pm*

London's first organic market draws a steady stream of devoted regulars, returning for fresh produce, organic meat, health foods and breads.

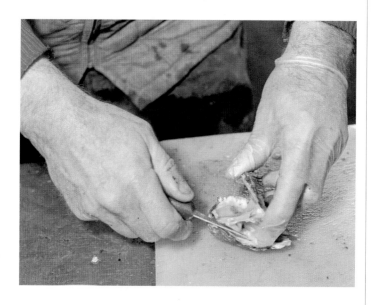

FARMERS' MARKETS

Farmers' markets (an idea imported from America, where farmers and food producers sell direct to local consumers) are growing in popularity throughout Britain. London is no exception with Islington hosting the first of the capital's farmers' markets, which opened in 1999. The capital now hosts a great number of farmers' markets, spread across the city. London Farmers' Markets (*www.lfm.org.uk*) run the majority of these, making sure that the foods on sale are produced within 100 miles of the M25. With around 35 stalls, Marylebone is one of the largest such markets, while the market at Stoke Newington specialises in certified organic and biodynamic produce.

Being able to buy seasonal produce at its best is obviously one of the attractions of the farmers' markets. In the summer months one might find English asparagus, garden peas, sweetcorn (which is at its best and sweetest the fresher it is) and soft fruit such as strawberries and gooseberries whereas in the autumn traditional English apple varieties, plums and root vegetables abound.

There is more on offer at farmers' markets, however, than simply fresh fruit and vegetables: meat, fish and shellfish, breads, cakes, cheeses and fruit juices are also sold. Regular stall-holders at a number of London's farmers' markets include Rowan Tree Goats' Farm selling their soft goat's cheese, yoghurt and milk, Purely Organic trout from Wiltshire, biodynamic produce from Perry Court Farm, the Exeter Street Bakery and Keith Bennett from Stockings Farm offering outdoor-reared pork and rare breed meats.

Blackheath SE3
2 Blackheath Village,
Blackheath Rail Station Car Park
Rail: Blackheath
Open: Sun 10am-2pm

Ealing W13
Leeland Road, West Ealing
Rail: West Ealing
Open: Sat 9am-1pm

Islington N1
Essex Road (opp. Islington Green)
Tube: Angel
Open: Sun 10am-2pm

Marylebone W1
Cromer Street Car Park
(off Marylebone High Street)
Tube: Baker Street
Open: Sun 10am-2pm

Notting Hill W8
Car park behind Waterstones
(access via Kensington Place)
Tube: Notting Hill Gate
Open: Sat 9am-1pm

Peckham SE15
Peckham Square,
Peckham High Street
Rail: Peckham Rye or Queens Road
Buses: 12, 36, 171, 345
Open: Sun 9.30am-1.30pm

Pimlico Road SW1
Orange Square, corner of Pimlico
Road and Ebury St, SW1
Tube: Sloane Square
Buses: 211, 11 & 239
Open: Sat 9am-1pm

Richmond TW9
Heron Square, Richmond
Rail/Tube: Richmond
Open: Sat 11am-3pm

Stoke Newington N16
William Patten School,
Stoke Newington Church Street
Rail: Stoke Newington; bus 73, 393
Open: Sat 10am-2pm

Swiss Cottage NW3
Finchley Road (near Homebase)
Tube: Swiss Cottage
Buses: 13, 82, 113, 268, 187
Open: Wed 10am-3pm (Eaton Av)
Open: Fri 10am-3pm (02 Centre
Car Park)

Twickenham TW1
Holly Road Car Park
Holly Rd (off King St),
Rail: Twickenham
Open: Sat 9am-1pm

Wimbledon Park SW19
Wimbledon Park First School,
Havana Road
Tube: Wimbledon Park
Open: Sat 9am-1pm

Tea & Coffee

CENTRAL

Algerian Coffee Store
- 52 Old Compton Street, W1
- ☎ 020 7437 2480
- Leicester Square LU
- 🕐 Mon-Sat 9am-7pm

A much-loved, vintage Soho institution, set up in 1887 by an Algerian businessman but now Italian-run for decades. The fragrant scent of coffee and spices wafts out of the door – a clue to the extensive range of coffees and teas inside, including Lebanese coffee with ground cardamom. Stock also includes an impressive range of coffee makers and delicious sweet treats, to enjoy after a meal with a cup of tea or coffee.

Angelucci
- 23b Frith Street, W1
- ☎ 020 7437 5889
- Leicester Square LU
- 🕐 Mon-Wed & Fri-Sat 9am-5pm; Thur 9am-1pm

This tiny family-run business, in these premises since 1931, is best-known for its in-house Mokital blend, used a few doors down by Bar Italia (see Italian London, p.164 for more details).

H. R. Higgins
- 79 Duke Street, W1
- ☎ 020 7629 3913
- Bond Street LU
- 🕐 Mon-Wed 8.45am-5.30pm,
  Thur & Fri 8.45am-6pm, Sat 10am-5pm

Founded in 1942 by Harold Higgins (known as 'the coffee man'), this family-run business continues to sell quality teas and coffees. The huge copper caddies, beautiful old scales and knowledgeable, courteous service provide a glimpse into another retail era.

Tea & Coffee

Monmouth Coffee Company

⌗ *27 Monmouth Street, WC2*

☏ *020 7379 3516*

🚌 *Covent Garden LU*

🕐 *Mon-Sat 8am-6.30pm*

With its high-backed, wooden booths and aromatic scent of coffee, this small coffee shop-cum-café is a much-loved Covent Garden institution. It offers a discerning range of ethically-sourced coffee, sold whole or freshly ground, as requested.

Monmouth Coffee Company

⌗ *2 Park Street, SE1*

☏ *020 7645 3585*

🚌 *London Bridge LU/Rail*

🕐 *Mon-Sat 7.30am-6pm*

Right by Borough Market, in a prime corner site, this is an attractively spacious café-cum-coffee shop (sibling to the Monmouth Street establishment) offering a carefully chosen range of coffees. Coffee drinkers can sit at a central table to enjoy their coffee along with a slice of baguette, jam and farmhouse butter and a selection of Sally Clarke's viennoiserie.

NORTH

Camden Coffee Shop

⌗ *11 Delancey Street, NW1*

☏ *020 7387 4080*

🚌 *Camden Town LU*

🕐 *Mon-Wed & Fri 9.30am-5.30pm, Thur 9.30am-2.30pm,*
  Sat 9.30am-5pm

"Fresh roasted coffee" reads a simple sign outside this small, old-fashioned shop, established in 1950. Inside the shop, George (who has run the business since 1978) roasts his coffees in batches in a small coffee-roaster, which clatters noisily as it turns, filling the air with the rich scent of roasting coffee. The choice is compact: ten coffees from Central and South America and Africa, ranging from light to dark roasts, and all very competitively priced. "I'm the only coffee shop left like this," remarks George thoughtfully, and he's absolutely right.

Angellucci's

W. M. Martyn

⌖ *135 Muswell Hill Broadway, N10*
☏ *020 8883 5642*
🚌 *Highgate LU, then 134 bus*
🕐 *Mon-Wed & Fri 9.30am-5.30pm,*
  Thur 9.30am-1pm, Sat 9am-5.30pm

The aroma of freshly-roasted coffee beans wafting down the Broadway marks the presence of this small, old-fashioned grocer's, which was established over 100 years ago. While best-known for its teas and coffees, the shop also stocks traditional groceries, from excellent dried fruits to sugar mice and bars of German marzipan. Staff are helpful and friendly.

MAIL ORDER

Union Coffee Roasters

⌖ *The New Roastery, Unit 2, 7a South Crescent,*
  London, EC16 4TL
☏ *020 7474 8990   fax 020 7511 2786*
🖃 *www.unionroasters.com*

Coffee afficionados Jeremy Torz and Steven Macatonia of Union Coffee Roasters specialise in hand-roasted coffee. Their carefully sourced coffees (which include organic, estate and decaffeinated) range from their popular Revolution Espresso blend to aromatic Yemen Mocha Matari. Union Coffee Roasters make a point of ethically sourcing their coffee from small family-owned farms.

Spices

The Spice Shop

- 1 Blenheim Crescent, W11
- ☎ 020 7221 4448
- 🚇 Ladbroke Grove LU
- 🕘 Mon-Sat 9.30am-6.30pm, Sun 11am-5pm

Birgit Erath runs this small, aromatic shop with enormous enthusiasm and energy, stocking an impressive range of spices and herbs for both culinary and medicinal purposes.

MAIL ORDER

Seasoned Pioneers

- 101, Summers Road, Brunswick Business Park, Liverpool, L3 4BJ
- ☎ 0800 0682348 (freephone)
- ✍ www.seasonedpioneers.co.uk

An intelligently chosen selection of over a hundred spices, spice blends and herbs are on offer from this mail order company. Spices are dry-roasted in small batches in-house and carefully blended to offer authentic flavours. In addition to more familiar spices, Seasoned Pioneers offer items such as rose petal masala, grains of paradise, sumac, chipotle chillies and curry leaves, with the spices ingeniously packaged in funky re-sealable foil packets.

Simply Spice

- Unit 1b, Repton Way,
  Chatham, Kent, ME5 9AP
- ☎ 0800 043 1016
- ✍ www.simplyspice.co.uk

A mail-order business offering an impressively comprehensive stock of Indian foodstuffs, including pulses, spices, rice, ghee and sweets.

Seasonal Treats

In Spring look out for:

Luscious Alphonso mangoes from India, sold by the box at competitive prices in Asian food shops in Ealing Road in Wembley, Green Street in Newham, Southall and Tooting.

In Summer look out for:

Deliciously salty fresh samphire, sold in good fishmongers.

English asparagus, sold in farmers' markets.

Wild salmon, sold in good fishmongers.

Durian, with its rich, powerful smelling yellow flesh, from Chinese and Thai food shops.

In Autumn look out for:

Game, one of the glories of British cuisine available from good butchers, such as Allen & Co. (page 13) or Moen's (page 19).

Flavourful wild mushrooms, from Booth's at Borough Market (page 56).

Fragrant quinces, from Greek or Turkish greengrocers.

In Winter look out for:

Fresh, ruby-red pomegranates, sold in Iranian shops.

Vacherin Mont D'Or cheese, from La Fromagerie (pages 21 &23) and other good cheese shops stocking French cheeses.

Goose, with its distinctive flavour and rich flesh, available from good butchers.

Assorted Turrons, both hard and soft, from Spanish shops such as Garcia (page 273) or Brindisa (page 270).

Smartly packaged panettone, from Italian delis such as I Camisa (page 164), Luigi's (page 172) or Valentina (page 175).

Best of British

Great British Food Shops

A British institution...
Fortnum & Mason *(p.45)*

Founded in 1707, this grand emporium, decked out with gilded wood, carpets and chandeliers continues to evoke a bygone age.

A must for British foodlovers...
A.Gold *(p.38)*

Attractively housed in an eighteenth century property, A. Gold stocks a discerning and witty selection of British foodstuffs, from sugar mice to mead.

Best British cheeses...
Neal's Yard Dairy *(p.21)*

Pioneering cheese shop noted for its fine British farmhouse cheeses, from prime examples of traditional territorials such as Colston Bassett Stilton, Montgomery's Cheddar and Kirkham's Lancashire to contemporary cheeses such as Beenleigh Blue.

A lovely loaf...
The Lighthouse Bakery *(p.10)*

This much-loved Battersea bakery, where the bread is freshly baked daily on the premises, is genuinely a community shop, offering a chance to enjoy treats from hot-cross buns to a truly delicious white tin loaf.

A gem of a grocer's...
W. M. Martyn *(p.63)*

A truly traditional grocer's shop, complete with dark wood fittings, selling delicious teas, own-roasted coffee and excellent dried fruits.

Tempting treats...
Melrose & Morgan *(p.30)*

Seriously meaty Cornish pasties, Chelsea buns and delicious apple juice are among the treats on offer at this modish contemporary deli.

The Lighthouse Bakery

Neal's Yard Dairy

A. Gold

A Taste of Britain: Eating Out

✗ Tea for two...
The Dorchester
- 53 Park Lane, W1
- ☎ 020 7629 8888
- 🚌 Hyde Park Corner LU, Marble Arch LU

Tea at the Dorchester is a deliciously classy affair, consisting of savoury finger sandwiches, warm scones with jam and clotted cream, cakes and tartlets served in the splendidly comfortable surroundings of the Promenade amid marble columns.

✗ A meal in a park...
Inn the Park
- St James's Park, SW1
- ☎ 020 7451 9999
- 🚌 Green Park LU, Piccadilly Circus LU

Stylishly housed in this elegant park, this airy café takes pride in sourcing top-notch British ingredients.

✗ Best of British grub...
Porters
- 17 Henrietta Street, WC2E
- ☎ 020 7836 6466
- 🚌 Covent Garden LU

Founded in 1979 by Richard, Earl of Bradford, who promised "real English food at affordable prices" this informal restaurant serves traditional dishes including steak and kidney pudding, savoury pies and classic steamed puddings such as spotted dick.

✗ Go for game...
Rules
- 35 Maiden Lane, WC2
- ☎ 020 7836 5314
- 🚌 Covent Garden LU

London's oldest surviving restaurant dates back to 1798. Game is a particular forte, with the menu offering classic English dishes such as potted shrimps and roast rib of beef with Yorkshire pudding.

✕ **Nose-to-tail eating...**

St John

▭ 26 St John Street, EC1

☎ 020 7251 0848

🚌 Farringdon LU

Just by Smithfields meat market, this austere restaurant, with its stripped-down surroundings, has a devoted following for its classic renditions of traditional British dishes. Signature dishes include roast bone marrow with parsley salad or chitterlings.

Five of the Best: Fish & Chips

✕ Golden Hind

▭ 73 Marylebone High Street, W1

☎ 020 7486 3644

🚌 Bond Street LU

Small, friendly vintage fish and chip shop in the heart of Marylebone.

✕ Sea Cow

▭ 37 Lordship Lane, SE22

☎ 020 8693 3111

🚌 East Dulwich Rail

Popular, contemporary fish and chip restaurant, complete with a display of fish on ice to demonstrate what's on the menu that day.

✕ Toffs

▭ 38 Muswell Hill Broadway, N10

☎ 020 8883 8656

🚌 Highgate LU, then 134 bus

Generous portions of spanking fresh fish are a trademark of this Muswell Hill institution.

✕ Two Brothers Fish Restaurant

▭ 297-303 Regent's Park Road, N3

☎ 020 8346 0469

🚌 Finchley Central LU

Both the restaurant and take-away are perpetually humming with customers, a tribute to the quality of the fish and chips served here.

African & Caribbean London

Back Home Foods, Brixton Market

In his monumental book, 'Staying Power', Peter Fryer points out that the first Black presence in Britain dates back to Roman times, when Black men were among the conscripts in the Roman army. The growth of a domestic Black community, however, was connected with Britain's slave trade, which was started in 1562-3 by the first 'triangular voyage' between Britain, Africa and the West Indies. The demand for sugar and the labour-intensive sugar cane plantation system in the Caribbean encouraged the slave trade's growth, making it enormously profitable to those running it.

Africans came to Britain as slaves until the slave trade was outlawed in 1807. Before this date some free Blacks, such as seamen, servants and street entertainers were established in Britain, with the London community living mainly along the Thames in Limehouse. But records such as that of freed slave Ukawsaw Gronniosaw, give a vivid picture of ill-treatment and discrimination, which forced many into destitution. After 1807 the Black community in Britain declined, although Black loyalists returned after fighting in the American War of Independence, and some seamen settled after serving in the Napoleonic Wars (1792-1815). In the late nineteenth century a small community of Somali seamen settled in the London docks.

The coming of the First World War meant a change of attitude towards the Black community. Instead of being rejected for work on racial grounds, their help was now needed in the munitions factories. Black seamen also filled the gaps in the Merchant Navy caused by conscription. By 1919 there were 20,000 Black people in Britain. But once the war was over the picture changed again, with the seamen's unions closing the door firmly against any Black labour.

A similar pattern occurred in the late 1940s and 1950s when, as Britain struggled to rebuild its war-torn economy, a call went out to the Commonwealth for workers to come to the 'Mother Country'. The 1948 Nationality Act granted British citizenship to people living in Britain's current and former colonies. For many West Indians this was an opportunity to be seized; unemployment was high in the West Indies and in 1951 a hurricane added to Jamaica's problems. Corporations such as London Transport actively recruited labour in Barbados in 1956, and by 1966 had also turned to Trinidad and Jamaica. Between 1945 and 1958, over 125,000 West Indians emigrated to Britain.

The different stages of African immigration into London in the post-war years have been triggered by the ebb and flow of African politics. The 1950s and 1960s saw an influx of West Africans made up largely of students and lawyers. During the 1970s, African and Asian Ugandans fled Idi Amin; while recent years have seen an increase in immigration from Ghana, Zaire and Ethiopia.

There is no single centre for the African community in London, with pockets of different African nationalities scattered throughout the capital. There are, however, focal points such as Brixton and Notting Hill for the West Indian community. Many of the first post-war Jamaican immigrants who sailed over on the Empire Windrush settled in Brixton, a formerly prosperous suburb which had become cheap and run-down. This community attracted further Jamaican immigrants during the 1950s and 1960s. Notting Hill, in which mainly Trinidadians settled, hosts the famous Carnival; what originated as a 1964 Bank Holiday street party for local children has since developed into Europe's largest open-air street festival. The costume parades and rhythmic steel drums all derive from Trinidad's own spectacular Carnival.

African & Caribbean Cuisine

'African food' is a blanket term covering a huge number of countries, each with their own characteristic cuisines. Certain staples, such as maize, cassava, plantain and beans, are shared across different African countries and crop up in Black cuisine in many parts of the world. Dried foods, such as smoked or salted fish and meat, are another common element in the African kitchen, reflecting the need to preserve food before the days of refrigeration or canning. Many of these ingredients are now used to add a distinctive flavour to dishes.

West African slaves brought their cuisine to the West Indies and its influence is still marked in today's Caribbean cooking. Many of the staples are the same (several brought from Africa): cassava, yams, taro, plantain, groundnuts. Dishes in common include coo-coo (cornmeal pudding) and fufu, the latter being a Fanti word used on the Cape Coast. In West Africa fufu is pounded yam, plantain and cassava dough dipped into a soup, while in Jamaica fufu now means both the pounded yam and the soup. The slaves' restricted diet also included salted meat and fish and these are still popular, although the latter is now something of a luxury.

Caribbean cooking is very much a melting pot of a cuisine, influenced by a series of colonisers and immigrants. Chillies were brought from South America by the Spanish colonisers and 'escovished fish', fresh pickled fish, originated from the Spanish dish escabeche. The arrival in Trinidad of indentured workers from India means that dishes like roti and curry goat are popular there today; a large proportion of the island's inhabitants have Indian roots.

The fertility of the Caribbean islands meant many plants could be introduced successfully. Staples now include breadfruit, which was introduced by Captain Bligh. Fresh seafood is characteristic of West Indian cuisine and increasingly fish such as colourful snappers are becoming available in Britain.

Glossary

Ackee: a red-skinned fruit that is only safe to eat when the fruit is fully ripe. The white, fleshy base called an aril is the part that is eaten. Fresh ackee is very rarely found but it is available in tins. Saltfish with ackee is one of Jamaica's famous dishes. The Latin name of the fruit, Blighia sapida, is a tribute to Captain Bligh, who introduced it to Jamaica.

Agbono: sometimes spelt ogbono, this is the inner kernel of the African bush mango. The kernel is the size and shape of an almond but browner and much harder. Available both whole and ground.

Allspice: peppercorn-sized berries, with a flavour that combines cloves, cinnamon and nutmeg – hence the name.

Annatto: small, orange-red seeds, used to add colour and flavour.

Arrowroot: a starch extracted from the underground stem of a water-plant.

Avocado: this green-skinned, soft-fleshed fruit is called 'pear' in the Caribbean.

Bananas: green bananas, which are the unripe fruit of certain varieties, and ripe yellow bananas are treated as both a vegetable and a fruit in Caribbean and African cuisines.

Bitter leaf: A distinctively flavoured African leaf, related to the lettuce family. Available dried or frozen.

Breadfruit: a football-sized fruit with thick, green, pimply skin and creamy flesh, used both as a starchy vegetable and in pies and puddings.

Callaloo: green leaves of the dasheen plant, used to make a famous eponymous soup. Available tinned and fresh.

Cassava: large, brown, hand-shaped tubers of the cassava plant, also called manioc or yucca. Bitter cassava, despite the fact it contains toxic prussic acid which must be removed by either cooking or pressing, is a staple food. Yellow-fleshed sweet cassava is eaten as a vegetable. Dried, ground cassava is used in Africa to make gari. Ground cassava meal is used in the West Indies to make a type of bread and the flavoured juice of grated cassava is used to make cassareep, a key ingredient of pepper-pot.

Catfish, dried: small blackened fish, with a distinctive large head, used to add flavour to soups and stews in West African cooking.

Cho-cho (christophene, chayote): a pear-sized member of the squash family, with a wrinkled skin ranging in colour from white to green, and watery white flesh.

Coconut: coconut flesh and milk are widely used in Caribbean cookery.

Cho-cho

Cornmeal: coarsely or finely ground dried corn kernels.

Crayfish, dried: although called 'crayfish' in Africa, these are a type of shrimp. Used whole or ground as flavouring.

Custard apple: apple-sized fruit with a knobbly, green skin. The white, sweet pulp has a custard-like texture, hence the name.

Dasheen: potato-sized fibrous tubers with white starchy flesh. Some varieties of dasheen have an acrid taste.

Eddoe: a small, rounded fibrous tuber with white starchy flesh.

Egusi: pumpkin seeds, which are available shelled, either whole or ground. Egusi is used in West African cooking, providing a nutty texture in soups and stews.

Fish: *flying fish*, a distinctive 'winged' fish; *king fish*, a firm-fleshed 'meaty' fish, often sold as steaks; *parrot fish*, a brightly-coloured fish with a beaky head; *snapper*, a popular, firm-fleshed fish, available in colours from grey to pinkish-red; and *trevalli*, a large, firm-fleshed oily fish. *Jacks* is the name given to the smaller fish of the same family.

Gari: coarsely-ground cassava, an African staple.

Guava: small, yellow-green, hard-skinned fruit with pinkish flesh filled with small seeds. It has a distinctive fragrance and is eaten raw or used to make jams and jellies.

Guinep: small, round, green fruit which grows in bunches. The pink flesh has a delicate flavour.

Irish moss: white, curly seaweed from which an eponymous drink is made. Available either dried or ready to drink.

Jackfruit: a large, green fruit with a pimply skin, similar in appearance to breadfruit.

Kenke: West African dumpling, made from fermented maize flour wrapped in corn husks or banana leaves and cooked.

Landsnails: giant snails, sold either alive, frozen, tinned or smoked. If bought alive, keep them and feed them on lettuce leaves for a few days before cooking to make sure they have excreted anything toxic.

Mango: this large, kidney-shaped fruit, with its succulent orange flesh and sweet, resiny flavour, comes in numerous varieties. One of the best-known West Indian varieties is the Julie mango.

Okra (ladies fingers, ochroes): finger-sized, ridged, tapering green pods, introduced into the Caribbean from West Africa.

Okra

Ortanique

Ortanique: a cross between an orange and a tangerine, this looks like an orange with a flattened end.

Palm hearts: tender palm tree hearts, usually found tinned.

Palm oil: a thick, orange-red oil, made from the fruit of the oil palm, which adds flavour and colour to African dishes.

Pawpaw: long, oval fruit, with soft orange flesh, varying in skin colour from green to orange.

Peppers: among the hottest and most flavourful of the peppers used in African and Caribbean cooking is the squat, rounded Scotch bonnet pepper, available in green, yellow and red varieties.

Scotch bonnet peppers

Pepper sauce: the sauce comes in a variety of textures from liquid to paste, but is always hot!

Pigeon pea (gunga): ridged pea pods, with every pea in its own section. Unusually, the peas within a single pod vary in colour from cream through green and brown. Available fresh, tinned or dried.

Plantain: similar in appearance to green bananas, plantain have starchy flesh and are cooked and eaten as a vegetable. They can be chipped, boiled or cooked in stews.

Plantain

Pomelo: often called shaddock, after the merchant ship captain who introduced the fruit to the Caribbean, this is a large, thick-skinned citrus fruit, similar in flavour to grapefruit.

Saltfish: preserved foods such as salted fish were brought over to the Caribbean to feed the plantation workers. It is now something of a luxury item. Stockfish is a popular salted fish.

Sapodilla (naseberry): a fruit very similar in appearance to kiwi fruit, with a brown, furry skin. Inside it has pinky-brown, granular flesh with a few glossy pips and a distinctive sweet flavour.

Sorrel (rosella): the red sepals of a flowering plant, used either fresh or dried to make a dark-red, aromatic drink, traditionally at Christmas.

Soursop: a large, oval-shaped fruit with a thick, green, spiny skin. The pinkish-white flesh inside is custard-textured with a delicate, tart flavour.

Sugar cane: similar in appearance to bamboo, this plant has played a considerable part in Caribbean history as the sugar cane plantations demanded extensive labour, provided by slaves. Short lengths of the woody stalk are either chewed and sucked for their sweet refreshing juice.

Sweet potato: a sweet-fleshed tuber, available in many varieties.

Sweet Potato

Yam: a family of large, brown-skinned, starchy tubers, which come in many varieties, both yellow and white-fleshed.

Food Shops

NORTH

The stretch of Stroud Green Road nearest to Finsbury Park tube station is home to a number of African and Caribbean food shops, ranging from greengrocers to halal butchers.

Engocha
- *143 Fortess Road, NW5*
- ☎ *020 7485 3838*
- *Tufnell Park LU*
- ⊘ *Daily 10am-8.30pm*

This tiny, frankincense-scented Ethiopian food shop has a meat counter and a small stock of basics, including green Ethiopian coffee beans, spices and tef (an Ethiopian grain). Home-made injeera (Ethiopian bread) is particularly popular.

France Fresh Fish
- *99 Stroud Green Road, N4*
- ☎ *020 7263 9767*
- *Finsbury Park LU/Rail*
- ⊘ *Mon-Sat 9am-7pm*

An eye-catching window display marks out this established shop, specialists in tropical fish and run by the same family who own Chez Liline, the Mauritian fish restaurant next door. Good things on offer include raw prawns, samphire (when in season) and exotic fish and seafood, including barracuda, conch and parrot fish.

K. M. Butcher's Grocer's
- *29 Stroud Green Road, N4*
- ☎ *020 7263 6625*
- *Finsbury Park LU/Rail*
- ⊘ *Mon-Sat 8am-8.30pm, Sun 9am-7pm*

A large store, complete with a counter piled high with goat meat and chickens, and groceries ranging from Mauby syrup drinks to bags of cornmeal.

Stroud Green Food Store

- 65 Stroud Green Road, N4
- 020 7272 0348
- Finsbury Park LU/Rail
- Daily Mon-Sun 8am-8pm

A neatly-arranged store with an attractive display of fresh fruit and vegetables outside, including breadfruit, mangoes, plantain and bunches of thyme, and grocery staples inside.

WEST

Portobello Road Market

- Portobello Road, W12
- Notting Hill Gate LU
- Mon-Sat 9am-5pm

Beyond the antique shops is a lively fruit and vegetable market. Several of the stalls here sell West Indian produce such as yams, Scotch bonnet peppers and okra.

Shepherd's Bush Market

- Uxbridge Road, W12
- Goldhawk Road LU, Shepherd's Bush LU
- Mon-Wed, Fri-Sat 9am-5pm, Thur 9am-1pm

A decade ago this was a larger, more food-orientated market. Among the fabric, lingerie and kitchenware stalls, however, one can find a handful of stalls selling Caribbean produce.

SOUTH-WEST

Brixton Market

- Brixton Station Road, Pope's Road, SW9
  Atlantic Road, Electric Road and Electric Avenue
- Brixton LU/Rail
- Mon, Tue, Thur-Sat 8am-5.30pm; Wed 8am-1pm

This is the best market in London for West Indian and African foodstuffs. Spread out through streets and arcades alongside a mixture of household goods, wig and fabric shops are a range of fruit and vegetable stalls, piled high with yams, red Scotch bonnet peppers, green and yellow plantains, breadfruit, mangoes, limes and bunches of thyme. Fishmongers here sell an array of tropical fish while the butchers (some with signs advertising 'meat so tender you don't need teeth') offer goat, offal, cow's feet and pig's trotters. Saturday is the busiest market day and the noise is tremendous: music blaring from the record shops and people exchanging greetings, catching up on news and arguing over prices.

Fresh Food City

- 256 Upper Tooting Road, SW17
- ☎ 020 8672 0414
- Tooting Broadway LU
- 🕒 Daily 9am-9pm

A large well-stocked store, catering for both the local Asian and Caribbean communities, complete with fresh produce section, halal meat and fish counters and grocery.

EAST

Queen's Market

- Green Street, E7 (on the corner of Queen Road)
- Upton Park LU
- 🕒 Tue, Thur-Sat 8am-5pm

Among the clothing and household goods are a number of stalls and shops selling Caribbean foodstuffs, such as tropical fish and halal meat.

Ridley Road Market

- Ridley Road, E8
- Dalston Junction Rail
- 🕒 Tue-Sat 9am-5pm

A large, bustling market with a mixture of English and West Indian fruit and vegetable stalls, fishmongers and halal butchers, alongside the fabric and hair-care stalls.

MAIL ORDER

Gramma's Pepper Sauce

- PO Box 218, East Ham,
  London, E6 4BG
- ☎ 020 8470 8751

Dawn Moore produces the best and hottest pepper sauce I have ever tried. She will supply jars of mild (seriously euphemistic), medium and super-hot pepper sauce.

Eating Places

CENTRAL

Calabash £££

- The Africa Centre,
  38 King Street, WC2
- ☎ 020 7836 1976
- Covent Garden LU

This basement restaurant offers a range of reasonably priced dishes from across the continent of Africa.

NORTH

Cottons £££

- 55 Chalk Farm Road, NW1
- ☎ 020 7485 8388
- Camden Town or Chalk Farm LU

Attractively decorated in bright tropical colours this funky restaurant serves up generous portions of excellent Caribbean food. Highlights include the banana leaf-wrapped ackee parcel and mixed jerk grilled fish (red snapper, squid, goat fish and mullet). Drinks include cocktails, sorrel and a serious range of rums.

Hummingbird £££

- 84 Stroud Green Road, N4
- ☎ 020 7263 9690
- Finsbury Park LU/Rail

This veteran Trinidadian restaurant is a relaxed place in which to try classic Trinidadian dishes such as rotis, curries and rice and peas, accompanied by delicious punches.

Lalibela £££

- 137 Fortess Road, NW5
- ☎ 020 7284 0600
- Tufnell Park LU

This small, friendly restaurant offers a chance to enjoy lovingly prepared classic Ethiopian dishes such as 'wot', richly-spiced stews and injeera, the flat, spongy, slightly sour bread with which one scoops up and eats the wot. Finish off with Ethiopian coffee, a pleasantly sensory, leisurely experience during which one inhales the fragrance of the freshly roasted beans, heated in a heavy metal saucepan, before being presented with a pottery flask of the freshly made coffee served with aromatic burning frankincense on the side.

Mango Room *£££*

⬚ *10 Kentish Town Road, NW1*
☎ *020 7482 5065*
🚌 *Kentish Town LU/Rail*

This attractive, mellow restaurant, perennially buzzing with a crowd of diners, offers contemporary Caribbean cuisine, with dishes featuring ingredients such as snapper, ackee and plantain.

WEST

BB's

▢ 3 Chignell Place,
Uxbridge Road, W13
☎ 020 8840 8322
🚇 Ealing Broadway LU

Hidden away down a tiny side-street this convivial restaurant, run by the genial Brian Benjamin, offers a menu of rich Grenadian food and rum cocktails. Eat with a crowd of friends and enjoy the party atmosphere.

Mandola ££

▢ 139 Westbourne Grove, W11
☎ 020 7229 4734
🚇 BayswaterLU, Queensway LU

This small, relaxed Sudanese restaurant, run with great charm by Yusuf and his wife, serves fresh, tasty food such as salata aswad (aubergine salad) and kustalata (lamb cutlets) at remarkably reasonable prices. Round off your meal with the delectable date mousse and traditional Sudanese coffee.

SOUTH-WEST

Asmara ££

▢ 386 Coldharbour Lane, SW9
☎ 020 7737 4144
🚇 Brixton LU/Rail

This small, homely restaurant serves up delicious, carefully cooked Eritrean food.

Cookbooks

Caribbean and African Cookery
Rosamund Grant
An informative and readable cookbook.

Caribbean Cooking
Elizabeth Lambert Ortiz
An excellent look at Caribbean cuisine.

Creole Caribbean Cookery
Kenneth Gardiner
A nicely written book with appetising recipes.

Nigerian Cookbook
H.O. Anthonio and M. Isoun
A very clear and informative book.

A Taste of Africa
Dorinda Hafner
A fascinating look at African and Caribbean cookery, written with exuberance and infectious enthusiasm.

Trade Wind: Caribbean Cooking
Christine Mackie
An evocative mix of text and recipes.

Asian London

Sira

The term 'Asian' covers what was once the Indian subcontinent but is today Bangladesh, India, Pakistan and Sri Lanka. An Asian presence in Britain can be traced back to the seventeenth and eighteenth centuries. Some early settlers were performers but many were servants brought back from India by the newly prosperous nawabs. Through the East India Company others came as lascars, Indian seamen.

A fascinating book, Across Seven Seas (edited by Caroline Adams), describes how many of these lascars were from one small, land-locked part of Bengal called Sylhet. There was a tradition in rural India of men leaving their villages to work and support their family. Work as seamen was offered at large ports such as Calcutta. In the words of Haji Kona Miah, "The Sylhet people were in the ship because these people follow each other, and some went there and others saw them and thought they could get jobs too". The serangs, agents who chose workers for the ships, preferred to employ people from their own village or locality. Once Sylhetis became serangs, a pattern of using Sylheti sailors was established.

Those who settled in London lived in the East End, near the docks. For many of them earning a living was difficult and in 1858 the 'Strangers Home for Asiatics, Africans and South Sea Islanders' was opened in West India Dock Road, Limehouse. The major growth in the Bengali community came this century in 1956, when passports were finally granted and thousands of people came to London. By 1962, the number of Bengali immigrants living in the East End had swelled from approximately 300 to 5,000.

Of course, it was not only Bengali seamen who came to London: doctors, politicians and lawyers were also among the immigrants. Indeed, three men pivotal to India's independence studied law in London at the turn of the century: Mohandas Karamchand (later Mahatma) Gandhi, Mohammed Ali Jinnah and Jawaharlal Nehru. In 1892 Dabadhai Naoroji, a campaigner for Indian rights, was elected as Britain's first Asian MP by a majority of three votes.

It was in the period following the Second World War that the Asian presence in Britain expanded considerably, the 1948 Nationality Act granted the right of British citizenship to Britain's colonies and former colonies. After Indian Independence the violent partition of India and Pakistan left thousands dispossessed. Britain officially encouraged mainly unskilled workers from India and Pakistan to come to Britain and by 1958 there were around 55,000 Asians in Britain. The next wave of immigration came in the late 1960s when Asians were expelled from Uganda, and in 1972, when Idi Amin expelled nearly 30,000 Ugandan Asians who arrived in Britain within the space of three months.

The Asian community today, like the complex Indian subcontinent, is made up of people from different countries who speak different languages and practice different faiths. Certain areas in London are linked to particular groups. Brick Lane, which over the centuries has housed different waves of immigrants, is now predominantly Bengali, the Sylhet seamen who first settled there having paved the way for others. The history of Brick Lane is encapsulated in the story of one building on Fournier Street, built as a Huguenot chapel in 1774, it later became a Methodist chapel, in 1898 it was converted into a Jewish synagogue, and nowadays it functions as the London Jamme Masjid mosque.

Wembley is a Gujarati area, while Southall is predominantly Punjabi and Sikh. There are various theories about Southall's roots. One is that workers brought in to construct the new airport at Heathrow settled near their worksite. Alternatively, it is thought that work was provided for Asian labourers in local factories and the community grew up around this. Southall today is a thriving community with everything from Sikh temples to bookshops and restaurants. In South London Tooting houses a diverse Asian community, including Sri Lankans, East African Asians, Pakistanis and Gujuratis. London's Hindu community, meanwhile, is justly proud of 'Shri Swaminarayan Mandir' (020 8965 2651), the traditional Hindu temple recently built in Neasden. The gleaming white marble temple, which rises like a mirage in an urban desert just off the North Circular, is unique in Europe as an example of traditional Indian temple construction. It is made from blocks of limestone and marble which were hand-carved in India then shipped over and assembled in London. There is an adjourning Haveli (community centre) decorated with intricate wooden carvings – visitors to the temple complex are courteously welcomed.

Asian Cuisine

The term 'Indian cuisine' is a catch-all phrase, covering the diverse cuisines of India, Pakistan, Bangladesh and Sri Lanka and a spectrum of regional, religious and cultural differences. The hallmark of all Indian cuisine is the emphasis on spices and herbs. These numerous flavourings, from aromatic crocus stamens (saffron) to pungent resin (asafoetida), are used in intricate and varying ways: dry-roasted, fried in hot oil or mixed with other spices to form a masala (spice mix). Underlying their culinary use is an ancient belief in the health-giving properties of spices. In the Holy Hindu Scriptures, the medicinal properties of herbs and spices are listed. Turmeric and cloves both have antiseptic properties. Asafoetida, a digestive which prevents flatulence, is added to lentil dishes. Spices are divided into 'warm', generating internal heat, and 'cool', lessening it.

Underneath this culinary umbrella are diverse cuisines influenced by religion (the main Indian faiths being Hinduism, Islam, Buddhism, Jainism and Sikhism), geography and culture. Religions have laid down rules and taboos as to what can or cannot be eaten. For example, the Hindus will not eat beef as the cow is a sacred animal. Some Hindus are vegetarian, while for strict vegetarians even the flavourings associated with meat (garlic and onion) are not permitted in cooking. For Muslims, pork is a forbidden meat.

When describing Indian cuisine in regional terms, it is possible to draw a crude north-south boundary, although there are exceptions. Flat wheat breads such as paratha and chapati are a staple in the north while rice is the staple in the south. Northern cuisine was influenced by Mogul rulers who came down to India through Persia. The Persian influence is apparent in the subtle spicing, the use of nuts and in dishes such as pullao, a descendant of the pilaff. From this luxurious court cuisine came techniques used today: korma (braising in a thick, often nut-based sauce); pot-roasting (in a traditional charcoal stove); and kebab, kofte and tandoori (dishes cooked in a tandoor oven). The Indian food that is most frequently served in restaurants is based on this Mogul cuisine. In Southern Indian cookery the coconut palm has an influential role, with sweet coconut milk used in many dishes. Rice is eaten not just as a grain but is ground, mixed with dal, and used to make light pancakes called dosai. As in other hot climates, fermentation is a well-used culinary technique.

Glossary

Angled loofah: a green gourd with distinctive raised ridges running down its length and a bitter flavour.

Asafoetida (heeng): a pungent brown resin, valued for its digestive properties, sold in either lump or powder form.

Bitter gourd (karela): a knobbly-skinned, cucumber-shaped green gourd with a distinctive bitter flavour and digestive properties.

Bitter gourd

Bottle gourd (dudi): a large, smooth, bottle-shaped, green-skinned gourd with marrow-like flesh.

Cardamom: a fragrant spice pod sold whole, hulled or ready-ground. The small green or white cardamoms are used in both sweet and savoury dishes while the larger wrinkled black cardamom is used only in savoury dishes.

Carom (ajwan): a tiny seed spice, like miniature fennel seeds, with a medicinal scent and sharp, thyme-like flavour.

Chickpea flour

Chayote (chow-chow): A pear-sized, wrinkled, green-skinned squash with a single large seed and marrow-like flesh.

Chenna: a ricotta-like curd cheese.

Chickpea flour (gram or besan): ground chickpeas are the basis for many breads and fritters. Madhur Jaffrey recommends fridge storage.

Chick–peas (channa): fresh chickpeas are small, puffy green pods which need peeling to reveal the kernel.

Chikoo (sapodilla): similar looking to kiwi fruit with fine brown, furry skin, pinky-brown granular flesh, glossy pips and distinctive sweet flavour.

Chillies: sold both fresh and dried. Long slim green chillies and dried red chillies are used in Indian cookery to add both pungent heat and a distinctive flavour.

Chilli powder: a hot red powder made from ground, dried red chillies.

Cluster beans (guar): fine, straight green beans.

Coconut milk: a thick white liquid made from grated coconut flesh and not, as is sometimes thought, from the cloudy liquid inside the coconut which is called 'coconut water'. Home-made coconut milk can be made by blending together dessicated coconut with hot water, then sieving it. Alternatively, tinned coconut milk is a convenient, ready-to-use product; Madhur Jaffrey recommends the Chaokoh brand. Creamed coconut or coconut milk powder needs diluting before use.

Coriander: both the aromatic green leaves (similar in appearance to flat-leafed parsley) and small rounded seeds are used extensively in Indian cookery.

Cumin: small, greenish, finely-ridged oval seeds, similar to caraway seeds, with a distinctive, slightly sharp flavour, widely used in Indian cookery. Black cumin, which is rarer, has a more pronounced herbal flavour.

Curry leaves

Curry leaf: a spicy-smelling leaf which resembles a small bay leaf. It's usually sold dried but sometimes branches of fresh curry leaves are available.

Dal: a generic term covering the three types of pulses (lentils, beans and peas) used in Indian cookery: *chana dal*, small yellow split peas; *masoor dal*, tiny pink split lentils (sometimes called red split lentils); *moong dal*, yellow split mung beans (sold both skinned and unskinned); *rajma dal*, red kidney beans; *toovar dal*, a large split yellow pea; *urad dal*, ivory-coloured hulled black gram beans (used in Southern Indian vegetarian cookery in dishes such as pancakes and fried dumplings).

Mung dal

Drumsticks: long, green, ridged pods with thick skin, fibrous pulp and a distinctive flavour. Usually available tinned but sometimes found fresh.

Drumstick

Fennel: aniseed-flavoured, greenish ridged seeds, valued as a digestive. Candied fennel seeds are eaten after a meal.

Fenugreek (methi): both the small, stubby, hard, yellow seeds and the spicy-smelling, bitter green leaves are used in Indian cookery. The seeds have a strong, bitter flavour and are used in pickles. The dark green trefoil leaves, which look similar to clover, are sold both fresh and dried.

Fenugreek

Fish: *hilsa*, a prized freshwater fish from Bangladesh; *pomfret*, a flat, round-shaped and white-fleshed fish.

Garam masala: a fragrant spice mix, available in many versions.

Ghee: clarified butter with a nutty flavour. Because of the clarification, ghee can be used for deep frying and stored at room temperature.

Ginger: this knobbly, lightbrown root is a key flavouring prized for its aromatic flavour and digestive qualities.

Guava: a fruit resembling a small, knobbly pear, with a distinctive aroma, pinkish flesh and several small, hard seeds.

Hyacinth bean (seim): a broad-podded, thick-skinned, curved green bean; a member of the hyacinth bean family.

Jackfruit: a huge fruit with a thick, green studded skin. The creamy-textured flesh inside is eaten as a vegetable when unripe and as a fruit when ripe.

Jaggery: a pale brown sugar with a rich, nutty flavour, made from sugar cane juice or palm sap, and used in Indian sweets.

Kohlrabi: a pale green or purple bulbous vegetable, resembling a sprouting turnip – but with a more delicate flavour.

Kokum: an inedible variety of mangosteen, sold in dried pieces and used as a souring agent.

Lemon crystals: light-coloured crystals used as a souring agent.

Mango: a kidney-shaped fruit, with succulent orange flesh and a sweet, resiny flavour, and enormously popular in India. Tart, green unripe mangoes are used to make pickles, chutneys and relishes while orange-red ripe mangoes are eaten on their own or used in desserts. Over a thousand varieties are grown in India, but the Alphonso mango is one of the best known in Britain.

Green mango

Mango powder (amchoor): sour, beige-coloured powder made from dried, unripe mangoes, used to add a tart flavour to food.

Mustard oil: a pungent yellow oil, made from mustard seeds, used extensively in northern India and Bangladesh.

Mustard seeds: tiny, black round seeds, often used in pickles.

Okra (bhindi, ladies fingers): a tapering, ridged green pod which exudes a sticky juice when cooked.

Okra

Onion seed (kalonji or nigella): tiny tear-shaped black seeds which, despite their name, are not related to onions. Used primarily in pickles but also on tandoori naan bread.

Panch phoran: a Bengali five-spice mix, containing cumin, fennel, onion seeds, fenugreek and black mustard seeds.

Paneer: a firm white cheese, made from pressed Indian curd cheese called chenna (which is similar to ricotta).

Panch phoran

Patra: large, green taro leaves which are spread with a gram flour paste, rolled and steamed to make a dish called 'patra'.

Phalooda (falooda): transparent, thread-like noodles made from wheatberry starch and flavoured with pine or rose essence, used in desserts, to garnish kulfi or in a drink of the same name.

Pistachio: green-fleshed, delicately-flavoured nuts, used in Indian sweetmeats and ice cream or as a nibble.

Pomegranate seeds (anardana): dried pomegranate kernels, used to add sourness.

Poppadums (papar): small round wafers made from split-peas and flavoured with garlic or spices. When fried in hot oil they puff up and become crispy.

Poppy seed (khas khas): minuscule white poppy seeds, used in ground form to thicken sauces.

Rice: the most famous and expensive of rice varieties grown in India is basmati, with its nutty aroma and flavour.

Rose essence: a delicate rose-scented essence used in desserts. Rose water is a diluted form of rose essence.

Saffron: the dried stigmas of a crocus variety, sold in both thread and powdered form.

Sevian: fine golden-brown wheat vermicelli, used in desserts.

Snake gourd: as the name suggests, a long, narrow, twisted green gourd with bland marrow-like flesh.

Spiny bitter gourd (kantola): a small, spiky, egg-shaped relation of the bitter gourd.

Asian London

Sweetmeats: many Indian sweetmeats are made from milk boiled down slowly until it thickens (rabadi) or until it takes on a fudge like consistency (khoya). Varieties include: *barfi*, a crumbly Indian fudge often flavoured with nuts; *gulub jamun*, deep-fried dumplings in syrup; *halwa*: nuts, fruits and vegetables cooked with ghee and sugar to a firm texture; *jalebi*: bright orange, crisp batter squiggles filled with syrup; *kulfi*, ice cream made from slow-cooked milk which gives a slightly grainy texture; and *rasmalai*: delicate, soft chenna dumplings served in *rabadi* (slow-cooked milk).

Tamarind

Tamarind: a brown fleshy pod with a sour-sweet flavour, used as a souring agent. Both tamarind pulp and tamarind paste are available.

Taro: the term applies to a whole range of fibrous tubers, recognisable by their brown hairy skins and white starchy flesh.

Tinda: a small, rounded member of the marrow family, with pale green skin and white flesh.

Tindola (tindori): walnut-sized 'ivy' gourds with variegated markings and a crisp, crunchy texture.

Tindola

Turmeric (haldi): a small-fingered, orange-fleshed root from which comes the powdered yellow spice powder of the same name.

Vark: fine edible foil, made from ground silver or gold, used to adorn dishes on special occasions.

White radish (mooli): long, thick white radish, with a mild flavour, used to stuff parathas in Pakistani cooking.

Yard-long beans: exceedingly long, thin green beans.

Yoghurt: traditionally made from buffalo milk, Julie Sahni suggests stirring a little soured cream into normal yoghurt to reproduce the necessary tangy flavour.

Food Shops

The range of stock in Asian food shops is huge, from fresh fruits and vegetables to staples like dals and flours. Often the emphasis is on bulk-buying and stocking up with large sacks of basmati or huge packets of spices. Area such as Southall, Tooting and Wembley have this kind of shop, sandwiched amongst stores selling alluring fabric and glittering jewellery. These shops often have a paan counter (a digestive made from shredded betel nut rolled up in a paan leaf).

NORTH

Tucked away behind Euston Station, the quiet backwater of Drummond Street is home to a number of excellent, good value Indian restaurants, and a few food shops.

Ambala

- 112 Drummond Street, NW1
- 020 7387 7886/3521
- Euston LU/Rail
- Daily 9am-9pm

Ambala have been selling Asian sweets since 1965, when their first small shop opened on this site. Ambala is now a thriving chain and the original shop has been revamped in bright colours with marble counters. Customers return again and again for excellent fudge-like barfis, sticky jalebi and takeaway packets of rasmalai. Savoury snacks include crisp vegetable samosas and packets of Bombay mix.

Indian Spice Shop

- 115-119 Drummond Street, NW1
- 020 7916 1831
- Euston LU/Rail
- Mon-Sat 9.30am-9.30pm, Sun 10am-9pm

Catering for both the local English and Indian communities, this is divided into an off-licence-cum-corner shop on one side and an Indian grocer's on the other which offers an excellent range of spices, chutneys, papads and dals, plus huge sacks of basmati.

Bina

⌨ *241 Golders Green Road, NW11*
☎ *020 8458 2366*
🕓 *Mon-Sun 8am-7pm*
🚌 *Golders Green LU*

This large Asian supermarket is strong on pre-packed goods, stocking assorted flours, spices, pulses, tinned fruits and vegetables, papads and chutneys.

Goodeats

⌨ *124 Ballards Lane, N3*
☎ *020 7349 2373*
🚌 *Finchley Central LU*
🕓 *Mon-Sat 9am-7pm*

This well-established, neatly arranged foodstore has an excellent range of stock. In addition to a good selection of Indian groceries, there is a fresh fruit and vegetable section, including fresh methi, mangoes and patra.

Q Stores

⌨ *19 Lodge Lane, N12*
☎ *020 8446 2495*
🚌 *Woodside Park LU*
🕓 *Mon-Sat 9.30am-5.45pm, Sun 10am-1pm*

Tucked away just off North Finchley's busy high street, this small, neat shop has a good selection of fresh Indian produce, from mangoes to methi, plus store cupboard staples.

NORTH-WEST

For an excellent choice of Indian food shops, especially greengrocers, visit Wembley's Ealing Road. Be warned, however, that it becomes very busy over the weekend and parking restrictions have made it hard to leave the car nearby.

Fudco

⌑ *184 Ealing Road, HA0*
☎ *020 8902 4820*
🚇 *Alperton LU*
🕐 *Daily 10.30am-6.30pm*

As importers and packagers, Fudco are a major supplier of foodstuffs from spices to dried fruits. Their own grocer's shop is a showcase for their own brand goods, stocking everything from chickpea flour to an assortment of dried chillies.

Royal Sweets

⌑ *280 Ealing Road, HA0*
☎ *020 8903 9359*
🚇 *Alperton LU*
🕐 *Tue-Sun 10am-7pm*

A friendly branch of the established Asian sweetmeat shop, selling brightly coloured halvas and savoury nibbles.

Sira Fruit–Veg

⌑ *288 Ealing Road, HA0*
☎ *020 8903 5769*
🚇 *Alperton LU*
🕐 *Daily 8am-8pm*

A roomy shop with a large fresh fruit and vegetable section, including okra, fresh curry leaves and bunches of methi. In addition, there is a selection of basic Asian groceries.

V. B. & Sons Cash and Carry

⌑ *218 Ealing Road, HA0*
☎ *020 8902 8579*
🚇 *Alperton LU*
🕐 *Mon-Fri 9.30am-6.45pm, Sat 9am-6.45pm, Sun 11am-5pm*

A huge, neatly-arranged store, aromatic with spices and bustling with customers tracking down the numerous special offers. V.B. specialises in groceries, with a huge range of spices, nuts, dried fruits, dals and flours. The freezer section contains yucca and mogo chips, samosas and samosa pastry.

Wembley Exotics
   133-135 Ealing Road, HA0
   020 8900 2607
   Alperton LU
   Daily 24 hours

Mounds of chillies, root ginger and peanuts under an awning mark this cavernous self-service store, which specialises in fresh produce. Inside is a staggering array of Asian fruits and vegetables, from guvar beans and pigeon peas to guavas and mangoes.

South-West
The main highway through Tooting is lined with a real variety of Asian food shops (halal butchers, greengrocers, foodstores and sweetshops) and a tempting choice of eateries, ranging from veteran South Indian vegetarian to Pakistani restaurants offering halal meat dishes.

Daily Fresh Foods
   152 Upper Tooting Road, SW17
   020 8767 7861
   Tooting Bec LU, Tooting Broadway LU
   Daily 8am-8pm

An eye-catching outdoor display of fresh fruit, vegetables and herbs, ranging from pumpkins and bunches of methi to passion fruit and mangoes, distinguishes this busy shop. Inside is a halal counter and a grocery section offering a limited choice of basics.

Deepak Cash and Carry
   953 Garratt Lane, SW17
   020 8767 7819
   Tooting Broadway LU
   Mon-Sat 9am-7.30pm, Sun 10am-4pm

An enormous, rather ramshackle supermarket with an extensive range of Asian foodstuffs, from provisions like poppadums and chutneys to fresh fruit and vegetables.

Asian Food Shops

Nature Fresh

▱ *126-128 Upper Tooting Road, SW17*
☏ *020 8682 4988*
🚌 *Tooting Bec LU, Tooting Broadway LU*
🕐 *Daily 7am-8pm*

This large, neatly arranged self-service greengrocer's has an excellent selection of good quality, reasonably priced produce, including patra leaves, yellow limes and chikoo.

Patel Brothers

▱ *187-91 Upper Tooting Road, SW17*
☏ *020 8672 2792*
🚌 *Tooting Bec LU, Tooting Broadway LU*
🕐 *Daily 9am-6.30pm*

A large store with a fresh fruit and vegetable section near the door. Stock includes shelves of pickles, curry pastes and spices, ghee and tinned foods. A side room is devoted mainly to rice, pulses and flours, including 32 kilogram sacks of chapati flour.

WEST

Southall, in London's western suburbs, is a busy Indian shopping area full of sari shops, jewellers, halal butchers, greengrocers and large-scale cash and carry stores, where the emphasis is on bulk-buying.

Ambala

🏠 *107 The Broadway, UB1*
☎ *020 8843 9049*
🚍 *Southall Rail*
🕐 *Daily 10am-8pm*

A branch of the established Asian sweet manufacturers.

Dokal & Sons

🏠 *133-135 The Broadway, UB1*
☎ *020 8574 1647*
🚍 *Southall Rail*
🕐 *Daily 9am-8pm*

What appears at first to be a small corner shop widens out into a huge store, filled with a comprehensive stock of groceries such as chutneys, flours, tinned vegetables, nuts and spices. Now coming up to its 30th year, it is run with friendly enthusiasm by Mr Dokal and his family.

Sira Cash and Carry

🏠 *128 The Broadway, UB1*
☎ *020 8574 2280*
🚍 *Southall Rail*
🕐 *Daily 8am-8pm*

A roomy shop with a good range of stock including flours, pulses, spices and chutneys. In addition there is an excellent, extensive greengrocery with an aisle of fruit including chikoo, limes, guavas and tiny green mangoes for pickling, and Asian vegetables such as karela, tindola and fresh chickpeas.

Branch: 43 South Road, UB1 (020 8571 4529); Open daily 8am-9pm

Asian Food Shops

EAST

Focal points for Indian shopping in the East End are the area around Brick Lane (home to the Bengali community) and, further out, Green Street at Upton Park.

Ambala

⊞ *55 Brick Lane, E1*

☎ *020 7247 8569*

🚇 *Aldgate East LU*

🕐 *Mon-Sat 10am-8pm, Sun 9.30am-7.30pm*

A branch of the Asian sweet manufacturers (see under Central for more details).

Taj Stores

⊞ *112-14a Brick Lane, E1*

☎ *020 7377 0061*

🚇 *Aldgate East LU*

🕐 *Daily 9am-9pm*

A comprehensive food store, serving the local Bengali community, which combines a halal meat counter, a greengrocery section and a mini-supermarket selling grocery items such as pulses and spices.

GREEN STREET, E7

This long East End road is characterised by a mixture of High Street chain stores, a jellied eel and mash shop and an assortment of Asian stores, selling everything from wedding saris and gold jewellery to bargain boxes of mangoes and sweetmeats.

Bharat

⊞ *4-6 Carlton Terrace, Green Street, E7*

☎ *020 8572 6393*

🚇 *Upton Park LU*

🕐 *Daily 9am-8pm*

This large store is aimed at those who buy in bulk, stocking things like huge 15 litre tins of ghee and 10 kilogram sacks of basmati. The freezers are jammed with Indian fast food, from halal kofta kebabs to spicy chicken nuggets. Fresh fruit and veg, such as aubergines and chillies, can be found at Bharat's small sister shop, over the road at No. 263.

Ambala

Green Village

⌗ *10a Carlton Terrace, Green Street, E7*

☎ *020 8503 4809*

🚇 *Upton Park LU*

🕐 *Daily 8am-7pm*

A large, neat greengrocer's, full of the smell of ripe mangoes at the time of my visit. Stock included more unusual items such as rolls of patra leaves, gunda (used in chutneys), sweet tamarind pods and Thai mangosteens.

Kishan The Mill Shop

⌗ *20 Carlton Terrace, Green Street, E7*

☎ *020 8471 0008*

🚇 *Upton Park LU*

🕐 *Mon-Sat 9am-7pm, Sun 10am-6pm*

A grocer's, with a large selection of spices, cooking oils, nuts, nibbles (such as cassava chips) and pulses, and brightly-coloured garlands of flowers hanging down behind the till.

Queen's Market

⌗ *Green Street, E7 (on the corner of Queen's Road)*

🚇 *Upton Park LU*

🕐 *Tue-Sat 8am-5pm*

Stalls here sell an assortment of goods, from curtain fabric to household wares. The presence of a local Asian community is reflected in halal butchers and stalls offering a huge range of Asian fruit and vegetables.

Sunfresh

⌗ *11-12 Carlton Terrace, Green Street, E7*

☎ *020 8470 3031*

🚇 *Upton Park LU*

🕐 *Daily 8am-7pm*

Funky music blares in this large store which offers an array of Indian fruit and veg as well as a grocery section with rice, pulses, chutneys and spices.

Eating Places

Over the last decade London's Indian restaurants have undergone a noticeable renaissance, with chic new restaurants offering regional Indian food, often presented in a Western style but with the emphasis on authentic flavours and spicing.

CENTRAL

India Club £££

⌨ *Strand Continental Hotel, 143 Strand, WC2*
☎ *020 7836 0650*
🚌 *Temple LU*

A long-established restaurant recommended by Indian friends, this is an unpretentious, friendly restaurant which offers good North Indian food at very reasonable prices.

Indian YMCA £

⌨ *41 Fitzroy Square, W1*
☎ *020 7387 0411*
🚌 *Warren Street LU*

The appetising smell of Indian cooking wafts out from this large building, adding character to its institutional air. On offer is good home-style food at student prices in a canteen atmosphere.

Malabar Junction £££

⌨ *107 Great Russell Street, WC1*
☎ *020 7580 5230*
🚌 *Tottenham Court Road LU*

A rather drab frontage hides a large airy restaurant complete with a glass-roofed dining room. South-Indian cuisine is the speciality here, from tangy idlee (steamed rice and black gram cakes) to spicy Keralan fish curry. Service is courteous and prices very reasonable given the standard of the cooking.

Ragam £££

⌨ *57 Cleveland Street, W1*
☎ *020 7636 9098*
🚌 *Goodge Street LU, Warren Street LU*

A small, modest and friendly restaurant serving excellent, good value food including South-Indian dishes such as avial or uthappam, and delicious breads.

Rasa Samudra £££

- 5 Charlotte Street, W1
- ☎ 020 7637 0222
- Goodge Street LU

An attractive Indian restaurant, specialising in Keralan seafood dishes such as kingfish and green mango curry, and crab in coconut milk.

Rasa W1 £££

- 6 Dering Street, W1
- ☎ 020 7629 1346
- Oxford Circus LU, Bond Street LU

Keralan vegetarian cuisine is on offer here, giving diners the chance to try distinctive spiced dishes such as green banana and mango curry and cashew nut patties. Round off your meal with Keralan desserts such as banana dosa (pancakes) or pal payasum (cashew rice pudding).

Veeraswamy £££

- 99 Regent Street, W1
- ☎ 020 7734 1401
- Piccadilly Circus LU

London's oldest Indian restaurant has shed its Raj image. Now owned by the Chutney Mary team it has become a sleek example of the new-wave of Indian restaurants, complete with vividly painted walls, smartly dressed staff and a menu featuring regional dishes.

NORTH

Diwana Bhel Poori House £

- 121 Drummond Street, NW1
- ☎ 020 7387 5566
- Euston LU/Rail

Tucked away behind Euston station this well-established, unpretentious South-Indian vegetarian restaurant serves up dosai, idlee and good value thali at remarkably reasonable prices.

Great Nepalese £L

⌧ *48 Eversholt Street, NW1*
☎ *020 7388 6737)*
🚇 *Euston LU/Rail*

A Euston institution, much-frequented by hungry commuters, which in addition to standard curry house fare serves a selection of Nepalese specialities.

Jai Krishna £

⌧ *161 Stroud Green Road, N4*
☎ *020 7272 1680*
🚇 *Finsbury Park LU/Rail*

An unpretentious restaurant offering cheap Indian vegetarian food. Refreshingly, the menu features less well known Indian vegetables such as tindora and dudi curries.

Majjo's £

⌧ *1 Fortis Green Road, N2*
☎ *020 8883 4357*
🚇 *East Finchley LU*

This small, smart, friendly take-away serves up superior Pakistani home-cooking. The meat is halal and there is a range of more unusual vegetarian dishes such as patra. Sample tastes are offered to those trying to choose from the array of dishes available.

The Parsee £LLL

⌧ *34 Highgate Hill, N19*
☎ *020 7272 9091*
🚇 *Archway LU*

Chef Cyrus Todiwala, himself a Parsee, offers Londoners a rare chance to sample authentic Parsee dishes such as lamb dhansak.

Raavi Kebab Halal Tandoori £

⌧ *125 Drummond Street, NW1*
🚇 *Euston Square LU*
☎ *020 7388 1780*

A small, unpretentious restaurant which specialises in delicious, chilli-hot kebabs, freshly grilled over charcoal.

Rani *££*

▣ *7 Long Lane, N3*
☏ *020 8349 4386/2646*
🚌 *Finchley Central LU*

Authentic Gujarati vegetarian cuisine. All dishes, from the home-made chutneys to the breads, are carefully prepared, and the exciting menu includes delights such as banana methi and tindora curry.

Ravi Shankar *£*

▣ *133-135 Drummond Street, NW1*
☏ *020 7388 6458*
🚌 *Euston LU/Rail*

A popular Indian vegetarian restaurant offering reasonably priced dishes such as masala or de luxe dosai.

WEST

Chutney Mary *££££*

▣ *535 King's Road, SW10*
☏ *020 7351 3113*
🚌 *Fulham Broadway LU*

This large, glamorous restaurant, complete with an attractive conservatory dining area, serves top-notch Indian cooking in an enjoyably buzzy atmosphere. The menu features carefully chosen regional specialities, with the chilli-marinated lamb chops and Alphonso mango ice cream being particular highlights.

NORTH-WEST

Karahi King *£*

▣ *213 East Lane, HA0*
☏ *020 8904 2760/4994*
🚌 *North Wembley LU*

Despite being distinctly off the beaten track, housed in a non-descript arcade of shops just off the North Circular, the Karahi King does excellent business – as the row of cars parked outside testifies. The decor is functional, but the service is polite and the food gutsy and tasty: from grilled kebabs to Karahi Lamb Chops – tiny, flavourful chops in a rich, thick tomato-based sauce. It's unlicensed but you can stock up next with booze at the off-licence next door.

Sakonis £

⌨ *119-121 Ealing Road, HA0*

☎ *020 8903 9601*

🚌 *Alperton LU*

This bright, cheery vegetarian diner attracts queues of would-be diners (many of them in family groups), waiting patiently by the paan stall and take-away counter to sit down in the back room. The menu promises a wide range of snacks, mains, drinks and desserts: seriously chilli-hot dosai, chilli paneer, falooda, chikoo ice cream and delicious, salty-sweet freshly-squeezed lime juice.

SOUTH-WEST

Lahore Karahi £

⌨ *1 Tooting High Street, SW17*

☎ *020 8767 2477*

🚌 *Tooting Broadway LU*

On Tooting's bustling high street, this down-to-earth café serves up tasty Indian food at low prices, pulling in a steady stream of customers.

Shree Krishna £

⌨ *192-194 Tooting High Street, SW17*

☎ *020 8672 4250*

🚌 *Tooting Broadway LU*

This large, well-established Gujurati restaurant is full of enthusiasts who appreciate both the good South Indian vegetarian food and the reasonable prices.

SOUTH- EAST

The Painted Heron £££££

⌨ *205-209 Kennington Lane, SE11*

🚌 *Kennington LU*

☎ *020 7351 5232*

This light, spacious modern Indian restaurant, complete with a large courtyard dining area, specialises in exemplary, refined contemporary dishes, using upmarket ingredients to elegant effect.

Asian Eating Places

EAST

Café Spice Namaste *££££*

🖃 *16 Prescott Street, E1*

☎ *020 7488 9242*

🚌 *Aldgate East LU, Tower Hill LU*

Chef Cyrus Todiwala is committed to bringing true Indian cookery, in all its variety and glory, to the London restaurant scene. From within a brightly-decorated old courthouse he serves up an extensive menu, including many unusual Goan and Parsee dishes.

OUTER LONDON

Madhu's *£*

🖃 *39 South Road, UB1*

☎ *020 8574 1897*

🚌 *Southall Rail*

A popular Southall eaterie, attracting Asians and non-Asians alike, which serves tasty Punjabi food such as Masala Fish and Karahi Chicken, with good breads.

New Asian Tandoori Centre (Roxy) *££*

🖃 *114-118 The Green, Southall, UB2*

☎ *020 8574 2597*

🚌 *Southall Rail*

This large, spic-and-span Punjabi eaterie offers both take-away food and a restaurant. Prices are cheap and this is a great place for group eating so that you can sample lots of dishes. The smooth, creamy lassi, ranging from salt to pistachio, is highly recommended.

Rita's Samosa Centre *£*

🖃 *112 The Broadway, Southall, UB1*

☎ *020 8571 2100*

🚌 *Southall Rail*

This cheery diner, complete with 'take-away' paan and kebab kiosks on the street, offers an assortment of snacks, chaats, curries, breads and rice. Drinks include sweet, thick mango juice and luridly pink, rose syrup-flavoured falooda.

Cookbooks

The Indian Kitchen
Monisha Bharadwaj
A well-illustrated and fascinating guide to Indian ingredients, plus simple recipes.

Madhur Jaffrey's Ultimate Curry Bible
Madhur Jaffrey
This wonderful cookbook lives up to its grandiose title, with Madhur Jaffrey exploring the curry around the world, from fish curry in Singapore to Pakistani-style kofta curry, in a succession of appetising and achievable recipes.

Madhur Jaffrey's Indian Cookery
Madhur Jaffrey
A clearly-written, accessible introduction to this great cuisine.

Fifty Great Curries of India
Camellia Panjabi
A beautifully-presented, illustrated guide which takes readers through the art of making curries clearly and in depth. Recipes range from classic dishes, such as Goanese pork Vindaloo, to less familiar ones such as Gujurati mango and yoghurt curry.

Classic Indian Cooking
Julie Sahni
A well-written Indian cookery book which is readable, practical and authoritative.

Classic Indian Vegetarian Cooking
Julie Sahni
An inspirational book filled with appetising recipes conveying the less well-known world of Indian vegetarian cuisine in all its subtlety.

Chinese London

Far East Bakery

The original points of entry for the Chinese community in Britain were Liverpool and London: the ports into which Chinese seamen with the East India Company arrived and settled. The Limehouse area, near the docks in the East End, was London's first 'Chinatown', with the first immigrants arriving during the eighteenth century when Britain's tea trade with China was booming. Sailors jumped ship and set up businesses running laundries, shops or becoming ship's chandlers. In the 1950s, the development of the laundromat and the domestic washing machine badly affected the laundry business, so catering became an alternative source of work.

Limehouse was practically destroyed in the Blitz, and post-war restrictive regulations imposed on non-British workers by the Seamen's Union hit affected Chinese seamen hard. So, both alternative livelihoods and accommodation had to be found. Soho, a run-down, derelict area with a bad reputation and low property prices, saw an influx of Chinese around the Gerrard Street area in the 1950s. The first Chinese restaurants in Soho were chop-suey outlets, opened in the 1940s to cater for American GIs and British servicemen who had acquired a taste for Chinese food overseas. Restaurants catering specifically for the growing Chinese community also opened in the area. The Communist revolution in China in 1949 meant a further wave of immigration from China into Britain in the 1950s and 1960s, mostly from the British colony of Hong Kong. As a result, the Chinese community in Soho expanded further.

The area bounded by Shaftesbury Avenue, Leicester Square, Charing Cross Road and Wardour Street is a rectangle of predominantly Chinese shops, businesses, gambling clubs and restaurants. Gerrard Street, now pedestrianised, comes complete with Chinese-style arches and pagoda-style phone boxes.

Two annual festivals have become major events in London, attracting people from outside the Chinese community. Chinese New Year, according to the Chinese lunar calendar, takes place either in late January or early February, and is celebrated with gifts to children of 'ang pow', money in lucky red envelopes, and a lion dance procession. Special dishes appear on menus in the restaurants. Each year is attributed to one of the twelve animals in the Chinese zodiac – with the Year of the Dragon being especially auspicious – and the New Year celebrations feature the animal to which the year belongs. The autumnal Moon Festival, around September, is marked by special moon cakes and a lion dance. During both these festivals, Chinatown is filled with Chinese of all generations, colourful lanterns and decorations and street-stalls selling snacks and gifts.

Chinese Cuisine

This ancient cuisine is both complex and various. Underlying it are the 'yin and yang' principles, translated in culinary terms into hot, cold and neutral, with ingredients allocated different properties. A huge range of ingredients is used, with nothing wasted. There is an old saying that 'A Cantonese will eat anything with four legs except for a piece of furniture and anything that flies apart from a kite'. Textures play an important role in Chinese cooking and include some that are foreign to Western sensibilities, with slippery, jelly-like textures being prized.

Each of China's regions has its own characteristic cuisine, influenced by climate and the availability of ingredients. It's customary, however, to group China culinarily into four broad geographical groups: Peking/Northern, Shanghai/Eastern, Sichuan/Western and Cantonese/Southern. The cuisine of the North is distinguished by its use of grains other than rice, such as wheat, corn and millet, in the form of breads, noodles, dumplings and pancakes. Because the ancient Imperial Court was situated in Peking, elaborate dishes such as Peking Duck are characteristic of this cuisine. The Mongols introduced lamb, which is eaten more widely here than in other parts of China.

Eastern cuisine is famous for its fresh fish and seafood. Rich, sweet seasonings are a hallmark and popular techniques include stir-frying, steaming, red-cooking (slow simmering in soy sauce) and blanching. Sichuan cooking, from the provinces of Hunan, Yunnan and Sichuan in Western China, is marked by its use of fiery chillies, garlic, ginger and Sichuan peppercorns producing a vigorous, strongly flavoured cuisine. Two regional foodstuffs are aromatic peppercorns and chilli-pickled mustard plant.

Cantonese cuisine is the best-known Chinese cooking outside China, because of the large numbers of Chinese from southern Canton who emigrated in the nineteenth century. Strong, overwhelming flavourings are avoided and, instead, a harmonious blend of colours, textures and flavours is sought. Stir-frying epitomises Cantonese cooking, with the freshness and colours of ingredients retained and a minimum of seasonings added. Dim sum, the small steamed and fried dumplings eaten at lunchtime, are another Cantonese speciality.

Glossary

Agar agar: a vegetarian setting agent obtained from seaweed which does not require refrigeration to set. Available either in powdered form or translucent strands.

Azuki beans: small red beans, used primarily in cakes and desserts and available both whole and in sweetened paste form.

Bamboo shoots: fresh bamboo shoots are occasionally available. Tinned bamboo shoots, either whole or sliced, are easily found.

Bean curd (doufu): a soya bean product which has always been a valuable source of protein in Chinese cooking. Fresh ivory-coloured bean curd has a firm custard texture and bland flavour. It is sold in the chilled section, packed in water. Deep-fried bean curd has a golden colour and spongy texture and is found in packets in the chilled section. Bean curd 'cheese', either red or white, is fermented bean curd with a strong, salty taste and is sold in jars. Dried bean-curd sheets are sold in packets.

Bean sprouts: white crispy sprouts of the mung bean; also available are the larger, nuttier soya bean sprouts, which should be cooked before eating.

Beche-de-mer: sea cucumber or sea slug, it is sold dried and prized as a delicacy.

Bird's nest: the key ingredient of the famous delicacy, bird's nest soup. The nests of a cave-dwelling species of swallow are coated with a gelatinous saliva and it is this which gives the soup its prized consistency. The nests are sold either whole or in fragments for high prices.

Black beans: small black soya beans, fermented with salt and spices, with a pungent flavour.

Chilli oil: a transparent oil, tinted red from chillies, sold in small bottles and with a powerful chilli kick.

Black beans

Chinese broccoli (gaai laan): a thick-stalked vegetable with large rounded leaves and white flowers.

Chinese cabbage (bok choy): similar in appearance to Swiss chard, with dark green leaves and thick white stems. Green bok choy, with green leaves and stems, is also available.

Chinese chives: long, dark green, flat leaves, with a stronger and more pungent odour and flavour than English chives; also sold blanched and complete with buds.

Bok choy

Chinese cinnamon: cassia bark, sold in sticks similar to cinnamon but larger and rougher with a stronger flavour.

Chinese flowering cabbage (choi sum): a leafy vegetable with rounded leaves, small yellow flowers and long stems.

Chinese leaves: a large tight head of white-green crinkly leaves with a crunchy texture; widely available.

Chinese mushrooms: black, dried shitake mushrooms with distinctive meaty flavour. Prices vary according to the size and thickness of the caps.

Chinese chives

Chinese sausages: these resemble small, fatty salamis, but they must be cooked before eating. There are two sorts: pork and pork and liver, the latter being darker in colour. They are found in packets or hanging up in bunches with other dried meats.

Coriander: this green herb, similar in appearance to flat-leaved continental parsley but with a distinctive sharp flavour, is one of the few herbs used in Chinese cooking.

Five-spice powder: fragrant, golden-brown powder made from five or sometimes six ground spices, with the four base spices being star-anise, Chinese cinnamon, cloves and fennel seeds. Sichuan peppercorns, ginger and cardamom are the additions.

Ginger: an aromatic root available fresh.

Glutinous rice: rounded rice grains with a sticky texture when cooked, used in both sweet and savoury dishes.

Ginger

Golden needles: long dried buds of the tiger-lily flower.

Longan: a small brown-skinned fruit, related to the lychee, with translucent flesh and glossy black seed (also known as 'dragon's eye' fruit). Available either tinned or fresh.

Lotus leaves: the large leaves of the water-lily plant, available dried and used to wrap food for cooking.

Lotus root: a crunchy root with a decorative tracery of holes, available fresh, in sausage-like links, or tinned.

Mooli: a large, long white radish, with crispy white flesh.

Mustard Greens (gaai choi): a green large-leafed plant. The bitter varieties are pickled rather than cooked.

Noodles: *cellophane noodles* (also known as beanthread, glass or transparent noodles): fine thread-like noodles made from mung beans which need soaking before they can be easily cut; *egg noodles*: made from wheat flour, egg and water, distinguished by their yellow colour; *rice noodles* and *vermicelli* are dried, white noodles of varying widths made from rice flour which need soaking before use; *river rice noodles* (sarhor noodles) are made from ground rice and water, steamed in thin sheets and cut into strips. Fresh-river rice noodles are sold in clear packets, and usually stored near the chilled section.

Egg noodles

Potato flour: fine white flour, made from cooked potatoes, used as a thickener.

Rice vinegar: mild vinegars, ranging from delicate white rice vinegar to sweet red rice vinegar and rich black rice vinegar.

Rice wine: made from glutinous rice, yeast and water, this is used for both drinking and cooking.

Sauces: *chilli bean sauce*, a hot, spicy, dark sauce made from soya beans and chillies; *chilli sauce,* a bright red sweet chilli sauce; *hoisin sauce*, a thick, brown fruity sauce; *oyster sauce*, a thick, brown sauce made from oysters; *soy sauce*, a dark brown salty liquid made from fermented soya beans (available as thin, salty Light Soy Sauce or as thicker, sweeter Dark Soy Sauce); and *yellow bean sauce*, a thick, brown sauce made from fermented yellow beans.

Sesame oil: a nutty, golden-coloured oil made from sesame seeds.

Shrimps, dried: small, shelled, dried pink shrimps, with a strong salty flavour.

Oyster sauce

Spring roll wrappers: white paper-thin wrappers, available in different sizes. Found in either the chilled or freezer sections.

Star-anise: dark brown, star-shaped pod with a distinctive liquorice flavour and scent.

Straw mushrooms: cone-shaped mushrooms, usually available canned.

Sichuan peppercorns: fragrant, reddish-brown 'peppercorns', which are the dried berries of a shrub.

Sichuan pickled vegetables: mustard green tubers, pickled in salt and hot chillies, which are a speciality of Sichuan province.

Tangerine peel: in its dried form, in dark-brown pieces, this is used as a flavouring in Chinese cooking.

Thousand-year-old eggs: preserved duck eggs, with a pungent flavour, which are in fact only about a hundred days old.

Water chestnuts: the crunchy bulbs of a waterplant. Fresh, brown-skinned bulbs are sometimes found, but tinned water chestnuts are easily available.

Water spinach (ong chai): a trian-gular-leafed plant with a mild, spinach-like flavour.

Winter melon: a large green gourd with white flesh, available whole or in pieces, and often used to make soup.

Water spinach

Wonton skins: small squares of yellow egg-noodle dough, used to wrap up dumplings. Found in either chilled or freezer sections.

Wood ears: black, crinkled, dried fungus with a beige underside.

Food Shops

For decades, Gerrard Street and its side-streets have housed Chinese food shops, an important and thriving part of London's Chinese community. Sadly however, as the book goes to press and despite protests from the Chinese community, developers have moved three Chinese food shops out from their current premises on Newport Court and Newport Place.

CENTRAL

Far East

⊞ *13 Gerrard Street, W1*
☎ *020 7437 6148*
🚏 *Leicester Square LU*
🕐 *Daily 10am-7pm*

During the day Far East functions as a friendly bakery-cum-tea-shop selling Chinese cakes and pastries freshly baked on the premises (including sticky, glazed char-siu buns, curry beef puffs and egg custard tarts). At night it metamorphoses into a restaurant.

Golden Gate Hong Supermarket

⊞ *14 Lisle Street, WC2*
☎ *020 7437 0014*
🚏 *Leicester Square LU*
🕐 *Daily 9am-8.30pm*

Boxes of fresh fruit and vegetables under a canopy signal this pleasant, neatly-arranged shop. The vegetables inside are labelled in English and there is a good basic stock.

Good Harvest Fish and Meat Market

⊞ *65 Shaftesbury Avenue, W1*
☎ *020 7734 4900*
🚏 *Leicester Square LU*
🕐 *Daily 11am-7pm*

From its new, much smaller Shaftesbury Avenue premises, this established Chinese fishmonger offers fresh scallops in their shells, live lobsters, raw king prawns and fish such as catfish and pomfret. Food writer Fuchsia Dunlop, author of Sichuan Cookery, recommends their 'very fresh' sea bass.

Loon Fung Supermarket

▢ *42-44 Gerrard Street, W1*
☎ *020 7437 7332*
🚌 *Leicester Square LU*
🕐 *Daily 10am-8pm*

Well over thirty years old, Loon Fung is the oldest and largest Chinese supermarket in Soho, occupying a key slot on Gerrard Street and always bustling with customers. Boxes of fresh fruit such as lychees, longans and persimmons, are displayed outside on the pavement with a large fresh vegetable section inside. A butcher's counter sells basic pork cuts plus more unusual items such as duck and chicken feet and duck tongues. All the staples are stocked across a wide range.

New Loon Moon Supermarket

▢ *9a Gerrard Street, W1*
☎ *020 7734 9940*
🚌 *Leicester Square LU*
🕐 *Daily 10.30am-8pm*

In the heart of Gerrard Street, this veteran food shop catches the eyes with an attractive display of consistently good quality fresh fruit and vegetables, such as gai lan and longans and Emperor lychees. Inside the busy shop is crammed with Chinese foodstuffs: noodles, sauces, tinned ingredients and teas. A large backroom contains chilled and freezer sections, cookware and an impressive range of spices.

See Woo

▢ *19 Lisle Street, WC2*
☎ *020 7439 8325*
🚌 *Leicester Square LU*
🕐 *Daily 10am-8pm*

This large, sprawling shop has an excellent, comprehensive stock of chilled, frozen, dried, tinned and bottled ingredients. There is a large fresh fruit and vegetable section, which regularly features more unusual items. A basement room contains bowls of all sizes, woks, steamers and other Chinese cookware.

Chinese Food Shops

Wonderful Patisserie

⌨ *45 Gerrard Street, W1*

☎ *020 7734 7629*

🚌 *Leicester Square LU*

🕐 *Daily 11am-7pm*

This bright and cheerful cake shop does a roaring trade in Chinese biscuits and cakes, both loose and pre-packed in packets, boxes and tins.

NORTH

Maysun Markets

⌨ *869 Finchley Road, NW11*

☎ *020 8455 4773*

🚌 *Golders Green LU*

🕐 *Mon-Sat 9am-7.30pm*

A small, pleasantly ramshackle shop, run with friendly cheerfulness by its owner, selling a mixture of household goods and Chinese foodstuffs. It has a basic stock of dried, bottled and tinned ingredients and some fresh produce.

Wing Yip (London) Ltd

⌨ *395 Edgware Road, NW2*

☎ *020 8450 0422*

🚌 *Colindale LU*

🕐 *Mon-Sat 9.30am-7pm, Sun 11.30am-5.30pm*

This enormous superstore at Staples Corner is the place for bulk-buying Chinese food. It has an impressive selection, ranging from freezers of dim sum to delicacies such as bird's nest and shark's fin. There is a small selection of fresh vegetables and foodstuffs such as bean curd and noodles.

SOUTH

Wing Thai Supermarket

⌨ *13 Electric Avenue, SW9*

☎ *020 7738 5898*

🚌 *Brixton LU/Rail*

🕐 *Mon-Sat 10am-7pm*

Tucked away behind the bustling fruit and veg stalls outside, this roomy store has a small fresh produce section and fish counter at the front but is particularly strong on bottled, tinned and frozen goods.

Eating Places

For many years, London's Chinese restaurants offered predominantly Cantonese food. As a result several places offer excellent dim sum – an assortment of steamed and fried dumplings traditionally served at lunchtime – which are a speciality of Canton. Today, however, the Chinese restaurant cuisine is beginning to reflect China's regional diversity, with, for example, restaurants and cafés offering Fujianese or Sichuan dishes beginning to appear.

With Chinatown overrun by tourists, standards have slipped in many of its restaurants, though some continue to offer excellent meals. If you enjoy good Chinese food, then you should also head for Bayswater, where a cluster of excellent Chinese restaurants attract enthusiastic and discerning diners.

CENTRAL

Café de HK *£-££*
⌨ *47-49 Charing Cross Road, WC2*
☎ *020 7534 9898*
🚌 *Leicester Square LU*

One of a new-wave of more contemporary, casual eateries opening up in Chinatown – good for a quick one-dish meal of rice, noodles or soup.

Joy King Lau *££*
⌨ *3 Leicester Street, WC2*
☎ *020 7437 1132*
🚌 *Leicester Square LU*

A Chinatown veteran, housed in a long narrow town house on a Soho side street and offering a classic Cantonese menu, with dim-sum especially popular.

Ecapital *£££*
⌨ *8 Gerrard Street, W1*
☎ *020 7434 3838*
🚌 *Leicester Square LU*

Unusually for London's Chinese restaurant scene, this smart, brightly decorated restaurant specialises in Shanghai rather than Cantonese dishes. These include classic cold starters such as pig's ear and jellyfish and beggar's chicken, complemented by a carefully chosen wine-list. The courteous staff are happy to explain the menu.

Fung Shing £££

⊞ 15 Lisle Street, WC2

☎ 020 7437 1539

🚌 Leicester Square LU

A peaceful, civilized restaurant noted for its authentic food, serving impeccable versions of dishes such as black bean braised hotpot and duck and plum sauce hotpot.

Golden Dragon ££

⊞ 28-29 Gerrard Street, W1

☎ 020 7734 2763

🚌 Leicester Square LU

Large, gaudily-decorated with splendid writhing dragons and efficiently staffed, this is a quintessential Chinatown restaurant. It's noted for its dim sum and is correspondingly busy at lunchtime on Sundays.

Hakkasan ££-£££

⊞ 8 Hanway Place, W1

☎ 020 7927 7000

🚌 Tottenham Court Road LU

Intriguingly situated down a back-street alley, this glamorous restaurant (set up by Wagamama founder Alan Yau) with its night-club décor and popular cocktail bar, is noted for its dainty lunchtime dim sum.

Hunan ££££

⊞ 51 Pimlico Road, SW1

☎ 020 7730 5712

🚌 Sloane Square LU

This upmarket veteran Pimlico-based restaurant, run with considerable charm by the velvet-gloved and iron handed Mr Peng offers a rare chance to sample deliciously fresh and flavourful Sichuanese food.

Imperial China ££

⊞ White Bear Yard, 25A Lisle Street, WC2

☎ 020 7734 3388

🚌 Leicester Square LU

Picturesquely tucked away in a courtyard, this upmarket restaurant offers excellent dim sum during the day.

Memories of China £££

▢ *65-69 Ebury Street, SW1*

☎ *020 7730 7734*

🚌 *Victoria LU/Rail*

Founded by acclaimed Chinese food writer Ken Lo, this elegant restaurant is home to the considerable cooking talents of Chef Butt. The cooking here, which showcases dishes from around China, is refined but flavourful, with signature dishes including lobster with hand-pulled noodles.

New World £££

▢ *1 Gerrard Place, W1*

☎ *020 7434 0396*

🚌 *Leicester Square LU*

Vast and invariably busy, New World is very much an old-style Chinatown restaurant, one of the few serving dim sum from trolleys, rather than à la carte.

Phoenix Palace £££

▢ *3-5 Glentworth Street, NW1*

☎ *020 7486 3515*

🚌 *Baker Street LU*

This spacious restaurant, perpetually filled to the brim with diners, is an impressively smooth-running operation, noted for its high-quality dim sum and a la carte menu alike.

Poons £££

▢ *4 Leicester Street, WC2*

☎ *020 7437 1528*

🚌 *Leicester Square LU*

A veteran Chinatown name, tucked away in a side-street, this restaurant continues to serve reasonably-priced, flavourful Cantonese food including speciality wind-dried meats.

Royal China £££

▢ *24-26 Baker Street, W1*

☎ *020 7487 4688*

🚌 *Baker Street LU*

See main entry p.128.

Yauatcha *££-£££*

▦ *15 Broadwick Street, W1*

☎ *020 7494 8888*

🚌 *Oxford Circus LU*

Restaurateur Alan Yau's latest basement restaurant is a wonderfully glamorous affair, complete with a long tank of eye-catching tropical fish, a light-studded ceiling and embroidered turquoise-coloured seating. Jewel-like dim sum, such as vegetarian shark's fin with gold leaf, look as good as they taste, with fresh seafood figuring prominently. The ground floor serves exquisitely presented East-West fusion patisserie and a rarefied selection of teas.

Yming *££-£££*

▦ *35-36 Greek Street, W1*

☎ *020 7734 2721*

🚌 *Leicester Square LU, Tottenham Court Road LU*

On a Soho street corner but away from the hustle of Chinatown itself, Yming is a peaceful, intimate restaurant, offering a very civilised Chinese dining experience. Staff are notably polite and helpful, happy to make recommendations and suggestions.

NORTH

Green Cottage *££*

▦ *9 New College Parade, Finchley Road, NW3*

☎ *020 7722 5305*

🚌 *Finchley Road Rail*

A down-to-earth restaurant offering Chinatown-standard Cantonese food in a North London setting.

WEST

Mandarin Kitchen *£££*

▦ *14-16 Queensway, W2*

☎ *020 7727 9468*

🚌 *Bayswater LU, Queensway LU*

Peering in through the large windows to the dimly-lit interior, one is reminded of an aquarium. Appropriately so, as this large, busy restaurant specialises in Cantonese seafood such as succulent steamed scallops in the shell, and fresh crab with ginger.

Royal China *££*

⌨ *13 Queensway, W2*

☎ *020 7221 2535*

🚌 *Bayswater LU, Queensway LU*

Such is the fame of the dim sum here that, at the weekend, queues start forming before the restaurant opens its doors at noon. Inside, the large, roomy restaurant is decorated with 70s opulence: shiny black tiled walls festooned with golden lacquerwork and masses of mirrors. Service is efficient, which is just as well considering how busy it gets. Dim sum dishes are spot on: from delicate mangetout dumplings (filled with pea-shoots) to soft, spongy char siu bau.

Branch: 24-26 Baker Street, W1

East

Shanghai *££*

⌨ *41 Kingsland High Street, E8*

☎ *020 7254 2878*

🚌 *Dalston Kingsland Rail*

What was formerly an eel and pie shop, complete with traditional tiles, has now been transformed into a busy Chinese restaurant. Good dim sum and a bargain lunchtime buffet pull in the punters.

Cookbooks

Sichuan Cookery
Fuchsia Dunlop
This elegantly written, attractively packaged cookbook offers a fascinating and appetising insight into Sichuan cuisine.

Chinese Cookery
Ken Hom
An accessible, basic introduction to Chinese cooking.

The Chinese Kitchen
Deh-Ta Hsiung
Offering a considerable insight into Chinese cuisine, this attractive, well-illustrated book offers both extensive information on Chinese ingredients plus a most appealing range of recipes.

Heart and Soul
Kylie Kwong
Kylie Kwong's appetising book combines personal recollections with tasty, clearly written recipes

Classic Chinese Cookbook
Yan-Kit So
A classic Chinese cookbook by a wonderful food writer who knew how to share her knowledge in the most accessible way. This is both lucidly written and well-illustrated with mouthwatering, workable recipes.

French London

French London

Maison Bertaux

London's first serious experience of the French was when it fell under Norman rule following the 1066 Conquest. French became the language both of the Court and local government. London saw an influx of merchant traders from northern France and a number of religious orders, including the influential Knights Templar, established themselves in the city.

The next major increase in London's French community was due to the arrival of French-speaking Protestants, known in France as 'Huguenots', who came to England to escape Catholic persecution. In France, the limited privileges granted to Huguenots by the 1598 Edict of Nantes were gradually eroded, with restrictions placed on Protestant worship. In 1680 many Huguenots fled, and Charles II offered them asylum in 1681. Four years later in France, the Edict of Nantes was revoked and Protestant churches were ordered to be destroyed. Following this, between 40,000 and 50,000 Huguenots moved to England, with half of them thought to have settled in London. By the year 1700, Huguenots formed around five per cent of London's population.

Spitalfields and Soho were the two main areas in London in which the Huguenots settled. Spitalfields (also home to a community of Flemish weavers) attracted the Huguenot weavers, who eventually contributed to a prosperous period in the British silk industry. In Soho, where the Huguenots took over a chapel built for Greek Christians and used it until 1822, the new immigrants were craftspeople, such as watch and clockmakers, bookbinders and gold and silversmiths.

Our popular perception of the French as stylish and fashionable was apparent even then, with a 1700 report declaring, 'The English have now so great an esteem for the workmanship of the French refugees that hardly any thing vends without a gallic name'. Huguenot merchants, alongside other immigrants, played an important part in London's financial life. When the Bank of England was setup in 1694, several of the founder directors were Huguenots. In addition to influencing crafts and business, Huguenot academics played a notable role in the worlds of science and technology, with many joining the Royal Society.

London's French community were joined by subsequent groups of refugees, with an influx of royalists fleeing the 1789 French Revolution, and political refugees escaping the 1870 Commune. Gradually, further institutions catering to French expats were set up, from a chapel in the French Embassy to French schools in Lisle Street in 1865. In 1867, the French Hospital and Dispensary in Shaftesbury Avenue was established, while 1893 saw the completion of the French Protestant Church in Soho Square. Paul Villars wrote in 1905 in 'Living London' of the French community that 'In London, as in France, they use the café as a club' – the Café Royal was a favourite haunt. During the eighteenth and nineteenth centuries, however, the French community slowly became assimilated into English society. Huguenot families such as the Courtaulds and Oliviers became established members of British society. Today, Spitalfields' Georgian houses and Huguenot names like Fournier Street are reminders of the area's former prosperity under the silk merchants.

During the Second World War, Soho, once home to the Huguenots, became a focal point for the French Resistance, with the York Minster pub acting as the headquarters of the Free French Forces. Generally known 'the French pub' it has now been renamed the French House; General de Gaulle used to shop for his coffee at Angelucci's around the corner on Frith Street.

Today, London's French enclave is in elegant, affluent South Kensington, with the French Lycée on Cromwell Road and the French Institute at Queensberry Place providing two focal points. Serving this community are a cluster of upmarket food shops and chic patisseries offering real croissants and delectable cakes.

French Cuisine

French cuisine has been highly influential throughout Europe, with Britain especially living in its shadow. As the current edition of the Larousse Gastronomique baldly states, 'At the beginning of the twentieth century, French cookery gained supremacy throughout the world.' Today the language of the kitchen continues to be French, from 'chef' to culinary terms such as 'sauté'.

Still a predominantly agricultural country, France has retained many of the regional ingredients such as cheeses, hams and herbs which give its cuisine character and flavour; local markets still abound selling locally-grown seasonal produce. Standards of produce have remained high and the simple pleasures of life, such as a decent loaf of bread and some good cheese, are easily found.

An enduring regionalism means that even in the twenty-first century local dishes are cherished, rather than discarded in a mass move

towards uniformity. As a result, French cuisine contains wonderfully contrasting strands: from the Mediterranean flavours of Provençal cooking, laden with tomatoes, basil and olive oil, to the cream, cider and calvados based dishes of Normandy.

French cooking can be divided broadly into 'haute cuisine', the cookery of grand restaurants and hotels; 'cuisine du terroir', regional cooking found in provincial restaurants; and 'cuisine grand-mère', the everyday food found in people's homes and in cheap, down-to-earth bistros. Haute cuisine has influenced chefs and cookery schools around the world. Naturally, it has followed trends and fashions. In the 1970s and 1980s 'nouvelle cuisine' – a move away from the over-rich dishes of the classic cuisine – was highly influential, although reviled in some quarters for its affectation. In contrast, regional and home cooking continues to stick to a traditional repertoire of classic French dishes, such as cassoulet or tarte tatin.

Glossary

Anchovy (anchois): a small seafish, generally available salted in cans or jars, filleted or whole. Its strong flavour plays a key part in dishes like tapenade and pissaladière.

Bayonne ham: a famous salt-cured, smoked ham, originally from Bayonne but now manufactured all over France.

Butter: pale, unsalted 'sweet' butter from Normandy is highly prized in French pastry-cooking.

Calvados: a spirit distilled from cider traditionally from Normandy. Pays d'Auge Calvados is a particularly high-quality brand.

Capers: the unopened buds of a Mediterranean shrub, used pickled either in brine or vinegar as a distinctive sour flavouring.

Celeriac (céleri-rave): the white, firm-textured, bulbous root of a variety of celery with a distinctive nutty flavour.

Cep (cèpe): a brown-capped, thick-stemmed edible wild boletus mushroom, valued for its rich flavour and meaty texture.

Cheeses: French cheeses are one of the glories of French cuisine. There are hundreds of different French cheeses, with the following only a tiny selection. *Banon*, a soft, small, round cheese, traditionally wrapped in chestnut leaves; *Beaufort*, a Gruyère-like hard cow's milk cheese from the mountain pastures of the Savoie; *Brie*, a circular, soft, unpressed cow's milk cheese, with its origins in the thirteenth century; *Brie de Meaux* is a classic brie, farm-made from unpasturised milk; *Camembert*, a round, flat, soft cheese, traditionally from Normandy; *chèvre*, goat's milk cheese (mi-chèvre refers to cheeses made with a mixture of goat's and cow's milks); *Comte*, a Gruyère-type cow's milk cheese from the Jura mountains; *crottin de chavignol*, a soft goat's milk, cheese made in Sancerre, shaped like a small flattened ball; *explorateur*, a mild, cylindrical, triple-cream cow's milk cheese; *Fourme d'Ambert*, a semi-soft, cow's milk veined cheese; *fromage frais*, fresh curd cheese made from cow's milk, used in cooking; *Livarot*, a soft Normandy cow's milk cheese; *lucullus*, a soft, cylindrical cow's milk cheese; *Munster*, a soft cheese from the Alsace with an orange-red rind; *Pont l'Eveque*, a square-shaped, soft cow's milk cheese from Normandy; and *Roquefort*, a famous veined, semi-soft sheep's milk cheese, ripened for three months in the limestone caves of Les Causses.

Chervil: a subtle-flavoured green herb, with fine fronds, resembling a delicate continental parsley.

Crème fraîche: soured cream containing a minimum of 30% butterfat.

Dandelion (dent-de-lion, pissenlit): a jagged-leafed, wild meadow plant, dismissed as a weed in England but eaten when young as a salad leaf in France.

Lard de poitrine: a fatty version of streaky bacon used for flavouring dishes such as stews; also available smoked.

Marrons glacés: sweet, glazed, syrup-poached chestnuts, eaten as a costly sweetmeat and used in desserts.

Marrons glacés

Available whole, in pieces or in purée form.

Mustard (moutarde): pale yellow Dijon mustard made from black or brown mustard seeds, verjuice and white wine; mild, aromatic dark-brown Bordeaux mustard; and grainy-textured Meaux mustard made from mixed mustard seeds.

Olive oil: Although a small producer, France's olive oil is well-regarded, with the best thought to come from Provençe.

Pâtés: *pâté de campagne*, coarse-textured pâté; pâté de foie, containing 15% pork liver and 45% fat.

French stick

Purslane (pourpier): a green salad vegetable with rounded, clover-shaped leaves.

Puy lentil: a prized small, green-brown lentil which retains its shape and has a good flavour when cooked.

Rocket (roquette): a peppery, jagged green salad leaf; a traditional element of Provençal mesclun (a wild leaf salad).

Salt cod (morue): dried, salted cod which needs pre-soaking before cooking and which is used in classic dishes such as brandade.

Saucisson sec: Dried sausages including: *Jésus*, a large, pork sausage; *saucisson d'Arles*, made from pork and beef; *saucisson de campagne*, made with pork, fat, garlic and spice; *rosette*, a slowly-matured pure pork sausage.

Sausages: *andouillette*, a thick, bumpy sausage, sometimes smoked; *boudin blanc*, a creamy white sausage containing meat such as veal, chicken or pork; *boudin noir*, a dark-skinned blood sausage made from pig's blood; *cervelas*: a short, stocky pork sausage;

Shallots

merguez, a spicy red-coloured Algerian lamb and beef sausage; *Toulouse*: a popular pork cooking sausage, used in cassoulet.

Shallot: a small, russet-skinned, mild member of the onion family.

Snails (escargot): an edible gastropod mollusc, enjoyed by the Gauls, available canned or frozen and sometimes found fresh.

Sorrel: a green, leafy herb with a distinctive sour flavour, used to flavour soups, omelettes and salads.

Tarragon: a fine-leafed green herb with a distinctively aromatic, faintly aniseed flavour.

Truffle (truffe): rare and costly black and white tubers, with a distinctive aroma and flavour. Black Périgord truffles are particularly prized.

Vanilla sugar: vanilla-flavoured caster sugar, available commercially but easily made at home by placing two or three vanilla pods in a jar of caster sugar and leaving it to infuse.

Wine vinegar: red and white wine vinegars are key flavourings in French cookery, essential in salad dressings. Orleans wine vinegars are particularly valued.

Food Shops

As one would expect from a country famous for its baking, several of London's best French food shops are elegant patisseries – offering Londoners an all too rare and welcome chance to enjoy decent croissants, delectable cakes and proper bread.

CENTRAL

Comptoir Gascon

- 61-63 Charterhouse Street, EC1
- 020 7608 0851
- Farringdon LU/Rail
- Mon-Fri 8am-8pm, Sat 9am-6pm

This discreetly smart shop, with its distressed walls, stone floor and dark wood shelving, boasts an excellent pedigree, linked as it is to the Michelin starred restaurant Club Gascon. Pride of place here goes to an array of home made foie gras, with the sweet wines stocked here specifically chosen as good accompaniments to foie gras. Own-made traiteur dishes range from pig's cheek in Armagnac to Gascony pies. On-site bakers produce very competitively priced viennoserie, a range of breads, cakes and pastries, including cannelle, a speciality from South Western France.

La Fromagerie

- 2-4 Moxon Street, W1
- 020 7935 0341
- Baker Street LU
- Mon 10.30am-7.30pm, Tue-Fri 9am-7pm,
  Sat 9am-7pm, Sun 10am-6pm

Discreetly positioned just off Marylebone High Street, Patricia Michelson's attractive food shop is filled with good things to eat. As the name suggests, cheeses are the shop's forte, stocked in a separate, temperature-controlled cheeseroom. Here are between 100 and 150 seasonal farmhouse cheeses, many of which are French with Alpine cheeses, such as Beaufort, being a speciality. Patricia, whose passionate enthusiasm for cheese is genuine and infectious, makes a point of sourcing cheeses herself, direct from small farms and suppliers. Other Gallic edibles include exquisite walnut oil, delectable jams and superb Normany cider and wines, chosen to complement the cheeses on offer. A tasting room at the back offers a chance to sample charcuterie and cheeses plus dishes made in the kitchen downstairs.

Madeleine

⌨ *5 Vigo Street, W1*
☎ *020 7734 8353*
🚇 *Piccadilly Circus LU*
🕐 *Mon-Sat 8am-10pm, Sun 11am-7pm*

A smart, roomy patisserie-cum-café with a tempting window display of French pastries and cakes such as tarte bonne femme, tarte tatin and religiouse, all freshly made on the premises.

Maison Bertaux

⌨ *28 Greek Street, W1*
☎ *020 7437 6007*
🚇 *Leicester Square LU*
🕐 *Mon-Sat 9am-8pm, Sun 9am-7pm*

Established for well over a hundred years, this small patisserie is the last food shop link to Soho's nineteenth-century French community. Tucked away down a side-street, it has a loyal clientele who enjoy the excellent pastries, good coffee and Bohemian atmosphere, lovingly sustained by Michelle, the manager. As one sits sipping coffee, trays of freshly made croissants or fruit tarts are brought out from the kitchen and regulars pause at the till for a few moment's gossip.

Najma

⌨ *17-19 Bute Street, SW1*
☎ *020 7584 4434*
🚇 *South Kensington LU*
🕐 *Mon-Fri 8am-7pm, Sat 9am-5.30pm*

This pretty, pale blue delicatessen, in the heart of francophone South Kensington, has its own café next door in which to sip Moroccan mint tea and sample French dishes. The shop's stock is French with a Moroccan twist. Nostalgic Francophiles can stock up on French sweets, biscuits, fromage frais and couscous, while the deli-counter offers traiteur dishes, cheeses, chacuterie and even pots of duck-fat.

Paul

⊡ *29 Bedford Street, WC2*

☎ *020 7836 3304*

🚌 *Covent Garden LU*

🕐 *Mon-Fri 7.30am-9pm, Sat-Sun 9am-9pm*

An alluring window display of fruit tarts draws the eye at this, the first London branch of a well-established French chain of bakers. Elegant in a very continental way, Paul's combines a bakery with a spacious salon de thé in which to indulge in a coffee éclair or sample a slice of authentic quiche Lorraine. All the goods are baked on the premises, indeed diners can watch the baker busy at work in the backroom bakery. Breads, which range from flute baguettes to rye and wheaten flour 'rustic' bread, are carefully made using traditional techniques.

Branch: 115 Marylebone High Street, W1 (020 7836 3304)

Poilâne

⊡ *46 Elizabeth Street, SW1*

☎ *020 7808 4910*

🚌 *Sloane Square LU, Victoria LU/Rail*

🕐 *Mon-Fri 7am-7.30pm, Sat 7.30am-6pm*

This small, dainty shop is the first London branch of a much-loved Gallic institution. An exact replica of Lionel Poilâne's famous bakery on Rue du Cherche-Midi in Paris, the shop's basement contains a huge, wood-fired brick oven where the master baker works through the night. Here one can buy the huge, distinctive tangy sourdough loaves (sold whole, halved, quartered or by the slice) for which Poilâne is famous as well as a select choice of viennoiserie, bags of Guerande seasalt and simple but utterly moreish punitions (biscuits).

Villandry

⊡ *170 Great Portland Street, W1*

☎ *020 7631 3131*

🚌 *Great Portland Street LU*

🕐 *Mon-Sat 8.30am-10pm, Sun 11am-4pm*

This swish deli-cum-eaterie has a strong Gallic element to its upmarket stock. Highlights are the excellent range of French farmhouse cheeses and huge assortment of French dairy products.

NORTH

La Fromagerie

- 30 Highbury Park, N5
- ☎ 020 7359 7440
- Highbury & Islington LU/Rail
- 🕓 Mon 11am-7.30pm,
  Tue-Sat 9.30am-7.30pm, Sun 10am-4.30pm

Under a dark blue awning, a window filled with appetising tarts and pastries marks the presence of this attractive shop. Inside, the shelves are packed with carefully chosen delicacies, with pride of place going to the cheese room at the back with its range of artisanal cheeses, a large proportion of which are French.

WEST

Bagatelle Boutique

- 44 Harrington Road, SW7
- ☎ 020 7581 1551
- South Kensington LU
- 🕓 Mon-Sat 8am-8pm, Sun 8am-6pm

This large, smart shop sells its own high-quality viennoiserie, patisserie, breads and cakes (all made with Normandy butter and French flour). In addition, there is a traiteur counter offering dishes such as salmon quenelles and home made foie gras. A counter of fine French chocolates completes the picture.

Filéric

- 57 Old Brompton Road, SW7
- ☎ 020 7584 2967
- South Kensington LU
- 🕓 Mon-Sat 8am-7pm, Sun 9am-7pm

This tiny, dainty patisserie and salon de thé, much frequented by the local French community, sells a small but select range of viennoiserie, patisserie and cakes.

Le Pascalou

- 🗎 *359 Fulham Road, SW10*
- ☎ *020 7352 1717*
- 🚇 *Fulham Broadway LU*
- 🕐 *Mon-Sat 8am-7.30pm, Sun 10am-6pm*

This distinguished and handsome shop, with its Gallic staff, sells an impressive range of foodstuffs. In front of the shop there's an eye-catching display of upmarket fresh fruit and vegetables, while inside are cheeses, charcuterie, French bread and chocolates, plus a separate fish room with an attractive display of seafood.

Maison Blanc

- 🗎 *102 Holland Park, W11*
- ☎ *020 7221 2494*
- 🚇 *Holland Park LU*
- 🕐 *Mon-Wed 8am-7pm, Thur-Fri 8am-7.30pm,*
  Sat 7.30am-7pm, Sun 8.30am-6pm

A striking display of elegant cakes draws customers into this attractive French patisserie-cum-salon de thé, the first London branch of this well-established chain. The baked goods on offer include rustic-style French breads and exquisitely stylish cakes and pastries including a classic tarte au citron. Bûches de Noel (at Christmas) and Tarte Bonne Femme are among the traditional French treats on offer.

SOUTH-WEST

Le Tour de France

- 🗎 *135 Sunnyhill Road, SW16*
- ☎ *020 8769 3554*
- ✑ *www.letourdefrance.co.uk*
- 🚇 *Streatham Rail*
- 🕐 *Mon-Fri 9am-8pm, Sat 10am-8pm, Sun 10am-2.30pm & 7pm-9pm*

Tucked away down a quiet residential Streatham side-street, this small, neat shop, knowledgeably run by its amicable owners Regine and Jean-Pierre Bruyas, is crammed with Gallic goodies. Luxury items include fresh Brittany oysters, goose fat, sel gris de Guerande and vintage Armagnacs, but it's also strong on basics such as vinegars, fruit juices and fresh sausages.

Eating Places

CENTRAL LONDON

Elena's L'Etoile £££

⊞ *30 Charlotte Street, W1*

☎ *020 7636 7189*

🚌 *Goodge Street LU*

In the heart of Fitzrovia this unashamedly cosy, unfashionably comfortable restaurant, with its red plush seating and signed celebrity portraits, is the sort of restaurant which inspires loyalty in its regulars. The rich, classic French food – such as scallops with celeriac purée – and charming service, presided over by famous maître d' Elena Salvoni, match the surroundings to perfection.

La Galette · ££

⊞ *56 Paddington Street, W1*

☎ *020 7935 1554*

🚌 *Baker Street LU, Bond Street LU*

This smart, attractive crêperie offers distinctly superior pancakes; both galettes with savoury fillings and sweet crêpes, such as crêpes Suzette.

Madeleine £

⊞ *5 Vigo Street, W1*

☎ *020 7734 8353*

🚌 *Piccadilly Circus LU*

In a side-street away from the bustle of Regent Street, this bright café, offers 'Les Snacks', including croque monsieur and a tempting range of patisserie, served by polite French staff,

Maison Bertaux £

⊞ *28 Greek Street, W1*

☎ *020 7437 6007*

🚌 *Leicester Square LU*

Vintage Soho café in which to enjoy a café au lait or freshly squeezed orange juice and a freshly baked pastry such as one of their famous almond croissants.

Mon Plaisir £££-££££

⊞ *21 Monmouth Street, WC2*

☏ *020 7836 7243*

🚌 *Covent Garden LU, Leicester Square LU*

London's oldest French restaurant, established for over 50 years, is a family affair, run with an eye for detail by Alain Lhermitte. Here one can enjoy well-prepared, classic dishes such as steak tartare or coq au vin in pleasantly old-fashioned, atmospheric surroundings.

Paul £

⊞ *29 Bedford Street, WC2*

☏ *020 7836 3304*

🚌 *Covent Garden LU*

Paul's backroom salon de thé is something of a haven; a civilized place in which to enjoy a slice of proper quiche Lorraine or a tempting pastry.

NORTH

Almeida ££££

⊞ *30 Almeida Street, N1*

☏ *020 7354 4777*

🚌 *Highbury & Islington LU/Rail*

Owned by Terence Conran, this Islington restaurant focuses on classic French food, hence hand-carved jambon du Bayonne with celeriac remoulade, superior steak au poivre, buttery potato gratin and a spectacular range of tarts, presented (tongue-in-cheek) on a trolley.

Le Crêperie de Hampstead £

⊞ *Corner of Hampstead High Street and Perrins Lane, NW3*

🚌 *Hampstead LU*

This corner stall is something of a Hampstead institution, serving excellent take-away sweet and savoury crêpes, such as classic crêpes Suzette. Customers stand mesmerised watching pats of butter sizzling on the griddles and thin pools of batter metamorphose into crêpes. Often attracts a queue, particularly when the pubs close.

WEST

Chez Max *££-£££*
- 3 Yeoman's Row, SW3
- 020 7590 9999
- *Knightsbridge LU, South Kensington LU*

A stylish basement brasserie-inspired restaurant, offering exemplary French bourgeois cuisine.

Racine *£££-££££*
- 239 Brompton Road, SW3
- 020 7584 4472
- *Knightsbridge LU, South Kensington LU*

An elegant, smooth-running restaurant serving classic French dishes with panache, rounded off with an impressive cheese board and fine wine list.

Cookbooks

Mastering the Art of French Cookery (Vols 1 & 2)
Simone Beck, Louisette Bertholle & Julia Child
A well-respected, practical classic.

French Country Cookery
Elizabeth David
An elegantly written, discriminating guide to traditional French cooking.

French Provincial Cookery
Elizabeth David
A classic cookbook by a master food writer.

Charcuterie and French Pork Cooking
Jane Grigson
A mixture of scholarly knowledge and practical food writing.

Larousse Gastronomique
A fascinating gastronomic encyclopaedia.

French Cookbooks

Greek London

Athenian Grocery

The Greek community in London today is about 160,000 strong and largely made up of Greek Cypriots; its growth has been a purely twentieth-century phenomenon. Historically, however, there was a small mainland Greek presence in London dating back to the eighteenth century. Bishop Timotheus Catsiyannis, of the Cathedral of Aghia Sophia on Moscow Road, has traced back the histories of such prominent Greek families as the Rallis. Pandias Ralli (1793-1865), a prosperous merchant from Chios, came to Britain to expand the family business. He was a leading figure in the early Greek community in Britain, becoming Consul of Greece in 1835.

The Greek community used the Russian Chapel for their religious services and ceremonies until 1837 when a Greek Chapel of Our Saviour was established at 9 Finsbury Circus, where the Ralli brothers had their business. As London's Greek community grew, Pandias felt this chapel to be inadequate and in 1843, proposed building a new church. Seven years later the Greek Church of Our Saviour was opened at London Wall – an historic moment for London's Greek community. This was followed, in 1878, by the completion of the imposing Cathedral of Aghia Sophia in Moscow Road.

The real growth in London's Greek community came much later, as a result of Britain's relations with Cyprus. This strategically important Mediterranean island was leased to the British government in 1878 by the Ottomans, and annexed as a colony by Britain in 1914. During the period of British rule, the lack of opportunities in Cyprus drove many Cypriots to Britain. In the 1930s, the Christian Cypriot Brotherhood was founded in London to offer support to this expat community. The number of Cypriots coming to Britain increased appreciably after the Second World World and during the 1950s. Many found work as kitchen hands and waiters, and in the garment industry. Soho, with its restaurants and cheap accommodation, was an early focal point. During the late 1940s, however, there was a shift to Camden Town and in 1948 Greek Cypriots took over the Church of All Saints on Pratt Street. In 1960, Britain withdrew from Cyprus and many of the jobs linked to the naval and military bases disappeared. The economic pull to Britain was at its strongest during 1961, when 25,000 Cypriots came to this country. The Turkish invasion of Cyprus in 1974 caused the next major influx, with hundreds of dispossessed refugees fleeing to Britain to seek refuge with family and friends.

During the 1960s the Greek community moved out from Camden, many of them heading north to Turnpike Lane, Wood Green and Palmers Green. Green Lanes, a long road in Haringey, was traditionally a focal point for Greek Cypriots, today, however, only a few veteran Greek Cypriot shops remain. Green Lanes now houses a Turkish and Kurdish community while the Greek community has dispersed through London's north-eastern suburbs.

 # Greek Cuisine

The cuisine of ancient Greece, chronicled by the second-century writer Athenaeus, has now been overlayed by other influences. A history of occupation by the Romans, Venetians and Turks has left distinct traces: pasta dishes, kebabs, coffee and honey pastries. There is a clear overlap between Greek and Turkish cooking, especially apparent in Cypriot cooking, and the debate over who originated which dish still continues today. There are also differences: alcohol and pork, prohibited to the Turks under Islam, are used in Greek cooking in dishes like stifatho and afelia. Easter, the most important religious festival in the Greek calendar, is marked by a host of traditional Greek dishes such as mayeritsa: a soup made from lamb head, heart, liver, lungs and intestines; and tsourekia: a braided loaf decorated with a red-dyed, hard-boiled egg, evoking the colour of Christ's blood.

The physical geography of Greece has influenced its cuisine. The long coastline of the mainland and the islands, shared between three seas, means an abundance of fish and seafood dishes. Mediterranean fish soups, such as bouillabaisse, may be Greek in origin. The lack of grazing ground meant that traditionally, meat was scarce and had to be ingeniously spun out: minced and layered with aubergine in moussaka or with macaroni in pastitio, or cubed and skewered in kebabs. Goats and sheep, able to thrive on the rocky hills, were more popular than cattle, with their need for pasture.

From Arcadia onwards this pastoral tradition has continued, and dairy products such as yoghurt and cheese still play an important, nutritious part in Greek cookery. The pungent flavour of sheep's, and goat's, milk provides a characteristic sharp note. In agriculture the olive and vine, able to flourish on the rocky hill tops, continue to dominate as they have done for centuries. Their products are essential to Greek cooking: olives on the table, mellow-flavoured olive oil, wine for drinking and cooking and vine leaves for dolmathes. The host of nut trees that thrive in Greece, such as almond, pistachio, walnut and stone pine, play their part, adding flavour and texture to both sweet and savoury dishes.

The lemon, also grown plentifully, sounds one of the keynotes of Greek cooking. Its fresh, sharp flavour characterises dishes such as avgolemono sauce and soup. The fragrant herbs that grow wild on the hill tops are another source of flavour. Athenaeus wrote of herbs being scattered on fish and grilled meat; rigani, or oregano, 'joy of the mountain' is especially popular. The hills are also the source of horta: wild green leaves such as dandelion, wild mustard and chicory, popularly eaten boiled with a dressing.

One Greek influence that has been embraced in kitchens all over the West stems from the Middle Ages. Cooks who entered the monasteries but continued their culinary vocation adopted tall white hats to distinguish themselves from the black-robed and hatted monks – hence the origin of the chef's white hat. The lavish feasts described by Athenaeus or Hesiod the Epicurean in one of the world's first cookbooks are no longer perceived as characteristic Greek cooking. Instead, Greek food is today valued for its flavourful simplicity.

Glossary

Bulgar

Bulgar (pourgori): parboiled, cracked wheat grains, available either coarse or finely ground.

Cheeses: *anari*, a soft cheese, similar to Italian ricotta; *feta*, a salty, crumbly white cheese made from cow's, sheep's or goat's milk, often stored in brine to retain its freshness; *halloumi*, a firm white cheese with a rubbery texture, often flavoured with mint.

Colocassi

Colocassi: a large, brown, fibrous tuber with a distinctive white stump, which is a staple of Cypriot cookery.

Filo: paper-thin pastry, sometimes spelled 'phyllo', used in both sweet and savoury dishes. It's usually available frozen, but occasionally fresh filo can be found. When using filo, be careful not to let it dry out and become brittle.

Glyko: preserved fresh fruit, such as quinces and cherries, in a sweet syrup. Traditionally offered to guests with coffee.

Kataifi: a vermicelli-like pastry, formed by pouring batter through a fine sieve onto a hot surface; usually found frozen.

Loundza: smoked pork loin, a traditional Cypriot Christmas food.

Louvana: a type of vetch, recognisable by its curly tendrils, eaten as a salad leaf.

Mahlepi: the fragrant kernel of the blackcherry stone, sold in husked form and added to sweet yeast breads.

Mastic: the fragrant resin of an evergreen tree, sold in powdered form for use in sweet yeast breads.

Olive oil: in Greek mythology the olive tree was a gift from Athena (the goddess of wisdom and warfare). The rich, fruity oil adds a distinctive flavour to Greek cookery.

Olives: *Kalamata*, named after the city, are the famous, large, purple-black olives. *Tiasis*, or cracked olives, are partially-crushed olives which have been marinaded, often with olive oil, lemon slices, garlic and cumin seeds.

Ouzo: clear, anise-flavoured liquor, distilled from grapes. When diluted, this potent aperitif becomes white and cloudy and is nicknamed 'lion's milk'.

Parsley: the flat-leafed, flavourful variety known as 'continental parsley' is a basic herb in Greek cookery.

Parsley

Pasta: dried pasta is a legacy of the Italian influence on Greek cookery. Shapes include *macarona* (long thick tubes of pasta), *manestra* (pasta kernels), and *vermicelli*, often cooked with bulgar.

Purslane (glysterida): a green salad vegetable with rounded clover-shaped leaves, sometimes called 'Cypriot watercress'.

Retsina: wine with a distinctive resin flavour, traceable back to the days when wine was kept in goat skins sealed with pitch.

Rocket (rocca): a green salad leaf with a distinctive peppery flavour, which is now very fashionable.

Sausages: *bastourma*, dark, short, spiced sausages; *loukanika*, thin sausages popularly flavoured with allspice, savory and orange peel or coriander seeds.

Savory: a peppery-flavoured herb, which looks similar to thyme.

Loukanika

Tahini: a smooth paste made from pounded sesame seeds.

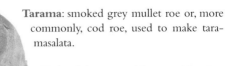

Tarama: smoked grey mullet roe or, more commonly, cod roe, used to make taramasalata.

Trahani: brown, stubby, crumbly tubes made from fermented cracked wheat and yogurt. They have a tangy flavour and should be soaked before using.

Vine leaves: large, distinctively-shaped leaves, used principally to make dolmathes. Occasionally found fresh but usually preserved in brine, when they need soaking to rinse off the excess salt.

Yoghurt: thick, creamy Greek yoghurt, made from sheep's or cow's milk.

Food Shops

NORTH

Clocktower Store

⌂   *52 The Broadway, N8*
☎   *020 8348 7845*
🚌   *Finsbury Park LU/Rail, then the W7 bus*
🕐   *Mon-Fri 8.30am-7pm, Sat 8.30am-6pm, Sun 10am-5pm*

This friendly, bustling Cypriot greengrocer, just by Crouch End's landmark Clock Tower, offers an excellent range of fruit and veg, from bunches of fresh herbs to huge watermelons. Inside are staples such as village bread, feta and olive oil.

Andreas Michli & Sons

⌂   *405-411 St Ann's Road, N15*
☎   *020 8802 0188*
🚌   *Harringay Green Lanes Rail*
🕐   *Mon-Thur 9.30am-7.30pm,*
    Fri 9.30am-8.30pm, Sat 9.30am-7.30pm, Sun 11am-3.30pm

Tucked away just off Green Lanes, this small, characterful row of shops sells everything from foodstuffs to barbecue equipment and Greek statuary. Andreas takes particular pride in the fresh produce, which includes delights such as bergamot lemons, myrtle berries, sweet, juicy un-waxed oranges and spanking fresh bunches of chard and spinach.

Halepi

⌂   *24 Grand Parade, Green Lanes, N4*
☎   *020 8800 9272*
🚌   *Manor House LU*
🕐   *Daily 9.30am-8pm*

This Greek bakery, which is well over 25 years old, is something of an institution, and especially famous among the Greek community for its monumental, multi-tiered, lavishly-iced wedding cakes, a display of which is kept upstairs.

Tony's Continental Stores

⊞ *140 High Road, N2*
☎ *020 8444 5545*
🚌 *East Finchley LU*
🕐 *Mon-Fri 8am-7pm, Sat 8am-6.30pm, Sun 10am-1pm*

From watermelons and figs in the summer to quinces and huge field mushrooms in the autumn, there is always a good range of produce at this self-service greengrocer, run with friendly courtesy by the Athanasiou family.

WEST

Adamou

⊞ *126 Chiswick High Road, W4*
☎ *020 8994 0752*
🚌 *Turnham Green LU*
🕐 *Daily 8.30am-6.45pm*

This Chiswick institution has an attractive display of fruit and vegetables outside, including pumpkins, colocassi, figs and wet walnuts. Inside, this large, old-fashioned shop offers an excellent range of general groceries.

Athenian Grocery

⊞ *16a Moscow Road, W2*
☎ *020 7229 6280*
🚌 *Bayswater LU*
🕐 *Mon-Sat 8.30am-7pm, Sun 9.30am-1pm*

Down the road from St Sophia is this charming corner shop, its blue-painted exterior and boxes of vegetables striking an attractive Mediterranean note. Established for well over 40 years, its stock includes seasonal items such as green almonds and fresh vine leaves, as well as basic staples. Banter is the name of the game here and insults are genially exchanged with regular customers, but service is friendly and heavy bags are carried out to waiting cars.

Andreas Michli & Sons

Eating Places

NORTH LONDON

Café Corfu £££

⌨ *7 Pratt Street, NW1*

☎ *020 7267 8088*

🚌 *Camden Town LU*

A contemporary bar-cum-restaurant offering above average Greek cooking and an excellent Greek wine list.

Daphne £££

⌨ *83 Bayham Street, NW1*

☎ *020 7267 7322*

🚌 *Camden Town LU*

An unreconstructed convivial Greek restaurant offering decent Greek food, popular for both romantic tête-à-têtes and parties of friends.

Lemonia £££

⌨ *89 Regent's Park Road, NW1*

☎ *020 7586 7454*

🚌 *Chalk Farm LU*

With its lively atmosphere, friendly staff and fresh-tasting food this is everyone's idea of what a Greek restaurant should be and accordingly, pulls in the revellers.

Vrisiaki £££

⌨ *73 Myddleton Road, N22*

☎ *020 8889 8760*

🚌 *Bounds Green LU*

Warmly recommended by Cypriot friends, at first sight this looks solely like a take-away kebab house. Venture in, however, past the busy charcoal grills and it opens into a large, popular restaurant. Those with gargantuan appetites should opt for mezedes, a seemingly never-ending array of dishes, starting with nibbles such as tahini and cracked olives and working up via seafood to a platter of grilled meats.

Cookbooks

Flavours of Greece
Rosemary Barron
An evocatively written collection of over 250 recipes for Greek dishes, ranging from aromatic giant beans to olive bread.

A Book of Mediterranean Food
Elizabeth David
A knowledgeable and evocative book which, although not solely about Greek cookery, captures the flavours of the Mediterranean.

Mediterranean Seafood
Alan Davidson
A fascinating and authoritative guide to Mediterranean seafood.

The Taste of Cyprus
Gilli Davies
A charmingly written cookbook, combining personal memories with straightforward recipes.

Mediterranean Cookery
Claudia Roden
A well-written and attractive book, dealing with Mediterranean cuisine as a whole.

The Greek Cook
Rena Salaman
Attractively and usefully illustrated with mouth-watering photographs this appetising cookbook offers a seasonal look at Greek cuisine.

Italian London

Tavola

Italian links with London date back to the Roman invasion in AD 43 and the creation of a settlement named 'Londinium'. Over subsequent centuries Italians came to live in London, but particularly so in the first half of the nineteenth century when waves of political refugees arrived in the capital. The community continued to grow through the turbulent times of Italian Unification and war with Austria – by 1900 there were around 10,000 Italians in London.

The historical Italian quarter, founded in the mid-nineteenth century, was in Clerkenwell and Holborn, known to outsiders as 'Little Italy' and to its residents as 'The Hill'. The nickname 'The Hill' came from two important streets in the community: Back Hill and Eyre Street Hill. St Peter's Church was the community's focal point, erected in 1864 with money donated by Italian immigrants; its importance in celebrating and commemorating the births, lives and deaths of the Italian community continues to this day. Although the Italian population has now dispersed from Clerkenwell, the legacy of this period is still visible in the area around King's Cross and Holborn where red, white and green signs over barbers, cafés and shops patriotically signal Italy.

Every year in July the Feast Day of Our Lady of Mount Carmel, a religious procession in her honour takes place through Clerkenwell from St Peter's, followed by a 'sagra' or fête. One of the few religious processions to take place in London, it has been enacted since the 1880s and older Italians have fond memories of attending it as children. Even today, the procession draws Italians back to Clerkenwell from all over Britain. There is a great sense of community, with the different generations all present and participating. Stalls are set up on the streets selling delicious Italian snacks such as polenta e salsiccie (cornmeal and sausages), freshly-roasted porchetta (pork) and slices of savoury tarts, with glasses of wine adding to the celebratory atmosphere.

The other traditional Italian area in London was Soho, which also saw an influx of Italians in the 1860s. Despite the internment of Italian residents as 'enemy aliens' during the Second World War and the tragic death in 1940 of 470 Italian internees being deported to Canada when the Arandora Star was sunk by the Germans, the Italian community continued to maintain its links with Britain. In the 1950s and 1960s, during the espresso bar boom, a wave of immigrants, mostly from the south of Italy, came to London seeking work and settled in Soho as waiters and restaurateurs.

Italian Cuisine

I talian cuisine is very much a regional affair; the different parts of Italy, united only in the last century, have their own dishes and even their own ingredients. The historical divide between the prosperous, industrial north and the poor, rural south also extended to foodstuffs. Rice, cornmeal polenta, and fresh egg pasta were the staples of the north while in the south factory-made, dried durum wheat pasta was eaten. Cooking fats varied: the north used butter, middle-Italy pig fat, and the south, olive oil. With the post-war migration of labour from south to north and the growth of mass-production, regional eating patterns became less rigid. Today the Mediterranean diet, stemming from the south, is valued for its health-giving qualities. Dried pasta and olive oil, low in saturated fats, are now eaten throughout Italy.

Despite this blurring of the north–south divide, regional charac-teristics are still apparent. Tuscan cuisine comprises rustic, peasant food such as bean soup (the Tuscans are nick-named 'mangiafagioli', bean-eaters), bruschetta and charcoal-grilled meat such as bistecca fiorentina, as well as T-bone steak traditionally from the Val di Chiana. Rice dishes are still popular in the north, where rice was traditionally grown, and in Lombardy you find risotto alla Milanese, flavoured with saffron, wine and stock. Roman cuisine is that of the 'quinto quarto', the fifth quarter, with the poor eating what was left after the rich had eaten, hence strongly-flavoured offal dishes. Sicily has a rich, varied culinary inheritance due to a history of invasions by the Greeks, Romans, Arabs and Normans. The Arab legacy is particularly noticeable, with sultanas, aubergines, pistachio nuts and spices being popular ingredients in Sicily.

Italian cooking is noted for its emphasis on clear, simple flavours. Good ingredients are the key to Italian cooking and seasonality is valued. Foods continue to be associated with the regions, towns or villages that have traditionally produced that ingredient: the best radic-chio from Treviso, with its annual radicchio festival; balsamic vinegar from Modena; prosciutto from Parma or San Daniele; fontina cheese from Val d'Aosta; and costly white truffles from Alba.

Glossary

Baccala: pungent salted, dried cod – needs soaking before cooking.

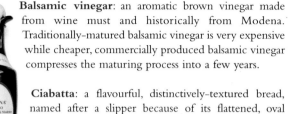

Balsamic vinegar: an aromatic brown vinegar made from wine must and historically from Modena. Traditionally-matured balsamic vinegar is very expensive while cheaper, commercially produced balsamic vinegar compresses the maturing process into a few years.

Ciabatta: a flavourful, distinctively-textured bread, named after a slipper because of its flattened, oval shape.

Colomba: a dove-shaped cake similar to panettone, but traditionally eaten at Easter.

Balsamic Vinegar

Foccacia: a flat, salty bread flavoured with olive oil and sometimes additionally with rosemary, onions or sage; known as schiacciata in Tuscany.

Fontina: semi-soft cow's milk cheese, traditionally from Val d'Aosta, and famously used to make fonduta, a fondue flavoured with white truffles.

Marscapone: an extremely rich cream cheese, an essential ingredient of the popular dessert tiramisu.

Mortadella

Mortadella: a large pink sausage, traditionally from Bologna, flavoured with peppercorns, garlic and pistachios. It can be eaten like a salami or used in cooking.

Mozzarella: a bland white cheese with a rubbery texture that is famously used on pizzas. Buffalo's milk mozzarella is more expensive than the more easily found cow's milk version. Baby mozzarellas are called 'bocconcini'.

Olive oil: a key ingredient in Italian cooking, olive oil is labelled according to its acidity levels. Extra Virgin must have no more than 1% acidity. As with wine, different regions produce different-flavoured olive oils, with Tuscan olive oil being famously piquant.

Pancetta: the Italian equivalent of bacon, this is made from the same cut of meat – pig belly.

Panettone: a light, brioche-style cake, containing sultanas, traditionally given at Christmas time, which is when London's Italian delis stock several varieties.

Olive Oil

Panettone

Parmesan: the best-known Italian cheese and also the largest and longest-matured cheese produced in Italy, this hard-grating cheese traditionally comes from around Parma. Grana padano is a similar cheese produced in Lombardy. Buy chunks of Parmesan and keep them refrigerated, wrapped in foil, to be used as required.

Parmesan

Pasta: this famous Italian staple comes both fresh and dried and in a multiplicity of forms. Fresh pasta, made with eggs, can be bought ready-made from delicatessens. Dried pasta should be made from durum wheat and popular Italian brands include Barilla and Da Cecco.

Pecorino: a hard sheep's milk cheese. Pecorino Romano is most commonly found but there is also Pecorino Sardo, from Sardinia, and Toscana, from Tuscany.

Polenta

Pine nuts: small ivory-coloured kernels from the stone pine tree, with a distinctive flavour.

Polenta: a Northern Italian staple made from maize, polenta flour is available in fine or coarse versions. Pre-cooked polenta flour, scorned by purists, is also available.

Porcini: wild Boletus mushrooms, prized for their flavour and priced accordingly. Dried porcini mushrooms, often in pieces, are easily found, while fresh porcini are much rarer.

Porcini

Prosciutto Crudo: the most famous of these salt-cured hams is Parma ham, cured for 14 months. San Daniele, cured for 12 months, is considered another fine prosciutto.

Ricotta: a light, bland sheep's whey cheese, drained in baskets which give it its distinctive woven markings. It is used in both sweet and savoury dishes.

Rocket: known as 'rucola', this peppery, jagged leaf is increasingly available as a chic salad leaf. Italians are fond of pointing out that in Italy it grows wild as a weed.

Rocket

Salami: ready-to-eat, salt-cured sausages, available in a range of sizes and flavours, such as fine-textured Milano or finocchiona, flavoured with fennel.

Salsiccie: Italian sausages, usually made from pork. Luganega is a mild sausage from Lombardy, sold in long narrow coils, while in the South chilli is often added as a flavouring.

Sun-dried tomatoes: as their name suggests, these are dried tomatoes, available either in their dry state or preserved in olive oil.

Truffles: these rare tubers with their overwhelming and distinctive flavour are astronomically expensive, especially when sold fresh. White truffles from Alba are particularly prized. Tinned and bottled truffles are available as is truffle-flavoured olive oil.

Food Shops

The older Italian delicatessens in London grew out of the community's needs, starting as everyday corner-shops supplying foods that had to be specially imported. In some cases the shop acted as an informal community centre, lending money, explaining English laws and providing advice. As the Italian community has become assimilated into British life this role has disappeared. With Italian food now enjoying a huge wave of fashionable popularity, newer, more upmarket delicatessens entering the market are now aimed primarily at the English.

CENTRAL

Angelucci

▢ *23b Frith Street, W1*

☎ *020 7437 5889*

🚇 *Leicester Square LU, Tottenham Court Road LU*

🕓 *Mon-Wed 9am-5pm, Thur 9am-1pm, Fri-Sat 9am-5pm*

A Soho institution, founded in 1929 by Signore Angelucci and based in these premises since 1931, this veteran coffee business is still run by the Angelucci family. This small old-fashioned shop, with its vintage old coffee-grinders on the counter, smells enticingly of roasted coffee, of which they sell 36 varieties at remarkably reasonable prices. The most popular is Mokital, for cappuccinos and espressos, which is freshly ground as required. If you want to sample Mokital, drop into Bar Italia two doors away and have one of their much-famed espressos or cappuccinos. Over the decades, customers have included General du Gaulle and numerous Dire Straits fans, drawn by the reference to Angelucci's in the song The Wild West End.

I Camisa & Son

▢ *161 Old Compton Street, W1*

☎ *020 7437 7610/4686*

🚇 *Leicester Square LU, Tottenham Court Road LU*

🕓 *Mon-Sat 9am-6pm*

On this bustling Soho thoroughfare, Gaby presides genially over this classic Italian deli. Established over thirty years ago, this small shop has a seemingly perpetual queue of loyal regulars, attracted by the quality of the cheeses (including excellent Parmesan), meats and delicious home-marinaded olives. Bags of fresh rocket and stunningly sweet Sicilian cherry tomatoes are another draw. Fresh, own-made pasta includes pappardelle, parma ham tortellini and gnocchi and there are home-made sauces such as pesto, lepre (hare) and porcini.

Carluccio's

⌨ *28a Neal Street, WC2*
☎ *020 7240 1487*
🚉 *Covent Garden LU*
🕐 *Mon-Thur 11am-7pm, Fri 10am-7pm, Sat 10am-6pm*

Set up by restaurateur and funghiphile Antonio Carluccio (also of the neighbouring Neal Street Restaurant) and his wife Priscilla, this sleek deli, their first food shop, offers an appetising selection of regional Italian foods, including a counter of ready-made dishes and fresh pasta. Everything, from the Calabrian stuffed figs to the rustic loaves of bread, is beautifully packaged and presented. Naturally, there is also a fine seasonal range of fresh wild mushrooms and truffles.

Gastronomeria Italia

⌨ *8 Upper Tachbrook Street, SW1*
☎ *020 7834 2767*
🚉 *Pimlico LU, Victoria LU/Rail*
🕐 *Mon-Fri 9am-6pm, Sat 9am-5pm*

This homely delicatessen is well-used by Italians and Spaniards from the local community. As well as a good basic stock of Italian ingredients, they sell tasty Italian snacks to cater to the lunchtime market.

Lina Stores

⌨ *18 Brewer Street, W1*
☎ *020 7437 6482*
🚉 *Leicester Square LU, Oxford Circus LU, Piccadilly Circus LU*
🕐 *Mon-Fri 7am-5.45pm, Sat 7am-5pm*

The pistachio-coloured façade and the 1930s lettering on the shop sign signal this is a vintage institution. Customers return as much for the friendly, leisurely atmosphere as for the delicious food. It is famous for its excellent fresh pasta, made on the premises every morning. The speciality is pumpkin tortelloni, a dish from Piacanza where the Filippi family come from. Groceries are wide-ranging – you feel you could ask for any Italian ingredient and it would be conjured up.

L. Terroni & Sons

- ⌂ *138-40 Clerkenwell Road, EC1*
- ☎ *020 7837 1712*
- 🚌 *Chancery Lane LU or Farringdon LU/Rail*
- 🕐 *Tue-Fri 9am-6pm, Sat 9am-3pm, Sun 10.30am-2pm*

Next to St Peter's Church – a focal point for London's Italian community – Terroni's was established in 1890 in the heart of Little Italy. The large shop retains its grocery store roots, offering a good selection of Italian foodstuffs. During the week it attracts a largely English clientele while Sunday mornings see it busy with Italians chatting and catching up on the news after the service at St Peter's.

Speck

- ⌂ *6 Thayer Street, W1*
- ☎ *020 7486 4872*
- 🚌 *Baker Street LU, Bond Street LU*
- 🕐 *Mon-Sat 10am-6pm*

A friendly café-cum-deli, with a communal table at which to enjoy sandwiches, pasta or savoury mains. Stock includes salami and cheeses, dried Italian pastas and store cupboard basics.

NORTH

Amici Delicatessen

- ⌂ *78 High Road, N2*
- ☎ *020 8444 2932*
- 🚌 *East Finchley LU*
- 🕐 *Mon-Sat 8am-7pm, Sun 10am-1pm*

A friendly, basic Italian deli, which draws in a lunchtime crowd for its freshly-made paninis and espressos.

A. Ferrari

- ⌂ *48 Cross Street, N1*
- ☎ *020 7226 1951*
- 🚌 *Angel LU, Highbury & Islington LU/Rail*
- 🕐 *Mon-Fri 8am-7pm, Sat 8am-6pm, Sun 9.30am-2pm*

Tucked away in an Islington side-street, this small family-run deli has been here for over 30 years. The stock is basic and unpretentious, with a good range of salamis, De Cecco and Barilla dried pasta and traditional cakes such as panettone at Christmas.

Giacobazzi's Delicatessen

⌗ *150 Fleet Road, NW3*

☎ *020 7267 7222*

🚌 *Hampstead Heath Rail*

🕐 *Mon-Fri 9.30am-7pm, Sat 9am-6pm*

The speciality here is ready-made fresh foods, of which there is an appetising display. The dishes are made on the premises by Raffaele Giacobazzi, who, acccording to his wife Renata, has a particular penchant for char-grilled vegetables ranging from radicchio to onions in balsamic vinegar. Home-made pasta, freshly made every day, includes upmarket treats such as gorgonzola, walnut and porcini, and white truffle tortellini.

King's Cross Continental Stores

⌗ *26 Caledonian Road, N1*

☎ *020 7837 0201*

🚌 *King's Cross LU/Rail*

🕐 *Mon-Sat 9am-7pm, Sun 10am-1pm*

Leo Giordani has run this pleasantly old-fashioned shop for over 30 years now. Customers who used to live locally but now live in other parts of London still return to catch up with Leo's news and you're more likely to hear Italian being spoken than English.

Flavours of Italy

▭ *318-322 Hornsey Road, N7*
☎ *020 7561 1251*
🕐 *Mon-Sat 8am-6pm*

With its green awning and marble and chrome fittings, this large, contemporary bar-cum-deli brings a touch of Italian style to North London. Deli goods include Italian dried pasta, wines and cold meats, while panini, own-made pasta sauces and take-out dishes are popular. A bakery counter, selling breads and pastries, completes the picture.

Mandara

▭ *20 High Road, N2*
☎ *020 8883 3777*
🚌 *East Finchley LU*
🕐 *Mon-Fri 8am-7pm, Sat 9am-6.30pm, Sun 10.30am-2.30pm*

Strategically positioned just over the road from East Finchley tube, this smart, bright deli has a basic range of foodstuffs and also serves cappucini and panini for hungry commuters.

Monte's

▭ *23 Canonbury Lane, N1*
☎ *020 7354 4335*
🚌 *Highbury & Islington LU/Rail*
🕐 *Mon-Fri 10am-7pm, Sat 10am-6pm, Sun 10am-4pm*

This is a New Wave Italian deli, with mauve walls, glossy black floor tiles, gleaming metal shelving and jazz playing in the background. The stock is distinctly upmarket, from large bowlfuls of marinaded olives and insalata di mare to fresh funghi ravioli. Groceries include several olive oils, balsamic vinegars and polentas.

Olga Stores

▭ *30 Penton Street, N1*
☎ *020 7837 5467*
🚌 *Angel LU*
🕐 *Mon-Fri 9am-8pm, Sat 9am-7pm, Sun 10am-2pm*

Run by the charming and knowledgeable Aida, this attractive deli founded in 1988 caters to its Islington clientele with a wide selection of foodstuffs, from marinaded olives to breads. Best-selling items include Aida's home-made lasagne, Portuguese-style salt cod fritters and her huge range of sauces, from tomato-based arrabiata and vongole to pesto.

Da Rocca

▭ *73 Highbury Park, N5*
☏ *020 7359 2670*
🚎 *Highbury & Islington LU/Rail*
🕐 *Mon-Sat 8am-7pm, Sun 10am-1pm*

Rocca's own home-made tortelloni and ravioli and fresh pasta are the stars of the show at this, old-fashioned, friendly shop, which is very much a neighbourhood store. Regulars return to stock up with Rocca's lasagne and pasta sauces; fans of Rocca's pasta include Tony Blair and a photo of him with Rocca takes pride of place on the walls alongside posters of the Italian football team.

Saponara

▭ *23 Prebend Street, N1*
☏ *020 7226 2771*
🚎 *Angel LU*
🕐 *Mon-Fri 8am-6pm, Sat 9am-6pm*

Run with friendly courtesy by brothers Marco and Vincenzo Saponara, this roomy deli-cum-bar offers a classic Italian mixture of delicious foodstuffs, from an excellent range of cured meats to their home-marinaded olives arrabiata. Specialities include home-made pesto "made the traditional way with pine nuts", pecorino with truffles and fine Italian wines. There are several tables at which to enjoy a cappuccino and panino, al' Italiano.

Salvino Ltd

▭ *47 Brecknock Road, N7*
☏ *020 7267 5305*
🚎 *Buses 29, 253 or 10*
🕐 *Mon-Sat 9am-7pm*

An agreeably down-to-earth shop run by the Salvino brothers. As importers of Italian food their stock is above average, with a good selection of cured meats, wines and aperitivos.

Italian Food Shops

WEST

La Bottega del Sole
▱ *323 Fulham Road, SW10*
☎ *020 7351 7370*
🚃 *South Kensington LU*
🕐 *Mon-Sat 8.30am-7pm, Sun 11am-5pm*

Inspired by her love of Italian cuisine, Patricia Hamzahee founded this pretty shop-cum-café (complete with marble counters and a back-room communal table) which serves Italian dishes, freshly cooked on the premises, to eat in or take away. The daily-changing menu includes dishes such as radicchio and gorgonzola risotto, arancini and sautéed fennel, with the emphasis on seasonality and authenticity. Stock include superior own-made fresh pasta and sauces and a carefully chosen range of artisanally produced foodstuffs such as pistachio pâté (for crostini), spelt pasta and mostarda di Cremona.

Emilia's Delicatessen
▱ *89 New King's Road, SW6*
☎ *020 7751 0189*
🚃 *Parsons Green LU*
🕐 *Daily 9am-8pm*

This smart shop, with strings of Italian flags fluttering from the ceiling, is crammed to the gills with an impressive range of Italian foodstuffs, with basics such as dried pastas, pulses and porcini stock cubes alongside luxuries such as truffle honey, fine Italian wines and excellent ham. Own-made, ready-to-eat dishes, including lasagne, risotto, frittata and chicken escalopes are a popular attraction.

Exeter Street Bakery
▱ *18 Argyll Road, W8*
☎ *020 7937 8484*
🚃 *High Street Kensington LU*
🕐 *Mon-Sat 8am-7pm, Sun 9am-6pm*

This smart shop does a roaring trade in authentically tasty slices of pizza, Illy espressos and classic Italian breads such as pane Pugliese and ciabatta.

I Camisa

Luigi's Delicatessen

▭ *349 Fulham Road, SW10*
☎ *020 7352 7739*
🚌 *Fulham Broadway LU*
🕐 *Mon-Fri 9am-9.30pm, Sat 9am-7pm*

This roomy, cheerful delicatessen attracts a steady stream of loyal customers. The stock is extensive and high-quality: 40 olive oils, an ample stock of quality Italian dried pastas and over 300 Italian wines, spirits and aperitivos. There is an appetising display of homemade sauces and dishes.

Manicomio

▭ *85 Duke of York Square, SW3*
🚌 *Sloane Square LU*
🕐 *Mon-Fri 8am-7pm, Sat 10am-7pm, Sun 10am-6pm*

Just off the King's Road, alongside smart boutiques, this spacious, elegant café-cum-deli offers an upmarket taste of Italy, showcasing Italian food importers Machiavelli's fine products. Popular items include the fresh Italian produce, such as prime red peppers and aubergines, Italian cheeses, including truffle-flavoured pecorino, cured meats and Machiavelli's coffee.

Negozio Classica

▭ *283 Westbourne Grove, W11*
☎ *020 7034 0005*
🚌 *Notting Hill LU*
🕐 *Tue-Fri 9.30am-8pm, Sat 9.30am-7pm, Sun 11am-4.30pm*

This sleek operation is a contemporary take on the Italian 'enoteca' or wine shop. Here one can sit at the chrome bar sampling wines, eating antipasti platters or sipping on an expertly-made cappuccino made from Saint Eustachio coffee. A large range of fine Italian wines, including top notch vin santo, are available, plus select artisanal foodstuffs including chestnut honey, trout cheeks in oil and Italian saffron.

La Picena

▱   *5 Walton Street, SW3*

☎   *020 7584 6573*

🚌   *Knightsbridge LU*

🕐   *Mon-Fri 9am-7.30pm, Sat 9am-5.30pm*

Tucked away behind Harrods is this refreshingly down-to-earth delicatessen. It is crammed full of good-quality Italian provisions including fresh pasta and excellent homemade pasta sauces.

Salumeria Estense

▱   *837 Fulham Road, SW6*

☎   *020 7731 7643*

🚌   *Parsons Green LU*

🕐   *Mon-Fri 10am-7pm, Sat 10am-5pm*

Now owned by Terroni's, this small, friendly shop offers basic Italian deli stock, including dried pasta, salamis and cheeses, and does a brisk business in take-away panini.

Speck

▱   *2 Holland Park Terrace, W11*

☎   *020 7229 7005*

🚌   *Holland Park LU*

🕐   *Mon-Fri 9am-8.30pm, Sat 8.30am-7pm*

This small, sleek shop carries upmarket stock, from an attractive display of home-made dishes such as marinaded grilled vegetables to a good assortment of balsamic vinegars, Cipriani dried pasta and fine olive oils.

Tavola

▱   *155 Westbourne Grove, W11*

☎   *020 7229 0571*

🚌   *Notting Hill Gate LU*

🕐   *Mon-Fri 10.30am-7.30pm, Sat 9.30am-5pm*

Alistair and Sharon Little's attractive food shop reflects their love of Italian cuisine with discerning products carefully sourced through their own personal contacts. Unusual Italian wines, fine balsamic vinegars and olive oils, truffle salami and artisanal dried Pugliese pasta are some of the Italian foodstuffs on offer. Alistair's own-cooked dishes, ready to take away, are often Italian-inspired, including an exemplary pasta e fagioli soup and chicken liver pâté flavoured with vin santo.

Italian Food Shops

SOUTH-WEST

Delicatessen Piacenza

▣ *2 Brixton Road, SW9*

☎ *020 7735 2121*

🚋 *Oval LU*

🕐 *Mon-Sat 9am-7pm, alternate Sundays 10am-5pm*

There has been an Italian deli on the site (which is a few doors away from the Chiesa della Redentore) for over 20 years. This small, traditional shop stocks a good range of basics.

I Sapori

▣ *146 Northcote Road, SW11*

☎ *020 7228 2017*

🚋 *Clapham Junction Rail*

🕐 *Mon-Sat 10am-7pm*

Distinctly stylish, this smart delicatessen is run by Michelin-starred Italian chef Stefano Cavallini. Traiteur dishes such as roast pigeon with cherry sauce are a particular highlight. Other home-made goodies include ravioli, pasta sauces and cakes and biscuits such as brutti ma buoni. Grocery items are upmarket: artisanal gelati, beautifully packaged chocolates, bottarga di tonno, flavoured honeys and unusual jams.

Salumeria Napoli

▣ *69 Northcote Road, SW11*

☎ *020 7228 2445*

🚋 *Clapham Junction Rail*

🕐 *Mon-Sat 9am-6pm*

A friendly corner shop with an appetising deli-counter containing olives, home-made red and green pesto sauces and a good selection of salamis and cured meats.

Tony's Continental Delicatessen

▣ *South Lambeth Road, SW8*

☎ *020 7582 0766*

🚋 *Vauxhall LU/Rail*

🕐 *Mon-Fri 7am-6.30pm, Sat 8am-5.30pm*

This down-to-earth corner deli has been serving the local Italian community for over 10 years now. On offer are deli basics, from dried pasta to chunks of Parmesan. There is fresh Italian bread and also panini, made up with salami and cheese from the deli counter.

Valentina

🖳 *210 Upper Richmond Road West, SW14*

☎ *020 8392 9127*

🚐 *Mortlake Rail*

🕐 *Mon-Fri 9am-7pm, Sat 8.30am-6pm, Sun 9.30am-3pm*

The Borfecchia's attractive, friendly delicatessen has a loyal local following. Particularly popular are the home-prepared dishes, from grilled vegetables to baked pasta dishes. There is a good range of grocery items and luxuries such as fresh truffles when they are in season.

South-East

La Gastronomeria

🖳 *135 Half Moon Lane, SE24*

☎ *020 7274 1034*

🚐 *Herne Hill Rail, North Dulwich Rail*

🕐 *Mon-Fri 9am-7.30pm, Sat 9am-6.30pm, Sun 10am-2.30pm*

This friendly, well-stocked Italian deli offers customers a solid range of basic groceries, from Italian dried pastas to packets of biscotti. Popular items on the deli counter include the home-made pastas and antipasti, made by their sister shop in West Dulwich.

Branch: 86 Park Hall Road, SE21 (020 8766 0494)

Mail order

✎ *www.esperya.com*

Specialising in artisanal Italian produce, Esperya impresses by its extensive range of products on offer and the quality of what's available. Efficient delivery completes a truly impressive picture.

Eating Places

Over the last 15 years London's Italian restaurant scene has undergone a transformation. A new wave of elegant and expensive restaurants have opened up offering authentic, delicious and regional Italian cooking – rather than the 'Britalian' fare previously on offer.

CENTRAL

Bar Italia   £
- 22 Frith Street, W1
- ☎ 020 7437 4520
- Leicester Square LU, Tottenham Court Road LU

Despite its cult status as the place for a late night espresso, Bar Italia remains thankfully down-to-earth, complete with fruit machines, a giant video screen for Italian football and the photo of the heavyweight boxing legend Rocky Marciano glowering down from behind the bar.

Carluccio's Caffe   ££
- 8 Market Place, W1
- ☎ 020 7636 2228
- Oxford Circus LU

The first in what is now a chain of successful café-cum-delis, this pleasantly stylish, family-friendly eatery offers excellent value Italian food, from spaghetti alla vongole with fresh clams to fresh lemon sorbet.

Manicomio   £££
- 85 Duke of York Square, SW3
- ☎ 020 7730 3366
- Sloane Square LU

Quality ingredients are at the heart of good Italian cooking and Manicomio's, set up by Italian fine food importers, has impeccable credentials on that front. The restaurant is smart in a pleasantly understated way and serves up excellent Italian food, with pasta a forte, complemented by a shrewdly chosen wine list.

Locanda Locatelli £ £ £ £

⌨ *8 Seymour Street, W1*
☎ *020 7935 9088*
🚌 *Marble Arch LU*

This sophisticated and elegant restaurant is a showcase for the considerable culinary talents of acclaimed Italian chef Giorgio Locatelli. Deftly executed dishes such as ravioli all'ossobuco or monkfish with walnut and caper sauce exhibit the flavourful simplicity of classic Italian cooking. Equally Italian is the welcome extended to children, with Saturday lunchtime particularly popular with families.

Oddono's £

⌨ *14 Bute Street, SE1*
☎ *020 7052 0732*
🚌 *South Kensington LU*

A small, bright gelateria, offering excellent, own-made Italian gelati with flavours including classics like pistachio, coffee and chocolate.

Passione £ £ £ £

⌨ *10 Charlotte Street, W1*
☎ *020 7636 2833*
🚌 *Goodge Street LU*

Chef Gennaro Contaldo's intimate Fitzrovia restaurant serves classically flavourful Italian food in attractive, atmospheric surroundings.

Sardo £ £ £

⌨ *45 Grafton Way, W1*
☎ *020 7387 2521*
☎ *Warren Street LU*

Sardinian specialities, including traditional pasta dishes such as spaghetti bottariga or malloreddus, are a feature in this intimate, friendly restaurant.

Spiga £ £ £

⌨ *84-86 Wardour Street, W1*
☎ *020 7734 3444*
🚌 *Tottenham Court Road LU*

A smart, rather hectic restaurant offering the chance to sample excellent pasta dishes (such as linguine with crab and chilli) and authentically thin-crust, wood-fired pizzas with sophisticated toppings.

La Spighetta £££
⌧ *43 Blandford Street, W1*
☎ *020 7486 7340*
🚌 *Baker Street LU*

Tucked away on a peaceful side-street this roomy restaurant serves first rate, authentically Italian pasta and pizza.

Strada ££
⌧ *15-16 New Burlington Street, W1*
☎ *020 7287 5967*
🚌 *Oxford Circus LU, Piccadilly Circus LU*

Pleasantly informal restaurant with a menu of pasta, grilled meat and (their speciality) flavourful Italian-style pizzas, cooked, as is traditional, in a wood oven with carefully chosen toppings ranging from speck to buffalo mozzarella.

Zafferano ££££
⌧ *15 Lowndes Street, SW1*
☎ *020 7235 5800*
🚌 *Knightsbridge LU*

A pioneer of fine Italian food in London, this rustically elegant restaurant continues to produce excellent Italian cooking

NORTH

Florians ££-£££
⌧ *4 Topsfield Parade, Middle Lane, N8*
☎ *020 8348 8348*
🚌 *Finsbury Park LU/Rail, then the W7 bus*

A pleasant, roomy bar-cum-restaurant offering regional Italian cooking, predominantly from the north, such as Venetian fish pie.

Marine Ices ££
⌧ *8 Haverstock Hill, NW3*
☎ *020 7485 3132*
🚌 *Chalk Farm LU*

A gelateria set up by Gaetano Mansi in 1930. He had been a fruiterer and the family myth goes that he began making water-ices from left over fruit. The business prides itself on its range of flavourful Italian ice creams, using ingredients such as dark-roasted Mocha. Grander desserts such as tartufo and cassata Siciliana have traditionally been purchased here for family occasions by London's Italian community. There is also a relaxed family-friendly restaurant area serving tasty pizzas and pasta.

La Porchetta Pizzeria *££*
⊞ *147 Stroud Green Road, N4*
☎ *020 7281 2892*
🚌 *Finsbury Park LU/Rail*

The gargantuan, tasty, bargain-priced pizzas on offer here ensure a busy, bustling atmosphere.

Refreshment House *£*
⊞ *Golders Hill Park, North End Road, NW3*
☎ *020 8455 8010*
🚌 *Golders Green LU*

Popular with families with young children and pensioners alike, this large Italian café serves up cappuccini, panini and a few pasta dishes. The star attraction, however, is their own gelati – fresh-tasting ice creams from refreshing melon to sweet, moreish marron, studded with pieces of marrons glacés.

WEST

Assaggi *££££*
⊞ *The Chepstow, 39 Chepstow Place, W2*
☎ *020 7792 5501*
🚌 *Notting Hill Gate LU*

Located above a pub this small restaurant is noted for its flavourful, authentic Italian food.

The River Cafe *£££££*
⊞ *Thames Wharf, Rainville Road, W6*
☎ *020 7381 8824*
🚌 *Hammersmith LU*

Informally stylish, this acclaimed restaurant, housed in a Richard Rogers-designed wharf complex by the River Thames, continues to thrive. Owners and chefs Ruth Rogers and Rose Gray make a point of using the finest quality, seasonal produce, from the best Italian cheeses and olive oil to the freshest of salad leaves. A number of best-selling 'River Café' cookbooks and a television series have ensured that the restaurant's fame has spread far beyond Hammersmith.

SOUTH- WEST

Eco Brixton Ltd £
🖃 *4 Market Row, SW9*
☎ *020 7738 3021*
🚌 *Brixton LU/Rail*

Tucked away amongst the hustle and bustle of Brixton Market, this tiny, relaxed pizzeria makes authentic Italian thin-based pizzas, generously topped with gourmet treats like fresh rocket or roasted red peppers. Food is served until 5pm in the afternoon.

Branch: Eco, 162 Clapham High Street, SW4 (020 7622 6848)

Pizzeria Castello ££
🖃 *20 Walworth Road, SE1*
☎ *020 7703 2556*
🚌 *Elephant and Castle LU/Rail*

An appetising waft of garlic signals this popular pizzeria. Regulars return for the excellent crisp pizzas and lively service.

Riva £££
🖃 *169 Church Road, SW13*
☎ *020 8748 0434*
🚌 *Barnes Bridge Rail*

A restaurant pioneer of regional Italian cooking, Riva continues to offer imaginative and tasty dishes in an elegant setting, and has a loyal clientele.

Cookbooks

Complete Italian Food
Antonio and Priscilla Carluccio
Attractively illustrated guide to Italian ingredients complete with
recipes by Italian chef Antonio Carluccio and his wife Priscilla.

The Classic Food of Northern Italy
Gastronomy of Italy
Secrets of an Italian Kitchen
Anna del Conte
Anna del Conte's books are at once wonderfully appetising and
informative.

Italian Food
Elizabeth David
Although first published in 1954, her comments on the essence of
Italian cookery remain perceptive and valid. A classic.

The River Café Cook Book
Rose Gray and Ruth Rogers
This stylish cookbook by the owners of London's famous River
Café restaurant features classic Italian dishes.

Italian Regional Cookery
Valentina Harris
A lively and informative recipe book.

The Classic Italian Cookbook
The Second Classic Italian Cookbook
Marcella's Kitchen
Marcella Hazan
Three wonderful cookbooks by a highly respected author: a great
source of knowledgeable writing about Italian cookery. Essential.

The Food of Italy
Claudia Roden
A beautifully written guide to the regions of Italy and their local
dishes; evocative and deliciously useable.

Japanese London

Fuji Food

Japanese Cuisine

The Japanese presence in London is a comparatively recent phenomenon. Japan's deliberate cultural isolation for hundreds of years was broken down in the seventeenth century by Portuguese traders and missionaries, but contact with the West remained limited. It was during Japan's post-Second World War business boom, as the country restored and developed its economy, that a community developed in London. It is primarily a business community, consisting of families on postings for large companies and banks. The temporary nature of most of these postings has kept the community transitory and relatively rootless. Social life, as in Japan, is conducted largely round the golf course and at business lunches.

It used to be said that the Japanese lived on the Northern Line, which provided access to all their needs, from the City for work to the leafy suburbs of Finchley and Golders Green for housing, with much-valued golf courses nearby. The presence of the Oriental City shopping plaza at Colindale was prompted by the growth of this North London community. The shifting of the Japanese School to Acton, however, has opened up a new area of suburban London for the Japanese community and the Northern Line is no longer the sole axis. Acton's Japanese community are now catered for by two kindergartens and primary schools, as well as Japanese food shops, book shops, property letting agencies and restaurants. The past decade has also seen a growing Japanese presence in the West End, with shops opening specifically to cater for the influx of prosperous Japanese tourists.

Japanese Cuisine

This highly refined cuisine, which developed in isolation for hundreds of years, is both aesthetic and ascetic. In Japan's codified society, a meticulously disciplined approach governs food preparation as well as other aspects of life. Presentation is all-important: small portions of foods are carefully arranged, delighting both the eye and the palate. Nouvelle cuisine borrowed greatly from Japanese culinary aesthetics.

'Kisetsukan' is the Japanese term for a sympathy with nature, important in Japanese culture. Dishes are designed to echo nature, perhaps creating a minature landscape or simply a natural gracefulness. A great value is placed on freshness and seasonality. Fish and vegetables, two key foodstuffs, are at their best fresh. Sashimi, raw fish served with a dipping sauce, epitomises this emphasis. Even though modern preserving techniques have robbed seasonality of its practical imperative, it continues to be valued. There is a whole range of dishes, such as cherry blossom rice or oden, eaten in appropriate months and seasons, with even preserved ingredients such as pickles and miso pastes changing according to the time of year. The flavour of individual ingredients is emphasised in the cooking rather than disguised. Even a Japanese stew retains the separate flavours of ingredients rather than blending them into a whole.

The range of seasonings in Japanese food is limited, falling into three broad categories: salty (provided by shoyu and dashi), sweet (from sugar, mirin and sake) and citrus (from yuzu and dai dai fruits). Shiso leaves and sansho provide an extra aromatic touch. These flavourings are used over and over again in different combinations. Pickles are carefully chosen to go with particular dishes. Fish and seafood, as befits a nation of islands, play a large part in the cuisine, from the basic soup stock to fishcakes and sausages. An extenstion of this love of seafood has been the use of seaweeds or sea-vegetables, a hallmark of Japanese cooking.

Many of the unique aspects of Japanese cuisine come from the fact that it developed to a great extent in isolation. However, over centuries, a number of foreign influences filtered through. China, between the sixth and eighth centuries, had an effect on many aspects of Japanese life including food – hence chopsticks, tea, the nutritious soya bean, rice and noodles. Zen Buddhism provided both the aesthetic criteria of Japanese cuisine and the emphasis on vegetables. It was only in the nineteenth century that the Japanese began eating red meat more widely. Certain dishes can be traced directly to outside sources, although most have been refined into something quintessentially Japanese. Portugese missionaries in the sixteenth century are said to have requested gambas fritta, fried prawns. From this developed the dish tempura: whole prawns and slices of vegetables cooked briefly in an exquisitely light batter so that the flavour and freshness of the ingredients are highlighted rather than disguised.

Glossary

Agar agar (kanten): a vegetarian setting agent obtained from seaweed, available either in powdered form or in translucent strands.

Azuki Beans: small dark red beans. In a sweetened paste form (*an*), they form a principal ingredient in Japanese cakes.

Bean curd (tofu): an ivory-coloured soya bean product with a firm custard texture, available either fresh or vacuum-packed. *Kinu* or silk tofu has a more delicate texture than *momen* or cotton tofu. *Koyadofu* is freeze-dried tofu, dull brown with a spongy texture. *Aburage* are thin deep-fried sheets of bean curd.

Bonito: dried bonito fish flakes, together with kombu seaweed, are used to make dashi soup stock and also as a garnish. *Dashi-no-moto* is an instant granule form of dashi stock, available in packets.

Burdock (gobo): a long slender root vegetable, available fresh and canned.

Chrysanthemum leaves (shungiku): the leaves of the edible garland chrysanthemum (not to be confused with our ornamental inedible one), used as a garnish and a vegetable.

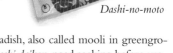

Dashi-no-moto

Daikon: a large, long, mild, white radish, also called mooli in greengrocers. Dried daikon strips, called *kiriboshi daikon*, need soaking before use.

Fish and Seafood: raw fish, either in sashimi or sushi, is one of the most famous elements of Japanese cuisine. Popular fish include mackerel (*saba*), salmon (*sake*) and tuna (*maguro*), with the latter graded according to its fattiness. Grilled eel (*unagi*) is a prized delicacy. Popular seafood includes abalone (*awabi*), horse clams (*mirugai*), scallops (*hotategai*), salmon roe (*ikura*), octopus (*tako*) and squid (*ika*).

Fishcakes and fish sausages: boiled, baked and deep-fried fishcakes and sausages come in various forms, and are often found in the deep freeze section. Popular varieties include: *naruto maki*, a fish sausage with a spiral pink or yellow pattern running through it; *satsuma-age*, oval-shaped fried fishcake; and *chukuwu*, a fish sausage.

Flours: rice flour (*joshinko*) is used for savoury doughs. Glutinous rice flour (*mochiko*) and soya bean flour (*kinako*) are used mainly for desserts.

Gingko nuts (ginnan): maidenhair tree kernels. Fresh gingko nuts (which need shelling) are ivory-cloured, while tinned, shelled gingko nuts are pale green.

Kabocha: Japanese pumpkin, often sold deep-frozen.

Kampyo: dried gourd or winter melon strips, used for tying food.

Kinome: prickly ash tree leaf, used as a garnish.

Konnyaku: a bland, glutinous substance made from the root of the devil's tongue plant, often labelled 'alimentary paste' and found in the chilled section or freezer. Konnyaku noodles, called *shirataki* (meaning white waterfall), are sold packaged in water.

Kabocha

Kuzu: a white starch made from the kuzu vine root, sometimes labelled 'kuzu arrowroot'.

Lotus root (renkon): a crunchy root with a decorative tracery of holes, available fresh, in sausage-like links, or tinned.

Mirin: a sweet Japanese rice wine, used as a glazing ingredient.

Miso: fermented soya bean paste, available in a variety of colours and flavours. In general, the light miso pastes have a more delicate flavour than the darker ones. It is usually found in the chilled or freezer section and should be stored in the fridge.

Mochi: cooked glutinous rice, pounded to a paste.

Mountain yam (yama no imo): a large, pale-skinned, sweet-flavoured tuber, which comes in different shapes.

Mushrooms: these include large, brown-capped *shitake* (available both fresh and dried), tiny white-capped clusters of *enokidake*, light brown *shimeji* and large, brown *matsutake*.

Natto: fermented soya beans with a pungent smell and sticky texture.

Noodles: *harusame*, fine cellophane noodles made from mung beans whose Japanese name means 'spring rain'; *soba*, brown buckwheat noodles; *somen*, fine wheatflour noodles, sometimes flavoured with green tea; *udon*, thick, white wheatflour noodles.

Pickles: *sudori shoga*, pickled ginger, traditionally eaten with sushi; *takuan*, pickled daikon, often bright yellow in colour.

Ponzu: a citric vinegar.

Sabo Noodles

Potato starch (kataturika): strongly binding sweet potato starch.

Rice: short grain, slightly glutinous rice is the staple. A very sticky glutinous 'sweet rice' is used to make desserts and cakes.

Rice vinegar (su): delicate rice vinegar, used in making sushi.

Sake: rice wine, both drunk and used as a flavouring in cooking.

Sansho: known as 'Japanese pepper' this is the seed of the prickly ash tree.

Seaweed

Seaweeds: *kombu*, a dark large-leafed seaweed used in making dashi stock; *nori*, thin green sheets of dried seaweed used for sushi, available untoasted or toasted; *wakame*, dried lobeleaf seaweed.

Shichimi togarashi: a piquant seven-spice mix containing chilli.

Shiso: the aromatic red or green leaves of the perilla or beefsteak plant, used to add both flavour and colour.

Shiso

Soya beans: raw soya beans (*edamame*), available frozen, are a poplar snack food. Dried soya beans (*daizu*) need long cooking.

Soy sauce (shoyu): Naturally brewed Japanese soy sauce, available both dark and light, has a different, more subtle flavour than Chinese soy sauce. Kikkoman is a reputable shoyu manufacturer.

Trefoil (mitsuba): a leaf herb, often found freeze-dried.

Umeboshi: small, deep red, pickled plums, with a tart flavour.

Warabi: young edible sprouts of bracken, picked before they have uncurled, available dried or vacuum-packed.

Wasabi: a pungent green root, compared to horseradish, sold in paste or powder form.

Wasabi

Wheat Gluten (fu): wheat gluten forms, often coloured, used rather like croutons in soups and simmered dishes.

Yuzu: an aromatic citrus fruit with a distinctive aroma and taste, used to flavour oil.

Food Shops

Japanese food shops, aimed at the ex-pat business community, demand high prices at which the Japanese themselves grumble. Many of the foodstuffs are imported from Japan and all of these are beautifully packaged, from rice-paper packets of ribbon-wrapped noodles to gaudy, wacky packets of sweets, shaped like robots or calculators. Fish and meat counters are a beautiful sight, with finely-sliced meat and aesthetic displays of seafood, from a gracefully-coiled octopus tendril to a mosaic of mackerel fillets, arranged skin-side up.

In general Japanese food shops are well ordered, with ingredients grouped together: flavourings, pickles, noodles. Often, the goods have small labels giving the English names.

CENTRAL

Arigato

▢ *48-50 Brewer Street, W1*
☎ *020 7287 1722*
🚇 *Leicester Square, Piccadilly Circus LU*
🕐 *Mon-Sat 10am-9pm, Sun 11am-8pm*

Neat and airy, this friendly supermarket-cum-take-away caters for office workers in the area. The stock covers basics from miso paste to soba noodles. The take-away sushi counter is especially popular.

Centre Point Food Store

▢ *20-21 St Giles High Street, WC2*
☎ *020 7836 9860*
🚇 *Tottenham Court Road LU*
🕐 *Mon-Sat 10am-10.30pm, Sun 12noon-8pm*

In the shadow of Centre Point's looming tower, the Centre Point Food Store is a large, well-stocked food shop, offering both Japanese and Korean foodstuffs. Stock is comprehensive, including freezers containing Japanese cuts of meat and fish, fresh vegetables and fruit, noodles, miso pastes and flavourings and a large choice of snacks and sweets. If the sight of all these Japanese ingredients gives you an appetite, simply head upstairs to the Sushi Café.

Japan Centre Food Shop

▭ *212 Piccadilly, W1*
☏ *020 7434 4218*
🚌 *Piccadilly Circus LU*
🕐 *Mon-Fri 10am-7pm, Sat 10.30am-8pm, Sun 11am-7pm*

In the heart of the West End, the Japan Centre has long been an important base for London's ex-pat Japanese, complete with a ground floor restaurant and travel shop, upstairs bookshop and a well-stocked, busy food shop, tucked away in the Japan Centre's basement. Brightly packaged sweets are an eye-catching element, while more functional foodstuffs are also well-represented, from fresh Japanese vegetables, fruit and herbs (such as kabocha and shiso leaves), noodles, teas, a Yoshino fish counter and freezers crammed full with seafood and fish cakes and sukiyaki beef. A deli-counter sells take-away snacks, including sushi.

Minamoto Kitchoan

▭ *44 Piccadilly, W1*
☏ *020 7437 3135*
🚌 *Piccadilly Circus LU*
🕐 *Mon-Fri & Sun 10am-7pm, Sat 10am-8pm*

This dainty shop specialises in Japanese confectionery: exquisite-looking concoctions made from red bean paste, rice flour and fruit and bean jelly, tastefully wrapped and packaged. Prices are high, reflecting the fact that these items are traditionally given as gifts. There is a small seating area where you can sit and enjoy green tea and a cake, such as their bestselling Tsuya (a soft round pancake filled with red bean paste).

NORTH

Atari-Ya Foods

▭ *15-16 Monkville Parade,*
Finchley Road, NW11
☏ *020 8458 7626*
🚌 *Golders Green LU, then bus 82, 102, 260*
🕐 *Mon-Fri 10am-6.30pm, Sat-Sun 10am-7pm*

This large, neatly arranged shop is particularly strong on store-cupboard staples such as rice, noodles, seaweeds and condiments, though there is a small fresh fish counter. Sunday's sushi counter is extremely popular with the local Japanese community.

Atari-Ya Foods

⌨ *595 High Road, N12*

☎ *020 8446 6669*

🚎 *West Finchley LU; Bus 263*

🕐 *Tue-Fri 10am-6.30pm, Sat-Sun 10am-7pm*

A neat shop dominated by a long fish counter, with the staff behind it expertly preparing the fish. In addition, there is a limited selection of groceries and a small chilled cabinet containing essentials such as fresh tofu.

Fuji Foods

⌨ *167 Priory Road, N8*

☎ *020 8347 91770*

🚎 *Finsbury Park LU, then W7 bus*

🕐 *Tue-Fri 9.30am-5.30pm, Sat-Sun 9.30am-5.30pm*

This small, immaculate shop offers an excellent range of Japanese food-stuffs, from frozen fish cakes to fresh tofu. Pride of place, however, goes to the fresh fish and sushi counter where Mr Fuji lovingly and expertly prepares his own sushi rolls, including piquant prawn and avocado coated in flying fish roe, nigiri sushi and marinaded fish, including black cod with miso.

Natural Natural

⌨ *1 Goldhurst Terrace, NW6*

☎ *020 7624 5734*

🚎 *Finchley Road Rail*

🕐 *Daily 9am-8pm*

A small shop, with fresh produce outside and Japanese foodstuffs inside.

Oriental City Supermarket

⌨ *Oriental City, 399 Edgware Road, NW9*

☎ *020 8200 0009*

🚎 *Colindale LU*

🕐 *Mon-Sat 10am-8pm, Sun 12noon-6pm*

Located in the shopping centre formerly known as Yaohan Plaza (which comes complete with a SegaDome), this is London's largest Japanese supermarket. Brightly spick and span, the store is well laid out and goods are clearly labelled in English. There is an excellent array of fresh produce, from burdock and lotus root to clusters of tiny enokidake mushrooms, and a fresh fish counter. Stock is comprehensive: from the aisles of noodles, teas, and condiments to the chilled counters with their neatly-packaged fresh fish and meat.

Unohana

⊟ *10 North End Road, NW11*

☏ *020 8201 8833*

🚌 *Golders Green LU*

🕐 *Mon-Sat 10am-8pm, Sun 11am-7pm*

Opposite Golders Green tube station, a few doors down from the Japanese Homes letting agency, this bright, tidy shop stocks an impressive range of Japanese foodstuffs. English customers are well-catered for with ingredients helpfully labelled with names and recipe pointers, while staff are friendly and happy to help. In addition to basic foodstuffs, including Japanese produce, bean curd, sauces and rice, there is a wide choice of ready-to-eat dishes, including croquettes, sukiyaki, fried fish and sushi, freshly prepared at the back.

Wing Yip (London) Ltd

⊟ *395 Edgware Road, NW2*

☏ *020 8450 0422*

🚌 *Colindale LU*

🕐 *Mon-Sat 9.30am-7pm, Sun 11.30am-5.30pm*

This massive Chinese supermarket, located just off Staples Corner, contains basic bottled and tinned Japanese ingredients: noodles, sauces, tea and sake.

WEST

Atari-Ya Foods

⊟ *7 Station Parade, Noel Road, W3*

☏ *020 8896 1552*

🚌 *West Acton LU*

🕐 *Tue 11am-6.30pm, Wed-Fri 10am-6.30pm,*
Sat 9am-7pm, Sun 10am-7pm

In West Acton's leafy suburbs, this corner food shop, across the road from a Japanese letting agency, serves West London's Japanese community with polite efficiency. Stock includes a selection of fresh fish and a good range of basic foodstuffs.

Natural Natural

⌂ *20 Station Parade, Uxbridge Road, W5*

☎ *020 8992 0770*

🕘 *Daily 9am-8pm*

This friendly, down-to-earth shop caters comprehensively for West London's Japanese community, with stock ranging from fresh fruit and vegetables in boxes outside to shelves of sake, freezers filled with frozen vegetables such as burdock and huge sacks of sushi rice stacked on the floor inside. Take-away foods such as tonkatsu and Japanese cakes are a popular draw with Japanese commuters returning home.

SOUTH-WEST

Japanese Kitchen

⌂ *9 Lower Richmond Road, SW15*

☎ *020 8788 9014*

🚌 *Putney Bridge Rail*

🕘 *Tue-Wed & Fri-Sat 11am-6pm, Thur 11am-7pm, Sun 11am-5pm*

Just by the River Thames, this tiny, pretty shop, decked out in red and white, has a small stock of basic foodstuffs, including frozen edamame and gyoza, pickles and sushi basics. Miso soup and own-made bento boxes cater for the lunchtime trade, while the rest of the shop is devoted to second-hand Japanese books and a quirky collection of Japanese toys.

Eating Places

Once Japanese restaurants in London were exclusive, expensive affairs. Two recent trends – the noodle bar and the conveyor-belt sushi restaurant mean that affordable, accessible Japanese food is now widely available.

CENTRAL

Abeno $\pounds\pounds$

⌗ 47 Museum Street, WC1

☎ 020 7405 3211

🚇 Holborn LU, Tottenham Court Road LU

Located on a peaceful Bloomsbury street, this small, tranquil restaurant offers a chance to sample 'okonomi-yaki': tasty Japanese pancakes made from a thick batter containing shredded cabbage, and topped with ingredients ranging from meat to seafood. Each okonomi-yaki is freshly cooked to order on a table griddle in front of the diner and the staff are charming and helpful.

Branch: Abeno Too, 15-18 Gt Newport Street, WC2 (020 7579 1160)

Gonbei $\pounds\pounds\pounds$

⌗ 151 King's Cross Road, WC1

☎ 020 7278 0619

🚇 King's Cross LU/Rail

A well-established restaurant which, despite its modest appearance, serves up prime sushi to an appreciative Japanese clientele.

Ikkyu $\pounds\pounds$

⌗ 67 Tottenham Court Road, W1

☎ 020 7636 9280

🚇 Goodge Street LU

Tucked away in a basement next to the Scientology Centre this pleasantly informal, veteran Japanese restaurant has a loyal following. Sushi is freshly prepared behind a counter while the set lunch menu includes bargains such as miso ramen, a huge bowl of garnished noodles in a flavourful stock.

Kulu Kulu *££*

⌨ *76 Brewer Street, W1*

☎ *020 7734 7316*

🚇 *Piccadilly Circus LU*

A classic example of a kaiten (revolving) sushi bar where diners graze on sushi plucked from a slowly moving conveyor-belt. The strength here is the quality of the fresh, handmade sushi.

Matsuri *£££-££££*

⌨ *15 Bury Street, SW1*

☎ *020 7839 1101*

🚇 *Green Park LU*

A classic, upmarket Japanese restaurant, aimed very much at the business community, and famed for its teppan-yaki grill cooking, carried out with impressive skill and dexterity.

Branch: 71 High Holborn, WC1 (020 7430 1970)

Satsuma *££*

⌨ *56 Wardour Street, W1*

☎ *020 7437 8338*

🚇 *Leicester Square LU, Piccadilly Circus LU*

From the Wagamama school of refectory-style dining: a sleek, stream-lined affair with long wooden tables and benches. Staff are lively and the food, ranging from chicken Teriyaki to sushi, is well-presented and tasty.

Ten Ten Tei *££*

⌨ *56 Brewer Street, W1*

☎ *020 7287 1738*

🚇 *Piccadilly Circus LU*

Tucked away from the hustle of Piccadilly, this friendly, relaxed restaurant serves up good value Japanese food with all the classics on offer, from sashimi to tempura.

Yoshino *££-£££*

⌨ *3 Piccadilly Place, W1*

☎ *020 7287 6622*

🚇 *Piccadilly Circus LU*

A civilised oasis, discreetly positioned in a side-street off Piccadilly, Yoshino serves first-class sushi, eaten either at the wide, comfortable bar or at the table.

NORTH

Jin Kichi   £££
⌦   *73 Heath Street, NW3*
☎   *020 7794 6158*
🚏   *Hampstead LU*

A friendly, long-established restaurant, specialising in yakitori dishes and so offering a large range of tasty salty-sweet skewered foods including chicken and prawns.

Oriental City Food Court   £
⌦   *Oriental City Plaza, 399 Edgware Road, NW9*
☎   *020 8200 0009*
🚏   *Colindale LU*

A busy, noisy indoor 'courtyard' dominated by a huge central TV with CNN news and the noise of vendors shouting out their clients' orders, surrounded by food stalls offering a host of Far Eastern cuisines including Japanese. The spanking fresh sushi from the sushi bar next to the supermarket is particularly good.

Sushi-Say   ££££
⌦   *33B Walm Lane, NW2*
☎   *020 8459 2971*
🚏   *Willesden Green LU*

In deepest Willesden, Sushi-Say, with its pretty, rustic décor is something of an oasis. It has a considerable regular clientele, drawn back by the delicious, freshly prepared Japanese food and the pleasantly relaxed and convivial atmosphere,

Wakaba   ££££
⌦   *122a Finchley Road, NW3*
☎   *020 7722 3854*
🚏   *Finchley Road Rail*

This restaurant's elegant façade, a curve of smoked glass, and its stark interior comply with one's expectations of Japanese aesthetics. The food is cooked with flair, including impressively fresh seafood.

WEST

Momo *£££*

⌧ *14 Queen's Parade, W5*

☎ *020 8997 0206*

🚌 *North Ealing LU*

With the Japanese School close by, this pleasant restaurant caters for the local Japanese community offering authentic food at reasonable prices.

Sushi-Hiro *££*

⌧ *1 Station Parade, Uxbridge Road, W5*

☎ *020 8896 3175*

🚌 *Ealing Common LU*

Handily situated just across the road from the tube station is this spick and span sushi restaurant, discreetly hidden behind a frosted glass façade, offering excellent value sushi either to eat in or take-away.

Cookbooks

Food of Japan
Shirley Booth
An illuminating, lucidly written look at Japanese cuisine with recipes and detailed ingredient information.

Step-by-Step Japanese Cooking
Leslie Downer and Minoru Yoneda
A clear introduction to Japanese cuisine.

Easy Sushi
Emi Kazuko
An illustrated, accessible guide to the joys of home-made sushi.

Japanese Cookery
Elizabeth Lambert Ortiz
A clearly-written cookbook; a useful introduction to the cuisine.

The Heart of Zen Cookery
Soei Yoneda
Guide to the centuries-old vegetarian cuisine of the Zen temples.

Jewish London

Platters

The Jewish presence in England dates back to the eleventh century when French Jews followed William the Conqueror and settled here. They were legally restricted to certain trades and professions but moneylending, forbidden to Christians, was allowed, indeed encouraged, and became the basis for a prosperous and established community. Persecution of the Jews grew, however, and in 1290 all Jews were expelled from England by Edward I.

Following the expulsion of Jews from Spain in 1492, some Sephardi Jews (Mediterranean Jews) accepted the Christian faith but continued to practise Judaism in secret. They became known as Marranos and a small community of them settled in London. In 1655 Rabbi Menassah ben Israel, resident in Holland, appealed to Oliver Cromwell to permit Jewish resettlement. In June of the following year Cromwell declared that Judaism would again be permitted in England and a small community of Sephardi merchants, bankers, bullion dealers and gem importers settled in London. The Sephardi community's first synagogue was in a house at Creechurch Lane in the East End. In 1701, when this had become too small, the Bevis Marks synagogue was built – and continues in use to this day.

The Jewish community was also expanded by the immigration of Ashkenazi Jews from Eastern Europe, who followed a different liturgy. In general they were artisans, peasants, tailors and shoemakers. By 1690, they had established their own synagogue in Dukes Place. George I encouraged German Jews to come to England and by the middle of the eighteenth century the Ashkenazi community outnumbered the Sephardi.

Aldgate and Houndsditch were popular Jewish areas, although in the first half of the nineteenth century a move took place among the established and prosperous Jewish families, such as the Rothschilds and Montefiores, who left St Swithins Lane for the fashionable West End. In 1858, a special parliamentary resolution enabled Lionel de Rothschild to take his seat in the House of Commons, which marked a watershed in Jewish emancipation in Britain. During the late nine-teenth century middle-class Jews moved into the new suburbs and by 1882, the St John's Wood synagogue was in operation.

For the poorer Jewish immigrants, however, the East End remained the focus. As Stephen Brook puts it in his fascinating book, 'The Club', 'Jews tend to live in enclaves not out of natural gregarious-ness but because they want to be close to institutions vital to the life of the community. Religious Jews will not ride or drive on the Sabbath so they wish to live within easy walking distance of a synagogue. They also needed convenient access to Jewish schools (there were seven in existence in 1851) and kosher butchers. Naturally new arrivals tended to join fellow Jews in the areas favoured by those who had arrived before them.'

Following the assassination of the liberal Russian Tsar Alexander II in 1881, a series of pogroms was unleashed in Russia and Poland, which continued into the early twentieth century. Thousands of Jews fled westwards, many aiming for and reaching America, but some staying in Britain instead of continuing their journey. Between 1881 and 1914 the Jewish population of the East End swelled by well over 100,000 people. These were Orthodox, Yiddish-speaking, semi-skilled or unskilled Jews; and the already established Anglo-Jews felt ambivalent about the influx, fearing an anti-Semitic backlash.

The Ashkenazi immigrants moved into the East End, especially around Whitechapel. Food shops sold the herrings and pickles of their homelands and the number of chevras (small synagogues) grew. The United Synagogues established dispersal committees to encourage Jewish immigrants to move out of the East End into the expanding suburbs of Dalston, Stoke Newington and Hackney. In the 1920s there was a move northwards from the East End into Stamford Hill and then into the newly established suburbs of Golders Green, Edgware and Ilford. The rise of anti-Semitism in the 1930s brought in around 70,000 Jews from Central Europe, with the influx increasing sharply after the 1938 Anschluss (unification) with Austria and the Kristallnacht pogrom. These were prosperous middle-class refugees who settled in north-west London in areas such as Hampstead, St John's Wood and Swiss Cottage. The decline of the Jewish East End community was hastened by the war, bombing destroying both families and property. Instead of return-ing after service or evacuation, many East End Jews opted for the suburbs with their by now well-established Jewish communities. By the 1970s the population of the East End Jewish community had shrunk to less than 5,000; today, around a third of Britain's Jewish population lives in north-west London.

Jewish Cuisine

Jewish cuisine reflects the widely dispersed Jewish community by containing a range of dishes and styles of cooking from around the world. Two broad and diverse strands stem from the culinary traditions of the Ashkenazi and the Sephardi. The former, influenced by long, cold winters, features preserved and pickled dishes such as rollmop herrings and smoked salmon; while the latter delights in aromatic spices and Mediterranean produce such as aubergines, peppers and olive oil. Common to all Jewish food, however, are the Kashrut, the strict dietary laws governing the preparation and consumption of food, which stem from biblical injunctions. They have been adhered to over the centuries.

Leviticus permits certain fish and meat: 'Any animal that has true hoofs, with clefts through the hoofs, and that chews the cud such you may eat' and 'Anything in water, whether in the seas or in the streams, that has fins and scales these you may eat'. Cattle, sheep and most fish, therefore, are permitted, but pigs, rabbits and shellfish are not, neither certain birds nor anything that crawls or swarms. Permitted animals and birds must be ritually slaughtered in a way that allows as much blood as possible to drain from the carcass. As the consumption of blood is forbidden, raw meat must be 'koshered' by being soaked in water, treated with salt, drained and then rinsed.

The injunction 'Thou shalt not boil a kid in its mother's milk' has been interpreted to mean that meat and dairy products may not be consumed together. Food containing dairy products may not be eaten after meat until at least three hours have passed. This extends to separating kitchen equipment used for meat products from that for dairy products. 'Pareve' means neutral and refers to foods that may be eaten with either meat or dairy products.

The commandment that 'On the seventh day thou shalt do no work, neither thy maidservant nor thy manservant' has produced a range of characteristically Jewish dishes that are prepared the day before they are eaten. Cholent is one of the most famous of these dishes: a Sabbath stew traditionally cooked slowly overnight. Harry Blacker, in his book of East End reminiscences Just Like It Was, writes of the cholent being 'carried to the nearest bakehouse, where for a small consideration (about 2 pence), the baker would put the pan in the oven to cook until the following midday'.

Religious festivals also influence Jewish cuisine. At Pesach (Passover), when wheat flour is banned, dishes are made with ground nuts, matzo meal or potato flour. Certain symbolic foods and dishes are eaten both during the weekly Shabbat (Sabbath) and the festivals. During Pesach, which celebrates the Jewish delivery from slavery to the Egyptians, a 'Seder' plate is assembled made up of symbolic ingredients such as haroset, a sweet fruit paste representing the mortar used by Jewish slaves when they worked on the Pharoah's cities, and a bitter herb, such as endive, representing the bitterness endured during slavery. Matzos, the unleavened bread used during Pesach, represents the bread which didn't have time to rise as the Jews fled.

Another element common to Jewish cookery across the continents is its ingenuity, born out of the poverty and lack of ingredients which Jewish communities often suffered. Meat, in particular, was eked out in resouceful dishes such as helzel, stuffed chicken neck skin, and koureven, stewed chicken gizzards.

Glossary

Bagels

Bagels: circular bread rolls with a distinctive, chewy texture which comes from being first boiled then baked. Increasingly available both plain and flavoured.

Bulka: the 'everyday' cholla loaf, made from the same dough as bagels but shaped differently.

Cholla: a symbolic plaited loaf made from an egg-rich dough, and with a brown glaze. It plays a prominent part in most Jewish festivals and is especially associated with Shabbat, the weekly Sabbath.

Chopped liver: a tasty mixture of finely chopped liver, onion and hard-boiled egg.

Falafel: small, savoury chickpea croquettes, now regarded as an Israeli national dish.

Gefilte fish: minced fish balls, either poached or fried.

Herrings: a staple fish, preserved by salting or pickling. *Chopped herring*, a sweet-sour mixture of herrings, onions, apple, sugar and vinegar; *rollmops* or *Bismarcks*, pickled herrings rolled around onion rings; *schmaltz herrings* or *matjes*, smoked young herrings, often ready-filleted.

Herring

Kreplach: triangular dumplings with a meat or cheese filling. The three corners symbolise the three patriarchs: Abraham, Isaac and Jacob. These can be found ready-made in freezer sections.

Latkes: shredded potato fritters associated with Chanucah.

Latkes

Lokshen: egg noodles, used in soups and also to make lokshen kugel, a rich baked pudding, traditionally baked overnight for Shabbat.

Matzos

Mandlen: from Yiddish for 'almonds', these are fried or baked dough 'soup nuts', used like croutons as a garnish.

Matzos: a flat unleavened bread, similar in texture and taste to a water biscuit. It is the main element in Passover cookery, which forbids the use of leavened grain. The entire process of matzo-making must take no longer than 18 minutes, otherwise fermentation may start.

Matzo balls (knaidlach): walnut-sized, matzo-meal dumplings.

Matzo meal: a binding element made from finely ground matzos.

Rye bread: bread made from rye, with a distinctively rich flavour.

Salt beef: boiled and pickled beef, usually brisket. Available freshly-made or in packets.

Smoked salmon (lox): traditionally served in a fresh bagel with cream cheese. Available pre-sliced or freshly sliced.

Food Shops

The food shop has always been important in Jewish life, both to satisfy religious dietary needs and as a focus of identity. The food that we find in Jewish shops in Britain is predominantly Ashkenazi rather than Sephardi. In 'East End Story', A. B. Levy remembers the aromas that 'wafted through the open fronts of delicatessen shops, from smoked salmon and roe, barrelled cucumbers and sauerkraut, and herrings in various guises, kippered, schmaltz, chopped and pickled.' These items continue to be familiar Jewish deli fare but nearly all the East End shops have gone and the delicatessens are now found in the North London suburbs.

Perhaps what is most baffling for a non-Jew are the varying degrees of kosherness. The Kashrut are strict dietary laws which govern the preparation and consumption of foods. Certain food shops display certificates to show that they are supervised or licensed by authorities such as the Kedassia, the Joint Kashrus Committee of the Union of Orthodox Hebrew Congregations, the Adam Yisroel Synagogue and the Golders Green Beth Hamedrash Congregation. These are the shops and eating places that I have called 'kosher' in my guide, but readers should satisfy themselves as to the standards of Kashrut observed. Some shops have a large range of kosher foodstuffs without being supervised while others carry a range of non-kosher Jewish foods. Interest in kosher food is reviving among younger Jews and the shops are responding to this. Kosher food, nowadays, is an increasingly sophisticated business and the range of kosher items available has increased enormously, from tandoori chicken to champagne.

NORTH

Amazing Grapes

▭ *94 Brent Street, NW4*

☎ *020 8202 2631*

🚇 *Hendon Central LU*

🕐 *Mon-Wed 9am-6pm, Thur 9am-7pm, Fri 9am-6pm in summertime (1$^1/_2$ hours before Shabbat in winter), Sun 10am-2pm*

This well-stocked kosher off-licence sells kosher wines from all over the world, reflecting the increasing range available. They stock Kiddush, the strong, sweet red wine used for sacramental purposes, and Israeli wines.

Carmelli Bakeries

　　128 Golders Green Road, NW11
☎　*020 8455 3063*
🚇　*Golders Green LU*
🕐　*Mon-Wed 7am-1am, Thur all night, Fri 7am-2pm, Sat all night through to Sun 11pm*

Smart and glitzy, this famous kosher bakery continues to attract crowds of customers. Noted for its bagels, it also offers a host of breads, cakes, pastries, quiches and biscuits. It is divided into a Pareve or 'non-milky' counter and a 'milky' counter, while behind-scenes bustles with bakers producing the goods.

J. A. Corney Ltd

　　9 Hallswelle Parade, Finchley Road, NW11
☎　*020 8455 9588*
🚇　*Golders Green LU*
🕐　*Tue-Thur 7.30am-5pm, Fri 7.30am-4pm, Sat-Sun 7.30am-1pm*

This well-established fishmonger's has been in the Corney family for over 40 years. It stocks a large range of fish, such as St Peter's fish and carp, plus minced fish (a mix of haddock, whiting and bream) – with more expensive fish minced on demand. Staff are friendly and knowledgeable.

Daniel's Bagel Bakery

　　13 Halleswelle Parade, Finchley Road, NW11
☎　*020 8455 5826*
🚇　*Golders Green LU*
🕐　*Sun-Wed 7am-9pm, Thur 7am-10pm, Fri 7am-1½ hours before Shabbat*

A busy kosher bakery noted for its top-notch bagels as well as its good range of cholla, rye bread and pastries.

Hendon Bagel Bakery

　　35-37 Church Road, NW4
☎　*020 8203 6919*
🚇　*Hendon Central LU*
🕐　*Mon-Thur 7am-11pm, Fri 8am-3pm, Sat 7pm until Sun 11pm*

A well-established and popular kosher bakery, selling bulka, dark and light rye breads and a wide choice of bagels. On Thursdays and Fridays, piles of freshly baked chollas lie temptingly on the racks.

Panzer's

⌨ *13-19 Circus Road, NW8*

☎ *020 7722 8162/8596*

🚇 *St John's Wood LU*

🕐 *Mon-Fri 8am-7pm, Sat 8am-6pm, Sun 8am-2pm*

Warmly recommended by Evelyn Rose, the doyenne of Jewish cookery, this large bustling delicatessen has been established since 1955, with Peter Vogel carrying on the family tradition. In its range and depth of stock, Panzer's is more like a supermarket than a deli, stocking everything from Hershey chocolate bars (for the area's ex-pat American community) to Israeli wine. Although not supervised, there is a large selection of kosher lines plus traditional Jewish foodstuffs. The large deli-counter offers six types of herring and four grades of smoked salmon among its delicacies, and its smoked salmon bagels are a must for afficionados.

Platters

⌨ *10 Halleswelle Parade, Finchley Road, NW11*

☎ *020 8455 7345*

🚇 *Golders Green LU, then bus 82, 102, 260*

🕐 *Mon-Sat 8.30am-4.30pm, Sun 8.30am-2pm*

This friendly, well-established business, run by the eponymous Platters family, offers a range of fresh, own-made, classic Jewish deli fare, from moreish fried gefilte fish to chopped liver. A particular highlight is the hand-carved smoked salmon, skillfully sliced by Len (now in his eighties), which attracts regular customers from as far away as Birmingham. *Branch: 83-85 Allitsen Road, NW8 (020 7722 5352)*

Sam Stoller and Son

⌨ *28 Temple Fortune Parade, NW11*

☎ *020 8458 1429*

🚇 *Golders Green LU, then bus 82, 102, 260*

🕐 *Mon 8am-1pm, Tue-Thur 7am-5pm,*
Fri 7am-1 hour before Shabbat, Sun 8am-1pm

Mr Sam Stoller opened his first fishmonger's in 1932. He took over this attractive tiled shop in 1947 and is known as a leading kosher fishmonger. The smoked salmon is particularly good, as is the 'prime kosher fish' such as St Peter's fish and Israeli carp.

EAST

Brick Lane Beigel Bake

⌨ *159 Brick Lane, E1*

☏ *020 7729 0616*

🚌 *Liverpool Street LU/Rail*

🕐 *Daily 24 hours*

This small, reasonably priced bakery is a culinary reminder of the East End's Jewish history. Piled high with bagels and chollas it remains enormously popular. A trip to Brick Lane market on a Sunday simply wouldn't be complete without one of their bagels – a fact confirmed by the perpetual, straggling queue.

Ilford Kosher Meats

⌨ *7 Beehive Lane, Ilford, IG4*

☏ *020 8554 3238*

🚌 *Gants Hill LU*

🕐 *Mon 6.30am-1pm, Tue-Thur 6.30am-6pm,*
   Fri 6.30am-1pm, Sun 7am-1pm

This large butcher's shop, run with genuine enthusiasm by Brian Brown, has an excellent selection of kosher meat products. Everything is made on the premises, from the lamb and mint sausages to the de-boned stuffed chicken. Traditional dishes include helzel (chicken neck stuffing) and Russian Verrainitz: (pastry-wrapped mashed potato, liver and onion) from an old recipe handed down by Mr Brown's grandmother.

OUTER LONDON

La Boucherie (Kosher) Ltd

⌨ *4 Cat Hill, East Barnet, EN4*

☏ *020 8449 9215*

🚌 *Cockfosters LU*

🕐 *Mon 8.30am-2.30pm, Tue-Thur 8.30am-5pm, Fri 8am-1pm,*
   Sun 8.30am-1.30pm and 3.30pm-7.30pm

This vast, sleek, scrupulously clean shop is one of London's leading kosher butchers and consequently bustles with customers. There are 40 staff altogether, including six chefs working behind the scenes on ready-made dishes such as Beef Wellington and the kofte kebabs for which La Boucherie is famous.

Platters

Louis Mann and Son Ltd

▭ *23 Edgwarebury Lane, WD6*

☏ *020 8958 4910*

🚌 *Edgware LU*

🕐 *Mon 7am-1pm, Tue-Thur 7am-5pm, Fri 7am-1pm, Sun 7am-1pm*

A smart, well-established kosher butcher, run with friendly efficiency by the Mann family. Salt beef, sold hot on Sundays, and hot roast chickens, sold daily, are especially popular.

Ivor Silverman

▭ *4 Canons Corner, London Road, Stanmore, Middlesex*

☏ *020 8958 8682/2692*

🚌 *Stanmore LU*

🕐 *Mon 8am-1pm; Tue-Thur 8.30am-5.30pm;*
   Fri 8am-1pm; Sun 8am-1pm

An elegant and upmarket kosher butcher which, in addition to freshly-cut meat and poultry, offers a large range of prepared meat dishes.

Steve's Kosher Kitchen

▭ *5 Canons Corner, London Road, Stanmore, Middlesex*

☏ *020 8958 9446*

🚌 *Stanmore LU*

🕐 *Mon-Wed 8.30am-5.30pm; Thur 8.30am-7pm;*
   Fri 8am-3pm (summer), 8am-1pm (winter); Sun 8am-1.30pm

A kosher delicatessen with an excellent selection of home-made foods. Specialities include chopped liver, salt beef and shallow-fried fish 'like granny used to do'.

Eating Places

CENTRAL

The Knosherie *£-££*

⌨ *12-13 Greville Street, EC1*

☎ *020 7242 5190*

🚌 *Chancery Lane LU*

Bustling and lively, this down-to-earth 'deli diner' specialises in generous portions of homely Jewish food, with salt beef sandwiches a particular forte.

NORTH

Blooms *££*

⌨ *130 Golders Green Road, NW11*

☎ *020 8455 1338*

🚌 *Golders Green LU*

Opened in 1965, this Golders Green institution has survived its better-known Whitechapel counterpart and continues to serve traditional kosher Jewish food. The salt beef is famous and portions are generous – homely food in a vintage atmosphere.

Chit Chat *££*

⌨ *85 Golders Green Road, NW11*

☎ *020 8731 6255*

🚌 *Golders Green LU*

A contemporary restaurant serving delicious Mediterranean Jewish foods: lots of the salads so beloved by Israelis and large portions of tasty grilled meats.

Harry Morgan's *£-££*

⌨ *31 St John's Wood High Street, NW8*

☎ *020 7722 1869*

🚌 *St John's Wood LU*

Dapper, well-established restaurant offering all the classics: chicken noodle soup with dumplings, salt beef and latkes.

Taboon £

▢ *17 Russell Parade, Golders Green Road, NW11*
☏ *020 8455 7451*
🚌 *Golders Green LU*

Thoroughly unpretentious, Taboon does a roaring trade in take-away falafel: deliciously juicy, freshly-fried chickpea rissoles garnished with good salad and tahini – a world away from the small, hard, dry rissoles normally on offer.

OUTER LONDON

Aviv ££

▢ *87 High Street, HA8*
☏ *020 8952 2484*
🚌 *Edgware LU*

A well-established kosher restaurant that specialises in Israeli food, hence there is a definite Middle Eastern flavour to the menu which offers mezze (including excellent houmous) and grilled meats.

Jewish Eating Places

Cookbooks

Jewish Cooking from Around the World
Josephine Bacon
A lively and accessible cookbook exploring both Sephardi and Ashkenazi cooking.

The Jewish Holiday Cookbook
Gloria Kaufner Greene
An informative look at festival and holiday dishes.

The Book of Jewish Food
Claudia Roden
A fascinating and absorbing look at Jewish food around the world, taking in both Sephardi and Ashkenazi traditions.

The Complete International Jewish Cookbook
Evelyn Rose
An excellent basic and reliable cookbook by a doyenne of Jewish cookery.

New Jewish Cuisine
Evelyn Rose
A straightforward look at Jewish recipes.

The Jewish Heritage Cookbook
Marlena Spieler
A well-illustrated cookbook filled with appetising recipes, including classics like gefilte fish, hamantashen and chopped eggs and onion.

Middle Eastern London

Zaman

The Middle Eastern community in London comprises several nationalities, drawn here at different times and for varying reasons. The Egyptians came to Britain in the 1940s and 1950s, both for education and work. The oil boom in the 1970s and the discovery by Arab countries of new sources of wealth and power resulted in an increasingly wealthy Arab presence in London, mainly focused around Mayfair and Kensington. A series of political disturbances has also contributed considerably to the Middle Eastern presence here. The overthrow of the Shah and the Iranian revolution brought in an influx of wealthy Iranian families who were able to use their money and connections to escape, many to America but some to London. They were followed by political opponents of the Ayatollah, seeking refuge. The civil war in Lebanon resulted in a substantial Lebanese presence in London. Edgware Road, Bayswater, Mayfair, Knightsbridge and Kensington together form the heartland of the Middle Eastern community, served by a splendid assortment of restaurants, fruit juice bars, cafés, banks, shops and clubs.

The Turkish community (which is included in this chapter because of the Ottoman Empire's culinary influence on Middle Eastern cuisine) is predominantly Turkish-Cypriot; many came to Britain because they were displaced following the Turkish invasion of Cyprus in 1974. They are mainly based in Islington, Hackney and Haringey, with the Stoke Newington end of Green Lanes being a particular focal point. Many of the cafés and kebab houses remain male preserves, with the sound of backgammon being played behind the scenes.

 # Middle Eastern Cuisine

This is an ancient cuisine, whose recipes can be traced back hundreds of years. An Egyptian recipe for melokhia soup, for example, dates from the time of the Pharoahs. The former spice routes which passed through the Middle East have left a fragrant legacy in the region's cooking.

Claudia Roden, an authoritative and knowledgeable writer on Middle Eastern cookery, identifies four main strands: Iranian or Persian, Arab, Ottoman Turkish and North African. Iranian cuisine is subtle and refined, a product of ancient Persia. Rice forms the heart of the cuisine and is carefully cooked and exquisitely garnished. The combination of meat with fruit or nuts is a hallmark of the Persian kitchen, shown in dishes such as koresh-e-fesenjan, chicken in walnut and pomegranate sauce. Arab cuisine is very flavourful, using strong-tasting herbs such as mint and coriander and fragrant spices such as cardamom, cinnamon and allspice. Grilled meats are popular, served with rice, burghul or flat breads.

During the Ottoman Empire, Turkish cuisine reached luxurious heights. Cooking at the Topkapi Palace in Istanbul followed a strict pattern of rules, still followed by chefs today. Ottoman food was spread through the Empire by the army and its followers, with shish kebab said to date back to these warlike days, when Turkish soldiers cooked over their camp fires. This culinary legacy includes numerous stuffed vegetables, such as imam bayaldi (an aubergine dish named after a priest who swooned with delight upon trying it); and layered nutty pastries in sweet syrups, beloved throughout the Middle East. North African cooking, in contrast to the other cuisines, has a fiery element, produced by hot sauces such as harissa. It is also a cuisine of subtle and delicate spicing.

The influence of Islam means that certain dietary laws are observed throughout the Middle East. Pork is forbidden and meat must be ritually slaughtered and drained of blood. Lamb is the most highly-prized meat throughout the region. Yoghurt is widely used: as a refreshing drink, in hot and cold soups, and in salads and marinades.

Glossary

Allspice: round berry, similar to peppercorns, with a flavour of nutmeg, cinnamon and cloves.

Apricot paste sheets (amretin): translucent orange sheets made from apricots which, when diluted with water, make a refreshing drink. Especially popular during the fasting month of Ramadan.

Apricot paste sheets

Arab bread (khoubz): flat round bread

Arab bread

Barberries (zerezhk): tart, red berries, used dried in Iranian cooking to add colour and flavour.

Burghul (bulgar): parboiled, cracked grains of wheat, available both coarse or finely ground.

Barberries

Coriander: a flat-leafed green herb, similar to continental parsley but with a distinctive sharp taste.

Couscous: fine yellow cereal made from semolina.

Dibbis: thick, dark brown syrup made from dates.

Dill: a caraway-scented herb with fine, feathery green fronds.

Dried limes

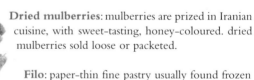

Dried limes (limoo): hard, brown, dried limes, used to add a distinctive flavour to Iranian and Iraqi soups and stews.

Dried mulberries: mulberries are prized in Iranian cuisine, with sweet-tasting, honey-coloured. dried mulberries sold loose or packeted.

Filo: paper-thin fine pastry usually found frozen but occasionally available fresh.

Dried mulberries

Freekeh: roasted green wheat.

Harissa: a fiery, red pimento paste.

Kashk: stony lumps of pungent dried buttermilk, used in soups and stews. Also available in powdered form.

Konafa (kadaif): a vermicelli-like dough, white in its raw state but resembling shredded wheat once cooked.

Labne (lebne): thick, strained concentrated yoghurt (usually sold bottled) which has been shaped into balls, and floats in oil.

Mahlab: small pale brown seeds which are the kernels of blackcherry stones, with a spicy fragrance.

Melokhia: a green, leafy vegetable, similar in appearance to mallow, used in making a famous eponymous Egyptian soup. Fresh melokhia is sometimes found, while dried is readily available.

Merguez: a spicy sausage from North Africa.

Okra: tapering, ridged green pods, available fresh, dried, tinned or frozen.

Onion seeds (sharmar): small, black teardrop-shaped seeds, not related to onions!

Orange–flower water: a fragrant flavouring made from orange flower essence, used in sweets, drinks and desserts.

Orange peel: fine strips of dried orange peel, traditionally from sour (Seville) oranges.

Nibbed pistachios

Pine nuts: small, ivory-coloured kernels, with the fine, long Lebanese pine nuts being particularly prized.

Pistachio: a small, green-coloured nut, indigenous to Iran.

Pomegranate syrup (pomegranate molasses): made from the concentrated juice of sour pomegranates and used in Iranian cooking.

Pomegranate

Pulses: black-eyed beans, with characteristic black markings; chickpeas, rounded yellow peas; Egyptian brown beans (*ful*), small brown broad beans.

Quince: a hard yellow-skinned fruit, resembling a large, craggy pear. Usually cooked, whereupon its flesh turns pink.

Quince

Rice: long-grain rice is a Middle Eastern staple. Fine quality Iranian rice is hard to get over here, with Basmati rice being the closest substitute.

Rose water: an essential scented flavouring made from rose essence and used in sweets and desserts.

Saffron: a costly spice made from the stigmas of a particular crocus variety, sold in thread or powdered form.

Salep: a thickening agent made from dried, crushed orchid roots, used in Iran to thicken ice cream.

Sumac: a dark red powdery spice, made from crushed berries, with a tangy flavour. Sometimes diluted and used as a lemon equivalent.

Tahini: sesame seed paste.

Tamarind: a brown pod with sour, dark brown, pulpy flesh and seeds. Available in de-seeded pulp form or as a paste. Also used to make a syrup, which is then diluted into a refreshing drink.

Turmeric: an orange-fleshed root, usually sold in its ground form as a yellow-orange powder. It has a harsh, flat taste and is used to add flavour and a distinctive yellow colour to dishes.

Vine leaves: large, distinctively shaped leaves of the vine. Occasionally found fresh, more usually sold in packets, preserved in brine, when they require soaking in water.

Yoghurt: tangy sheep's and goat's yoghurt as well as cow's yoghurt is widely used in Middle Eastern cooking.

Zahtar: a spice mix made from thyme, salt, sumac and sometimes roasted sesame seeds, often baked on the top of breads.

Food Shops

Attractive greengrocers-cum-delis selling everything from bunches of fresh herbs to pretty pastries, as well as bakers and halal butchers all serve the Middle Eastern community in London.

CENTRAL

Bustling Edgware Road is lined with Middle Eastern grocers, cafés and restaurants, and is well worth exploring if you're at all interested in Middle Eastern food. Drive up it late at night and you'll see a lively, metropolitan scene with drivers pulling in to get a take-away kebab and people sitting on pavement tables watching the world go by.

EV Delicatessen

⌂ *97-99 Isabella Street, SE1*
☎ *020 7620 6194*
🚇 *Waterloo LU/Rail, Southwark LU*
🕐 *Mon-Fri 7.30am-10pm, Sat 9am-9pm, Sun 11am-9pm*

Spectacularly housed in a railway arch, this stylish delicatessen stocks an impressive range of Turkish foodstuffs, and is part of the Tas chain (which also has a restaurant and bar in neighbouring arches). Organic grains, black tea and pulses, large-grained Turkish couscous, herbal teas, spices (including sumac) are all part of the line up as well as brightly coloured packets of Turkish delight. An in-house bakery produces a range of breads, including traditional, flat 'pide'. An attractively styled café dining area offers a chance to sample mezze and Turkish fruit juices.

Green Valley

⌂ *36 Upper Berkeley Street, W1*
☎ *020 7402 7385*
🚇 *Marble Arch LU*
🕐 *Daily 8am-10pm*

Warmly recommended by cookery writer Claudia Roden, this spacious Lebanese shop just off the Edgware Road has an eye-catching array of pastries, arranged temptingly in the window. Stock is impressively comprehensive: fresh produce, groceries, a halal meat counter and an in-house bakery. Customers with a sweet tooth are well-catered for with an ice-cream counter, pastry counter and a huge assortment of prettily packaged nougats, candied nuts and Turkish delight. There's even a small coffee counter at which to enjoy an aromatic cardamom-flavoured Lebanese coffee.

NORTH

Antepliler

⌖ *47 Grand Parade, Green Lanes, N4*
☎ *020 8809 1004*
🚌 *Manor House LU*
🕓 *Daily 8am-10pm*

Bright and cheery, this bakery-cum-café is famous for its high quality Turkish pastries. These are truly luxurious nut-filled, syrup-laden concoctions such as pistachio baklava which are baked on the premises.
Branch: 33A Newington Green, N16 (020 7226 9409)

Hormuz

⌖ *5 Ashbourne Parade, Temple Fortune, Finchley Road, NW11*
☎ *020 8455 8184*
🚌 *Golders Green LU, then bus 82, 102, 260*
🕓 *Daily 9am-9pm*

Next door to an Iranian bookshop of the same name, this neatly arranged Iranian grocery is recommended by Claudia Roden as having "a lot of good things". Inside there is a pleasing cross-section of Iranian foodstuffs: jams (including barberry), teas, pulses, flower waters and syrups, pastries, pickles and dairy products.

Phoenicia

⌖ *186-188 Kentish Town Road, NW5*
☎ *020 7267 1267*
🚌 *Kentish Town LU/Rail*
🕓 *Mon-Sat 9am-8pm, Sun 11am-4pm*

This large, bright, halal food hall was deliberately named Phoenicia by its owner Ghassan to reflect its Mediterranean stock. Foodstuffs here range comprehensively across the Mediterranean, so Italian pasta can be found beside couscous and Bulghur wheat, assorted Lebanese and Iraqi flatbreads nestle alongside ciabatta. One side of Phoenicia is a café, with a counter laden with Lebanese pastries (baklava and mamoul), a nut counter and Italian ice creams, plus a sandwich bar. Customers stock up on everything from halal meat from the butcher's counter to fruit syrups and juices, a process helped by the fact Phoenicia has a customer car park behind the shop.

Sahand

⌖ *74 Ballards Lane, N3*
☎ *020 8343 3279*
🚌 *Finchley Central LU*
🕐 *Mon-Sat 8am-9pm, Sun 9am-9pm*

This small, neatly arranged Iranian food shop offers a useful cross-section of Iranian ingredients: packets of tea, bottles of scented waters and syrups, pulses and an array of pastries. The courteous manager is happy to offer advice.

Yasar Halim

⌖ *493-495 Green Lanes, N4*
☎ *020 8340 8090*
🚌 *Manor House LU*
🕐 *Mon 8am-9.30pm, Tue-Sun 8am-10pm*

'Haringey's best supermarket!' declares a sign inside this bustling, well-established Turkish food store, which usefully combines a bakery, green-grocer's, deli and halal meat counter. Here one can find everything from fresh green almonds and spanking fresh flat-leafed parsley to tubs of sheep's yoghurt and jars of quince jam. The bakery here remains a bustling focal point, with customers queueing up for the freshly baked, huge, round loaves of village bread and sweet and savoury pastries such as guzleme, brought into the shop still warm from the oven. Fresh filo and kadaif is also on sale. Staff are numerous and friendly.

WEST

Del' Aziz

⌖ *24-28 Vanston Place, SW6*
☎ *020 7386 0086*
🚌 *Fulham Broadway Rail*
🕐 *Mon-Sat 7am-8pm, Sun 8am-6pm*

Dominating an entire Fulham side-street, Del'Aziz is an eye-catching operation, with one window filled with a colourful display of Moroccan ceramic tableware and another with an appetising range of patisserie and sweets. Inside, Del'Aziz operates as a deli-cum-café, with a central dining area and a long counter, offering own-cooked dishes, from pastries to salads. Diners sit surrounded by a picturesque assortment of foodstuffs, including confectionery, preserves and oils.

Lebanese Food Centre

⊞   *153 The Vale, W3*

☎   *020 8740 7365*

🚌   *Acton Central Rail*

🕐   *Daily 8am-10pm*

A large down-to-earth shop resembling a small supermarket, complete with a halal meat counter and an adjoining kebab restaurant. The stock is strong on basics such as pulses, spices and dried herbs with a small selection of fresh fruit and vegetables outside on the pavement.

Maroush Deli

⊞   *45-49 Edgware Road, W2*

☎   *020 7723 3666*

🚌   *Marble Arch LU*

🕐   *Daily 8am-midnight*

The Maroush restaurant chain's new food shop is a magnificent affair, splendidly fitted out with marble, mirrors and chrome. Stock ranges from a halal meat counter (offering cuts such as lamb's tongues), a fresh fish counter, attractively arranged fruit and vegetables, assorted pastries and grocery items. The delicatessen counter offers a chance to sample mezze dishes, such as tabbouleh and sambousek, prepared by the Maroush kitchens.

Le Marrakech

⊞   *64 Golborne Road, W10*

☎   *020 8964 8307*

🚌   *Ladbroke Grove LU*

🕐   *Mon-Sat 8.30am-7.30pm, Sun 10am-4pm*

An attractive front-of-shop display of earthenware tagines indicates this food shop's Moroccan roots. Inside, there are delights such as olives with kumquats, pomegranate molasses and pickled lemons, with cookware including couscoussiers and gilded tea-glasses. Lanterns, chandeliers and wall-hangings create something of a bazaar atmosphere – compounded on my visit by one of the staff pulling out a box of Moroccan leather slippers and offering them to an interested punter.

Middle Eastern Food Shops

Reza Patisserie

⌨ *345 Kensington High Street, W14*

☎ *020 7602 3674*

🚇 *Kensington High Street LU*

🕐 *Daily 8.30am-9pm*

A tempting assortment of pastries are on offer here, including both Arabic pastries, characterised by nuts and honey, and Iranian, which are simpler and more subtle. The freezer contains Iranian ice creams, flavoured with rose water and saffron, while the shelves carry an array of nuts, sweetmeats and dried fruit, such as Iranian sour cherries.

Sara Super Market

⌨ *7 Hereford Road, W2*

☎ *020 7229 2243*

🚇 *Bayswater LU, Notting Hill Gate LU, Queensway LU*

🕐 *Daily 8am-11pm*

Tucked away down a side-street, Massooud's small, neat, friendly shop offers fresh fruit and vegetables such as pomegranates and sour cherries and a selection of Iranian basics including nuts, cheeses, pickles and syrups. In addition, the shop is famous within Britain's Iranian community for its stock of Iranian music (both classical and popular) and films.

Zaman

⌨ *347-349 High Street Kensington, W8*

☎ *020 7603 8909*

🚇 *Kensington High Street LU*

🕐 *Daily 9am-10pm*

This attractive shop's Iranian roots are clearly signalled with a bright fluorescent sign saying 'Persian Caviar' in the window, a colourful fresh fruit and vegetable display in front of the shop, including hand-picked pomegranate kernels and sweet lemons, and the sound of Persian music floating through the door. En route to a downstairs halal meat counter, stock includes an eye-catching self-service counter of nuts, seeds and dried fruit such as mulberies and figs, a chilled cabinet with labne and yoghurt drinks and an assortment of pickles with their characteristic sour scent. Non-edible items on sale include inlaid backgammon boards, splendid Iranian teapots and tea-glasses and a basement room of CDs and tapes.

Pomegranates

SOUTH-WEST

Mediterranean Food Centre

⌂ *45 A & B Streatham Hill, SW2*

☎ *020 8678 1385*

🚌 *Streatham Hill Rail*

🕓 *Daily 6am-1am*

This large corner store serves the local community by offering, as its sign declares, 'English, Turkish, Greek, West Indian Food'. Fresh fruit and vegetables include quinces and pumpkins alongside chow-chows and yams. The comprehensive stock also features pulses, dairy products, dried fruit, nuts and spices. Next door is the bakery, selling freshly baked pide, and a halal butcher's counter.

EAST

Turkish Food Centre

⌂ *89 Ridley Road, E8*

☎ *020 7254 6754*

🚌 *Dalston Junction Rail*

🕓 *Mon-Sat 9am-7.30pm, Sun 8.30am-7pm*

A large, down-to-earth, competitively-priced Turkish supermarket. The shop offers a halal meat counter selling lamb, mutton and quails; and a cheese counter and piles of fresh fruit and vegetables – including bunches of leafy greens, vine tomatoes and watermelons. The large bakery section does a roaring trade in kibbeh and loaves of flat 'pide' bread.

Eating Places

London's thriving Middle Eastern restaurants cater very much for the ex-pat community and as a result, standards are generally high. The range is such that you can enjoy simple but good street food such as a succulent lamb kebab washed down with fresh fruit juice, or a leisurely meal of sophisticated Lebanese mezze in elegant surroundings.

CENTRAL

Al–Hamra *££££*

▢ *31-33 Shepherd Market, W1*
☎ *020 7493 1954*
🚌 *Green Park LU*

Elegant décor, efficient service and fine Lebanese food combine in one of London's best-known Lebanese restaurants, with prices reflecting the affluent location. The mezze are superb (including delights such as walnut-stuffed baby aubergines) but the atmosphere and service can be on the chilly side.

Al Sultan *££££*

▢ *51-52 Hertford Street, W1*
☎ *020 7408 1155*
🚌 *Green Park LU*

This intimate, upmarket Lebanese restaurant is an excellent place in which to sample exemplary mezze, from smooth-as-silk hummus Shawarma, topped with pine nuts and tender pieces of lamb to gutsily garlicky foul mkala. The dainty dessert pastries are similarly not to be missed.

Ali Baba *££*

▢ *32 Ivor Place, NW1*
☎ *020 7723 5805*
🚌 *Baker Street LU*

This modest café, with its bargain-priced food, is recommended by Claudia Roden for its 'real Egyptian' food, in particular the melokhia and the falafel.

Efes Kebab House *££*

- *80 Great Titchfield Street, W1*
- *020 7636 1953*
- *Great Portland Street LU, Oxford Circus LU*

This enormous Turkish restaurant – something of an institution – continues to run with smooth efficiency. The menu caters for carnivores, with charcoal-grilled kebabs much in evidence.

EV Restaurant & Bar *££-£££*

- *97-99 Isabella Street, SE1*
- *020 7620 6191/6192*
- *Southwark LU, Waterloo LU/Rail*

The latest addition to the Tas restaurant chain is eye-catchingly housed under the railways arches near Waterloo. One arch is given over to a smart, spacious bar, while the next arch is home to a similarly stylish restaurant, serving tasty Turkish food, with mezze being especially popular.

Original Tagines *££*

- *7A Dorset Street, W1*
- *020 7935 1545*
- *Baker Street LU*

A small and charming restaurant, serving up carefully cooked tagines, ranging from chicken with preserved lemon to lamb with caramelised pear.

Sofra *££*

- *36 Tavistock Street, WC2*
- *020 7240 3773*
- *Covent Garden LU*

This spacious Turkish restaurant operates on a successful formula: good, simple Turkish food served by polite staff at very reasonable prices, especially given the West End location.

Tas *££*

- *33 The Cut, SE1*
- *020 7928 2111*
- *Waterloo LU/Rail*

This large, New Wave Turkish restaurant offers reasonably priced, tasty Turkish food.

NORTH

Hafez $\pounds\pounds$

⌨ *559 Finchley Road, NW3*

☎ *020 7431 4546*

🚌 *Finchley Road LU*

Recommended by Iranian friends for its authentic food, this is the more glitzy sister restaurant of the Hereford Road branch in West London.

Mangal II $\pounds$

⌨ *4 Stoke Newington Road, N16*

☎ *020 7254 7888*

🚌 *Stoke Newington Rail*

With its relaxed, friendly atmosphere and seriously flavourful Turkish food at bargain prices, this Stoke Newington institution has built up a loyal following.

Yayla $\pounds$

⌨ *429 Green Lanes, N4*

☎ *020 8348 9515*

🚌 *Manor House LU*

Small, cheery corner café serving tasty Turkish food, from kebabs to pide, at remarkably reasonable prices. Bread is freshly made on the premises before your eyes.

WEST

Adams Café $\pounds\pounds$

⌨ *77 Askew Road, W12*

☎ *020 8743 0572*

🚌 *Buses 12, 207 or 266*

Operating as a café by day and a restaurant by night, this relaxed restaurant draws a loyal crowd of regulars by offering good-value, tasty Tunisian food at reasonable prices. Freshly fried brik make an excellent starter and there is an impressive array of couscous from which to choose.

Alounak $\mathcal{LL}$

🖃 *10 Russell Gardens, W14*

☎ *020 7603 7645*

🚌 *Kensington Olympia LU/Rail*

Originally housed in a portacabin in an Olympia car park, Alounak has expanded into more conventional premises. Still on offer, however, is gutsy Persian food – excellent lamb kebabs and flavourful stews.

Branch: 44 Westbourne Grove, W2 (020 7229 0416)

Hafez $\mathcal{LL}$

🖃 *5 Hereford Road, W2*

☎ *020 7221 3167 or 020 7229 9398*

🚌 *Bayswater LU, Notting Hill Gate LU, Queensway LU*

A pleasantly laid-back Iranian restaurant offering classic dishes such as Persian bread, freshly baked to order in an impressive tiled oven, grilled meats and Persian stews.

Maroush $\mathcal{LLLL}$

🖃 *21 Edgware Road, W2*

☎ *020 7723 0773 or 020 7262 1090*

🚌 *Marble Arch LU*

Very much an Edgware Road institution, this smart Lebanese restaurant serves high-quality food, complete with live entertainment at weekends.

Mohsen $\mathcal{LL}$

🖃 *152 Warwick Road, W14*

☎ *020 7602 9888*

🚌 *Earls Court LU, Kensington Olympia LU/Rail*

Despite an unprepossessing location opposite a huge Homebase, this small Iranian restaurant, with its outside courtyard area, is warmly recommended by food writer Margaret Shaida. Diners here can enjoy Persian dishes, including kebabs and stews, at their flavourful best.

Ranoush Juice Bar $\mathcal{L}$

🖃 *43 Edgware Road, W2*

☎ *020 7723 5929*

🚌 *Marble Arch LU*

Gleamingly glitzy with its black marble interior, this take-away bar serves fresh fruit juices and tasty Lebanese snacks with panache. Pay first, then order your food.

Middle Eastern Eating Places

Yas *££-£££*

▢ *7 Hammersmith Road, W14*

☎ *020 7603 9148*

🚌 *Kensington Olympia LU/Rail*

Bright and cheerful, this friendly, well-established Iranian restaurant serves freshly baked Iranian breads, dips, kebabs and Persian stews business is brisk, especially in the early hours of the morning.

EAST

Anatolya *£*

▢ *263a Mare Street, E8*

☎ *020 8986 2223*

🚌 *Hackney Central Rail*

A friendly down-to-earth Turkish caff, serving generous portions of gutsy food.

Cookbooks

Lebanese Cuisine
Anissa Helou
An appetising cookbook offering an insight into the glories of Lebanese cuisine.

The New Book of Middle Eastern Food
Claudia Roden
An invaluable and classic book on Middle Eastern cookery, evocatively and authoritatively written, with tempting recipes.

The Legendary Cuisine of Persia
Margaret Shaida
An elegant and well written book charting the history of Persian cuisine and filled with excellent recipes.

Polish London

Korona

Polish London

From the eighteenth century onwards, Poland's history of partition, invasion and resistance, created a Polish presence in London – a self-contained, close-knit community, with a military bias. Following the collapse of communism in Poland, however, business opportunities for British-born Poles have increased, and the former sense of exile which marked the ex-pat Polish community has diminished. London's Polish community, however, retains and cherishes a very strong awareness of its Polish roots.

In 1765, Poland was divided up between Austria, Prussia and Russia. Many Polish émigrés fled to France and a few to England, so starting a pattern of political exile. A succession of failed insurrections in 1830-31, 1848 and 1863-64 brought more exiles to Britain. In Highgate Cemetery, White Eagle Hill is the resting place of the leaders of the failed 1863-64 uprising. The author Joseph Conrad emigrated first to France and then to Britain after his father's arrest in the period prior to that rebellion. Some Poles came to Britain for purely economic reasons, taking on jobs as artisans or labourers. By the late nineteenth century, a Polish Christian community in London was centred around the Polish Catholic church on Devonia Road in Islington, Our Lady of Czestochowa. Large numbers of Polish Jews entered Britain during this period but they became assimilated into the Jewish community.

The real increase in Britain's Polish community – swelling its numbers from 5,000 to tens of thousands – came with the Second World War. Following the German invasion in September 1939, over 30,000 Poles from the government and the military came to Britain and a Polish Government-in-Exile under Prime Minister Sikorski was declared. Operational headquarters were set up around South Kensington and the Polish Air Force fought alongside the RAF. Their contribution was extensive: during the Battle of Britain one in seven of the German planes shot down was dispatched by Polish airmen. A memorial to the 1,241 Polish airmen who died stands on the edge of Northolt Airport.

The Soviet occupation of Poland and the Treaty of Yalta dispossessed thousands of Poles by handing over Eastern Poland to the Soviet Union, so many Poles who had come to Britain to fight in the war stayed on. The British government offered free domicile to the 250,000 Poles (and their families) who had fought under British command, and over 150,000 accepted. Offers of British nationality were usually refused by Poles on patriotic grounds, in an effort to keep the political situation in Poland a 'live' issue.

Post World War II, high property prices created a move west from Kensington to Earls Court, with Cromwell Road becoming known as the 'Polish Corridor'. Polish clubs founded during the war, such as the magnificent White Eagle Club in Knightsbridge and the aristocratic Ognisko on Exhibition Road, had provided community focal points, but again rising costs edged the Polish community out into Balham, Chiswick and Ealing. Many of the upper and middle-class Poles (who constituted the majority of the community) had to adapt to difficult circumstances following the war.

The completion in 1982 of POSK, the Polish Social and Cultural Centre, at considerable expense, was a source of pride to London's ex-pat Polish community and remains an important focal point for it. The Catholic Church, too, strengthened existing bonds, with around 12 Polish Catholic centres and churches in London.

Polish Cuisine

The popular perception of Polish cuisine as hearty winter food is a realistic one. The bitter Polish winters mean that many of the essential ingredients are those that can be stored or preserved: grains, root vegetables, sauerkraut, dried mushrooms, and salted and pickled herrings. Flavourful, warming stews and soups are popular, with soups such as krupnik (barley soup), yellow-pea soup and barley soup dating back to the Middle Ages.

Polish food is often described as Russian-influenced. This is a generalisation resented by the Poles, although the cuisines do share many dishes, ingredients and characteristic flavours. Other influences on Polish food, however, include Italian (traceable back to the 1518 marriage of King Sigismund to Bona Sforza) and French, with one of the earliest cookbooks published in Poland, 'The Perfect Cook', being translated from the French.

Meat has always been highly valued in Polish cookery, a sad irony during the post-war years when meat was rationed and scarce. Every bit is used, producing the famous sausages, hams, black puddings, tongues and brawn. The Poles also enjoy game, traditionally hunted in their homeland's numerous forests. Bigos, or huntsman's stew, is a famous dish, made from game, sauerkraut and sausages. When Bona Sforza and her Italian retinue came to live in Poland, they were reputedly horrified at the amount of meat consumed by the Poles. The

Italians introduced salads and certain vegetables, and even today 'wloscyzna', the word for basic green vegetables, means 'things Italian'.

Grains and cereals have always been important crops for the Poles, and rye bread is a staple. In her fascinating book 'Old Polish Traditions in the Kitchen and at the Table', Maria Lemnis writes, 'The popularity of bread in Poland is manifested in the numerous old sayings, e.g. 'bread unites the strongest', 'bread cries when eaten for free', 'bread obtained for labour is tasty and filling', or, sharper in tone, 'whomever bread harms, a stick can cure'. Cereals such as millet, barley and buckwheat are used widely in dishes from soups to kasha, a purée of cooked grains.

The Catholic Church has had a marked influence on Polish cooking. Catholic festivals such as Christmas and Easter are celebrated with a host of special dishes and cakes. The austerity of the various fasts laid down by the church is also an influence, with fish and mushroom dishes eaten instead of meat at certain times of the year. Christmas Eve, for example, is traditionally celebrated with a feast including carp or pike.

Because of the grim economic situation and political isolation following the Second World War, Polish cookery remained frozen in time, restricted by severe food shortages and closed to foreign influences. The recent political changes and the opening up of trade means that Polish cuisine is developing in Poland, with 'modern Polish' cooking offering sophisticated versions of traditional classic dishes.

Glossary

Buckwheat

Buckwheat: a triangular brown-green grain. Buckwheat flour is used in blinis.

Cakes: Cakes and pastries are an important feature of Polish life, and a huge variety are made, with some traditionally eaten at Christmas and Easter. *Babka*, a famous Easter yeast cake with a distinctive fluted shape; cheesecake, traditionally baked and not oversweet; *makowiec*, poppy-seed roll; *mazurek*, flat, traditionally rectangular cakes eaten at Easter; and *paczki*, Polish doughnuts, often filled with plum jam.

Caraway seeds: tiny, ridged brown seeds, with an aniseed flavour.

Curd cheese: a slightly tangy soft cheese made from curds, used in pierogi and cheesecake.

Dill: a caraway flavoured herb with delicate, feathery fronds.

Dried mushrooms: hunting for wild mushrooms is a national pastime in Poland. Fresh wild mushrooms are rarely found in the shops, but both dried and pickled mushrooms are widely available.

Juniper berries: aromatic, blue-black berries, used with game.

Kohlrabi: a plump, rounded vegetable, either pale green or deep purple, called a 'cabbage-turnip' by Jane Grigson.

Kohlrabi

Pierogi: filled pasta pouches, often called Polish ravioli.

Pinhead barley: fine-grained barley.

Polish Glossary

Polish pure spirit: a powerful spirit – 168 proof – used to make vodka.

Sauerkraut

Poppy seeds: tiny white or purple-blue seeds, used in vast quantities in Polish baking.

Rye bread: a Polish fundamental. Rich-flavoured, dark brown Ukranian rye is distinctive.

Sauerkraut: pickled, shredded cabbage with a sharp flavour, available fresh or bottled.

Sausages: *boiling ring*, loops of spicy sausages; *kabanos*, long, thin pork sausages; *kielbasa*, pork and beef sausage flavoured with garlic; *krakowska*, garlic sausage, eaten as a salami.

Kielbasa

Vodka: flavoured vodkas in Poland include: honey, lemon, *sliwowica* (prune), *winiak* (matured in wine barrels), *wisniak* (cherry), and *zubrowska* (bison-grass, easily identifiable because of the blades of long grass in the bottle).

Polish Glossary

Food Shops

Polish food shops have been an important part of the self-contained Polish community in London. As one Polish lady said, 'We Poles like our food', and the shops provide essentials such as rye bread, sausages and cakes as well as acting as a local meeting place. Rumour has it that one Polish shop had a sign declaring 'English Spoken Here'.

NORTH

Austrian Sausage Centre

- 🏠 *10A Belmont Street, NW1*
- ☎ *020 7267 3601*
- 🚇 *Chalk Farm LU*
- 🕐 *Mon-Fri 7am-5pm, Sat 7am-1pm*

Hidden away on an industrial estate, this functional retail outlet attracts East European ex-pat and English old age pensioners, drawn by the huge array of sausages and cooked and cured meats from brawn to kielbasa.

Polish Delicatessen

- 🏠 *32 Crouch Hill, N4*
- ☎ *07970 112 489*
- 🚇 *Finsbury Park LU/Rail*
- 🕐 *Mon-Sat 9.30am-8pm, Sun 9.30am-4pm*

This small, basic shop, despite space constraints, offers a large range of Polish foodstuffs, all imported directly from Poland. These include sausages (naturally), rye breads, cakes, smoked fish (including eel and halibut), fresh pierogi, dairy products and even Polish eggs.

Sahand

- 🏠 *74 Ballards Lane, N3*
- ☎ *020 8343 3279*
- 🚇 *Finchley Central LU*
- 🕐 *Mon-Sat 8am-9pm, Sun 9am-9pm*

Unusually this Iranian food shop also stocks a large range of Polish foodstuffs, including sausages, jams and canned foods.

WEST

Polanka

- 258 King Street, W6
- 020 8741 8268
- Ravenscourt Park LU
- Mon-Sat 10am-10pm, Sun 11am-8pm

A shop-cum-restaurant with a delicatessen counter selling Polish sausages, sweets, cakes, Krakus jams and pickles.

Enca Foods

- 2 Salisbury Pavement, Dawes Road, SW6
- 020 7385 5762
- Fulham Broadway LU
- Mon-Fri 7am-6pm, Sat 8am-5pm

Hidden away among Fulham's backstreets is this well-established, family-run Polish food supplier. It is famous for the 30 types of sausages and cooked and cured meats made on the premises – an appetising, savoury smell permeates the shop. Raw carcasses are delivered to the back door to be transformed into specialities such as pork brawn or roasted pork poledwica. There is also a basic grocery stock of Central European foodstuffs: rye breads, cakes, pickles and jams.

Parade Delicatessen

- 8 Central Buildings, The Broadway, W5
- 020 8567 9066
- Ealing Broadway LU/Rail
- Mon-Fri 9.15am-6pm, Sat 9.15am-5pm

There's been a Polish food shop on these premises for well over 50 years now. This appetising delicatessen carries an excellent range of Polish foods, from sausages and cured meats, plus a variety of herrings, curd cheese and pierogi. Also on offer is a good choice of groceries, from biscuits and sweets to packet soups and Polish jams.

Polish Food Shops

Prima Delicatessen

⌂ *192 North End Road, W14*

☎ *020 7385 2070*

🚌 *West Kensington LU*

🕐 *Mon-Thur and Sat 9.30am-6pm, Fri 9.30am-7pm*

Founded in 1948, this old-fashioned corner shop is warmly recommended by Polish friends. It has an excellent stock of Polish ingredients: a large counter is filled with sausages and smoked meats, rye breads, cakes and pastries. The chilled section offers pickled wild mushrooms and there is a rack of pulses and seeds incuding buckwheat and poppy seeds.

SOUTH-WEST

Korona Delicatessen

⌂ *30 Streatham High Road, SW16*

☎ *020 8769 6647*

🚌 *Streatham Hill Rail; Bus 159, 109 or 133*

🕐 *Mon-Fri 9am-7pm, Sat 9am-6pm, Sun 9.30am-2.30pm*

Run with knowledgeable helpfulness by Mr and Mrs Wicinska, this well-established, pleasantly old-fashioned food shop offers a fine selection of Polish foodstuffs and has a loyal local following. The range of stock reflects the increased range of Polish foods now available, including a particularly impressive range of assorted pickled herrings. Polish bakery items, including plum jam doughnuts, poppyseed cakes and babka, are popular, as are the home-made pierogi (filled with curd cheese), meat, sauerkraut and wild mushrooms. Luxuries include an impressive range of vodkas, such as bright pink, rose petal vodka, and gold-flecked gold wasser liqueur.

Panadam Delicatessen

⌂ *2 Marius Road, SW17*

☎ *020 8673 4062*

🚌 *Balham LU/Rail*

🕐 *Tue-Fri 9.30am-5.45pm, Sat 9.30am-4pm, Sun 10am-1.30pm*

A charming 25 year-old delicatessen serving Balham's large Polish community. The deli-counter offers a good selection of Polish sausages, meats and herrings, and there is a range of rye breads and cakes. The Sunday opening is explained by the presence round the corner of the Polish church of Christ the King.

Eating Places

Some of London's best-known Polish eating places continue to be housed in veteran clubs or institutions, characteristic of the close-knit Polish commmunity.

CENTRAL

Baltic *££££-£££££*
📇 *74 Blackfriars Road, SE1*
☎ *020 7928 1111*
🚇 *Southwark LU/Rail*

Smart, contemporary East European restaurant and vodka bar serving an elegant, haute-cuisine version of traditional Polish food and a spectacular range of vodkas.

NORTH

Zamoyski *££*
📇 *86 Fleet Road, NW3*
☎ *020 7794 4792*
🚇 *Belsize Park LU, Hampstead Heath Rail*

A veteran Polish eaterie, complete with a pleasant and intimate wine bar and restaurant offering traditional Polish food and vodkas.

WEST

Daquise *££*
📇 *20 Thurloe Street, SW7*
☎ *020 7589 6117*
🚇 *South Kensington LU*

This sedate café has been a popular Polish meeting place since it was founded in the 1940s and is now an institution. The furniture and fittings, the elderly Polish clientele and the veteran staff, complete the impression that nothing much has changed since the 1950s. The menu offers homely, reasonably priced Polish food such as pierogi and apple strudel.

Café Grove £

⬚ *65 The Grove, W5*
☎ *020 8810 0364*
🚍 *Ealing Broadway LU/Rail*

A pretty café serving Ealing's Polish community and offering a tempting range of savoury dishes and classic Polish cakes.

Lowiczanka Polish Cultural Centre (POSK) ££

⬚ *238-46 King Street, W6*
☎ *020 8741 3225*
🚍 *Ravenscourt Park LU*

Inside the Polish Social and Cultural Centre this large restaurant serves a typically Polish menu. Service can be slow so be prepared for a leisurely meal. Prices are reasonable, especially the set lunch.

Ognisko Polskie £££

⬚ *Polish Hearth Club,*
   55 Princes Gate, Exhibition Road SW7
☎ *020 7589 4635*
🚍 *South Kensington LU*

Housed in an elegant high-ceilinged room, the restaurant at this famous Polish club is a bastion of first-rate Polish food. The menu offers classic dishes including barszc, bigos or pierogi, which can be washed down with flavoured vodkas.

Patio ££-£££

⬚ *5 Goldhawk Road, W12*
☎ *020 8743 5194*
🚍 *Goldhawk Road LU, Shepherd's Bush LU*

This intimate, unpretentious restaurant attracts a loyal following for its generous helpings of tasty Polish food and convivial atmosphere.

Wodka £££

⬚ *12 St Albans Grove, W8*
☎ *020 7937 6513*
🚍 *Kensington High Street LU*

A sleek New Wave Polish restaurant serving distinctly upmarket food at corresponding prices. As the name implies, a huge range of flavoured vodkas is also on offer.

Cookbooks

The Food and Cooking of Eastern Europe
Lesley Chamberlain
A clearly written, overall look at East European cookery.

The Polish Kitchen
Mary Pininska
A well-written, knowledgeable book on Polish cookery, with appetising recipes.

South–East Asian London

Tawana

South-East Asian London

The South-East Asian community in London is widespread and diverse, reflecting the variety of its national origins. The term 'South-East Asia' encompasses Indonesia, Malaysia, the Philippines, Singapore, Thailand and Vietnam. There is no obvious centre, an equivalent to Gerrard Street for the Chinese community, but Peckham and Dalston are focal points for the Vietnamese, while Earls Court is a centre for the Filipino community. Wat Buddhapadipa in Wimbledon, the UK's first Buddhist temple, is an important focal point for the Thai community. April sees Thai New Year celebrations at the temple, a characteristically friendly affair offering a chance to sample street-style Thai food from assorted stalls.

South-East Asian Cuisine

The term 'South-East Asian cuisine' is the blanket term used to describe the cuisines of Indonesia, Malaysia, the Philippines, Singapore, Thailand and Vietnam – a simple way to describe a complex set of overlapping national cuisines. Seemingly no dish has a single recipe in South-East Asia: variations abound from country to country, region to region and family to family. Satay in Thailand may be served with toast and a sweet chilli-based dipping sauce, whereas the Malaysian version comes with a spicy peanut sauce, cucumber and cubes of compressed rice. Differences stem from race and religion with, for example, pork avoided by the Muslim Malays but enjoyed by the Chinese. These variations help create a rich and diverse set of cuisines, but there are certain shared characteristics across the region.

Both Chinese and Indian cuisines have influenced South-East Asian food in cooking techniques and ingredients. From China comes the balancing of five flavours: sweet, sour, hot, salty and bitter, and from India, the use of spices and curry pastes. Like both Chinese and Indian cuisine, South-East Asian cuisine is mainly rice-based.

Certain ingredients provide unique flavours that distinguish South-East Asian cooking. Coconut milk, extracted from the flesh of the versatile coconut, is a key ingredient. It is widely used in both savoury and sweet dishes as a marinade, a stock, a curry base and a dairy equivalent. Fragrant aromatics have a citrus quality: lemon grass, lime juice, kaffir lime leaves and rind. To the Asian trinity of onion, garlic and ginger are added the more subtle rhizomes: galangal and krachai. Chillies, introduced by the Portuguese and Spanish in the sixteenth century, provide a chracteristic South-East Asian 'hot' kick.

Seafood is important in South-East Asian cooking and found in abundance. In its dried and fermented forms, seafood is used to add saltiness to food. Fish sauce often replaces soy sauce in Thailand, the Philippines and Vietnam, while pungent dried paste is used throughout South-East Asia.

Indonesian and Malay cooking are often grouped together, as the dominant religion in both countries is Islam. Singapore is distinguished culinarily by Nonya or Straits Chinese cuisine, a unique blend of heavily spiced dishes combining Chinese and Malay ingredients and techniques. Thai cooking, with its emphasis on aesthetic presentation, is marked by its use of aromatic herbs such as coriander, Thai mint and several varieties of basil. Filipino cuisine stands out from the rest of South-East Asia, as it was influenced by the Spanish colonization of the country from 1521 to 1898 and subsequent American occupation until 1946. The Spanish influence is apparent in Filipino dishes such as adobo and paella while American influences crop up in a predeliction for condensed milk and apple pie. Brightly coloured rice cakes and desserts are also popular in the Philippines, made with ingredients such as maka-puno, soft-fleshed coconut. Vietnamese cuisine, influenced by Chinese and French cuisines, is noted for its subtlety and characterised by the generous use of fresh herbs, including basil, coriander and mint.

Glossary

Agar agar: a vegetarian setting agent obtained from seaweed which does not require refrigeration to set. Available in either powdered form or translucent strands. Filipino agar agar (*gulaman*) comes in bright pink and yellow to add colour to desserts.

Annatto (achuete): small red seeds which impart an orange colour.

Banana leaves: used to wrap foods in the way that kitchen foil is used, with the added virtue of also adding flavour to whatever is cooked within.

Thai basil

Basil: a herb used in Indonesian, Thai and Vietnamese cuisines. In Thailand one finds *bai horapa* (similar to European sweet basil), *bai mangluk*, and *bai garapo* or holy basil.

Bean curd (tahu, tokua): a nutritious soya-bean product. Fresh ivory-coloured bean curd has a firm, custard texture and bland flavour and is sold packed in water. Deep-fried bean curd has a golden colour and spongy texture. Both are found in the chilled section.

Betel leaves (La lot): the large, heart-shaped, dark green leaves of a climbing pepper plant. With a distinctive flavour, these are used as an edible packaging in South-East Asian cooking. Wipe the leaves with a damp cloth before using them.

Candlenuts (kemiri, buah keras): large, white, waxy nuts, used to thicken curry pastes, sold unshelled. Raw macadamia nuts are the closest substitute.

Chilli paste (nam prik pow): a thick sauce made from chillies, onions and sugar.

Chillies (prik, cabe, sili labuyo): introduced from South America by the Portuguese and Spanish in the sixteenth century, chillies are an essential ingredient in South-East Asian cookery. Generally the smallest are the hottest, for instance, the tiny Thai bird's eye chillies.

Coconut milk (santen): this thick white 'milk' is made from the grated flesh of the coconut and not from the cloudy water found inside the coconut. In South-East Asia freshly-made coconut milk is sold in markets; here, tinned coconut milk is the best option widely available. Creamed coconut and coconut milk powder, both of which need mixing with hot water, are the other options.

Coconut milk

Coriander (cilantro, Chinese parsley, daun ketumbar, pak chee): this green flat-leafed herb, similar in appearance to continental parsley, has a distinctive sharp flavour. Both the seeds and the leaves are used throughout South-East Asia.

Custard apple (sweet-sop): an apple-shaped, green-skinned fruit with creamy flesh and plentiful small seeds.

Duku (long kong): a fawn-skinned tropical fruit, related to the lychee, which grows in clumps and contains small, separate, juicy segments with a delicate, pomelo-like flavour.

Long kong

Durian: a notorious large, spiky, green-skinned fruit, prized as a delicacy throughout South-East Asia. It is notable for its pungent smell, described as a cross between Camembert and turpentine and, as a result, is banned on airlines.

Fish sauce (nam pla, nuoc mam, patis): a thin, brown salty liquid, produced from compressed shrimps or small fish, and used similarly to soy sauce as a salty flavouring.

Fish sauce

Galingal (Siamese ginger, kenguas, languas, ka): a fleshy rhizome, resembling a creamy-coloured root ginger with pink nodules, and a sharp, medicinal aroma. Available fresh or dried, either in pieces or in powder form (Laos powder).

Ginger: a brown-skinned rhizome, noted for its aromatic flavour and digestive qualities. Lesser ginger (krachai in Thai) is a milder relation and, while similarly-coloured, comes in clusters of small 'fingers'.

Galingal

Jackfruit: bulky, football-sized fruit with a thick green skin covered in prickles, similar in appearance to durian. Yellow jackfruit flesh is available tinned.

Kafir lime leaves

Kaffir limes (jeruk purut, makrut): large limes with a bumpy, dark-green skin. The glossy lime leaves, sold in bunches or packets of loose leaves, are used in South-East Asian cooking and add a distinctive citrus flavour.

Kaffir lime

Kalamansi: small, round, green citrus fruits used in the Philippines to make a refreshing drink.

Kangkong: water-convolvulus leaves, eaten as a green vegetable.

Lemon grass (serai, sereh, takrai): a fibrous grey-green grass with a white bulbous base and subtle citrus flavour.

Long coriander (ngo gai, saw leaf herb): a herb with a fragrance similar to that of coriander, used particularly in Vietnamese cookery.

Macapuno: a type of coconut with soft, slightly sticky flesh, used in Filipino desserts.

Mango: an orange fleshed, fragrant fruit, eaten fresh and used in desserts. Pale orange Thai mangoes are particularly prized for their delicate flavour and scoopable flesh.

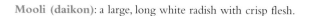

Mangosteen

Mangosteen: an apple-sized fruit with thick purple skin which, despite its name, is no relation to the mango. Inside, it contains white pulpy segments with a delicate, perfumed flavour.

Milkfish (bangus): a bony, white-fleshed fish, cultivated and eaten extensively in the Philippines.

Mooli (daikon): a large, long white radish with crisp flesh.

Noodles: *cellophane noodles* (also known as beanthread, glass or transparent noodles) are fine threadlike noodles made from mung beans, which need soaking before they can be easily cut; *yellow egg noodles* (available fresh and dried); *dried white rice noodles* and *vermicelli*; *river rice* or *sarhor* noodles, made from ground rice and water. Fresh river rice noodles are sold in clear packets, usually stored near the chilled section.

Palm sugar (gula melaka): a caramel-flavoured, dark brown sugar made from the coconut palm flower, sold in small, hard cylinderical blocks.

Pandan leaves: long, thin, dark green screwpine leaves, sold fresh in bunches. They add a unique, slightly nutty flavour and green colouring to desserts.

Pawpaw (papaya): a gourd-like fruit, which comes in varying sizes and colours from deep green to orange. Green pawpaw is used in salads by the Thais.

Pea aubergine: tiny pea-sized aubergines with a sharp, bitter taste, used especially in Thai cooking.

Pomelo (shaddock): the largest of the citrus fruits, resembling a huge grapefruit with a flattened end; used in Thai salads.

Pea aubergine

Prawn crackers (krupuk): flat wafers which puff up when fried. Emping are a slightly bitter Indonesian version, made with melinjo nuts, and used to garnish gado gado salad.

Rambutan: a fruit resembling a hairy, red egg – the name comes from 'rambut', Malay for 'hair'. Inside is a translucent, juicy egg-shaped fruit, prized for its refreshing qualities.

Rice: long-grain rice is commonly used, with the best coming from Thailand. The phrase 'perfumed rice' is an indicator of quality. Short-grained white and black glutinous rice is also used in both savoury and sweet dishes.

Rice paper wrappers: round, triangular or square rice flour wrappers, sold dried. Dip them in hot water for just a few seconds before using them as a wrapping.

Shrimps, dried: small, shelled, dried pink shrimps, with a strong salty flavour.

Shrimp paste (blachan, terasi, bagoong, kapee, mam tan): a paste made from fermented shrimps, available in many forms, from solid, brown blocks to bottled pink-grey liquid. It has an extremely pungent smell and should be stored in an airtight container.

Shrimp paste

Soy sauce: a dark brown, salty liquid made from fermented soya beans, available as thin, salty Light Soy Sauce or as thicker, sweeter Dark Soy Sauce. Kecap manis is a thick, sweet Indonesian soy sauce.

Starfruit (carambola): a ridged, fleshy fruit which when sliced produces star-shaped slices.

Straw mushrooms: cone-shaped mushrooms, usually available canned.

Tamarind (asam, mak kum): a bean-like fruit from the tamarind tree, available in lumps of de-seeded pulp, and used to add tartness to dishes. Tamarind sauce, although slightly salty, is a convenient version. 'Tamarind slices', from a different fruit with similar qualities, is also available.

Tempe: a pressed fermented soya bean product, with a nutty taste.

Turmeric: a slender, brown-skinned rhizome, with a deep orange flesh. Widely available in dried powdered form, or occasionally found fresh.

Yam bean

Ube: a bright purple, sweet yam used in Filipino cookery.

Yam bean: a brown-skinned, turnip-shaped tuber, with dense white, slightly sweet crunchy flesh, a traditional ingredient in rojak salads.

Yard-long beans: as the name implies, these are long green beans, commonly cut into short lengths before cooking.

South-East Asian Glossary

Food Shops

Traditionally the more established Chinese supermakets have acted as umbrella suppliers, carrying basic South-East Asian ingredients. With the recent boom in Thai cookery, major supermarket chains are also starting to stock ingredients such as tinned coconut milk and fresh lemon grass. For the more unusual items, especially vegetables and herbs, it is necessary to track down a specialist South-East Asian shop.

CENTRAL

Mari-Mari
- 🏠 *41 Snowfields, SE1*
- ☎ *020 7403 4600*
- 🚌 *London Bridge LU*
- 🕐 *Mon-Wed 11am-3pm, Thur-Sat 11am-6pm*

Run as a sister business to the stylish restaurant Champor-Champor, Mari-Mari bills itself as a "one-stop Asian food emporium". Here you can find herbs, curry pastes, teas and coffees alongside striking tableware and authentic South-East Asian kitchenware.

New Loon Moon Supermarket
- 🏠 *9a Gerrard Street, W1*
- ☎ *020 7734 9940*
- 🚌 *Leicester Square LU*
- 🕐 *Daily 10.30am-8pm*

As you enter this pleasantly old-fashioned shop you're greeted by an attractive display of good quality fresh Thai produce, including fresh Thai basil, pea aubergines, green mangoes and papayas and petai beans. The grocery section includes a good range of South-East Asian ingredients, including coconut milk, chilli sauces and, in the back room, an impressive range of curry pastes.

See Woo
- 🏠 *19 Lisle Street, WC2*
- ☎ *020 7439 8325*
- 🚌 *Leicester Square LU*
- 🕐 *Daily 10am-8pm*

Although a veteran Chinese supermarket See Woo is a reliable stockist of South-East Asian ingredients including fresh flavourings such as kaffir lime leaves and galingal.

NORTH

Maysun Market

⌖ *869 Finchley Road, NW11*
☎ *020 8455 4773*
🚍 *Golders Green LU*
🕒 *Mon-Sat 9am-7.30pm*

This small, old-fashioned shop stocks a selection of South-East Asian ingredients (predominantly tinned, bottled, frozen or dried) which range from frozen seafood and packets of pig's blood to tins of Alphonso mango pulp.

Wing Yip (London) Ltd

⌖ *395 Edgware Road, NW2*
☎ *020 8450 0422*
🚍 *Colindale LU*
🕒 *Mon-Sat 9.30am-7pm, Sun 11.30am-5.30pm*

This enormous supermarket at Staples Corner contains an impressive range of South-East Asian ingredients, and is particularly strong on bottled, tinned, dried and frozen foods. The greengrocery section, although small, stocks more unusual items such as pandan leaves, Thai basil and fresh tamarind.

WEST

Masagana Filipino Groceries

⌖ *30 Queensway, W2*
☎ *020 7229 1966*
🚍 *Bayswater LU*
🕒 *Daily 10am-8.30pm*

A few doors down from Bayswater tube, this small, narrow shop looks like a phone card kiosk from the front. Inside, however, its shelves are filled with jarred and canned goods, including bagoong (fermented salted shrimp paste), sliced macapuno shreds and packets of annatto, while a freezer at the back contains milk fish.

Manila Supermarket

⌨ *11-12 Hogarth Place, SW5*

☎ *020 7373 8305*

🚌 *Earls Court LU*

🕐 *Daily 9am-9pm*

As the name and the stacks of The Filipino newspaper near the door suggest, this friendly, roomy store specialises in Filipino foodstuffs such as purple yam jam, coconut spread and pork sausages, but also stocks an excellent range of general South–East Asian ingredients. One room contains freezers of grated cassava, fresh coconut milk, sweet potato leaves and a variety of fish and seafood. Greengrocery items include chillies, galingal and banana leaves.

Muay

⌨ *8A Hogarth Place, SW5*

☎ *020 7341 3599*

🚌 *Earls Court LU*

🕐 *Mon-Sat 9am-8pm, Sun 10am-8pm*

This small, cluttered Thai food shop (above a basement hairdressers) sells an excellent selection of fresh Thai vegetables and herbs, attractively arranged in baskets. Pretty Thai cakes, fresh mangosteens and packets of fresh, moist yellow durian segments when in season are among the treats on offer.

Sri Thai

⌨ *56 Shepherd's Bush Road, W6*

☎ *020 7602 0621*

🚌 *Shepherd's Bush LU*

🕐 *Daily 9am-7pm*

This clearly arranged shop, run with friendly courtesy by Mr and Mrs Threpprasits, has a great stock of Thai ingredients, with the excellent selection of fresh Thai produce being a particular forte. Tuesday is the best day to visit for fresh vegetables and herbs jetted in from Thailand, such as bitter melon, fresh Thai basils and galingal.

Tawana

⌨ *16-20 Chepstow Road, W2*

☎ *020 7221 6316*

🚌 *Bayswater LU*

🕐 *Daily 9.30am-8pm*

"There were only two Thai restaurants in London when we started," muses owner Mr Farooqi. Today, Thai cuisine is popular and his roomy, well-stocked shop does a roaring trade in Thai staples such as kaffir lime leaves, coconut milk and lemon grass. Wednesdays and Saturdays are the best days for fresh produce flown in from Thailand, including pea aubergines, banana leaves and holy basil. Next door, the 'Oriental Delicatessen' offers take-away Thai dishes including fishcakes, noodles and a wide choice of dainty Thai cakes.

Branch: 243-245 Plaistow Road, E15

SOUTH-WEST

Amaranth
⊞ *346-348 Garrett Lane, SW18*
☎ *020 8871 3466/8874 9036*
🚌 *Earlsfield Rail*
🕓 *Mon-Sat 11am-9pm*

An extension of the popular Thai restaurant next door, this small food shop stocks basic Thai ingredients, including home-made curry pastes. Tuesday is the best day for fresh Thai produce, such as holy basil or lime leaves, as deliveries from Thailand arrive on Monday evening. The shop's particular forte, and one which pulls in the local commuters, is its home-made, frozen ready-to-cook savouries, such as dainty spring rolls or red duck curry. Staff are friendly and helpful and happy to offer cooking advice.

Talad Thai
⊞ *320 Upper Richmond Road, SW15*
☎ *020 8789 8084*
🚌 *Putney Rail*
🕓 *Daily 9am-8pm*

Upstairs functions as a Thai take-away while downstairs is a basement supermarket with a small back room of fresh vegetables, herbs and fruits such as Thai basil and pea aubergines. The large freezer section contains meat and seafood while the shelves are lined with noodles, condiments, tinned vegetables and coconut milk. The manageress is friendly and helpful and there are Thai cookery demonstrations every Sunday morning.

Paya Thai

⊞ *101-103 Kew Road, TW9*

☎ *020 8332 2959*

🚌 *Richmond LU/Rail*

🕐 *Daily 10am-7pm*

This large store has every thing you could want for Thai cooking, from fresh pea aubergines and fragrant Thai basil to bottles of fish sauce and tins of coconut milk.

Wing Thai Supermarket

⊞ *13 Electric Avenue, SW9*

☎ *020 7738 5898*

🚌 *Brixton LU/Rail*

🕐 *Mon-Sat 10am-7pm*

Tucked away behind the bustling fruit and veg market stalls outside, this roomy store has a small fresh produce section, but is very strong on bottled, tinned and frozen goods with a selection of Vietnamese products such as dried rice wrappers.

EAST

Alan's Chinese & Vietnamese Grocery

⊞ *199 East India Dock Road, E14*

☎ *020 7515 8909*

🚌 *All Saints DLR*

🕐 *Daily 10am-10pm*

A small Vietnamese grocery, warmly recommended by American food-writer and pho-fan Marlena Spieler, with an excellent range of Vietnamese foodstuffs, from bunches of fresh dill, mint and coriander to a wide selection of dried noodles and rice pancakes.

Hoang–Nam

⊞ *185 Mare Street, E8*

☎ *020 8985 9050*

🚌 *London Fields Rail*

🕐 *Daily 9am-9pm*

A large, well-established Vietnamese supermarket offering hard-to-find Vietnamese herbs and vegetables. Stock ranges from store-cupboard staples (rice, noodles, condiments) to frozen seafood, taking in jade jewellery and underwear en route.

Eating Places

While Thai food seems to have established a pub restaurant niche, authentic South-East Asian food in London is pretty scarce. With delicious ingredients such as lemon grass, lime leaves and coconut milk to use, it's not so much that the majority of food on offer is unpleasant – rather that it lacks the depth of flavour and gutsiness of the genuine article.

CENTRAL

C & R *£*
- 4-5 Rupert Court, W1
- ☎ 020 7434 1128
- Leicester Square LU

This bright, cheerful café, hidden down a back alley, does a roaring business in bargain Singaporean and Malaysian dishes, including Hainanese chicken rice, laksa and ice kacang.

Champor-Champor *£££-££££*
- 62 Weston Street, SE1
- ☎ 020 7403 4600
- London Bridge LU/Rail

Tucked away down a quiet side-street, this vibrantly decorated, intimate restaurant offers an imaginative take on South-East Asian cuisine. Malay chef Amran Hassan prepares beautifully presented, creative and flavourful dishes drawing on ingredients and cooking techniques from across the region.

Nahm *££££*
- The Halkin, Halkin Street, SW1
- ☎ 020 7333 1234
- Hyde Park Corner LU

In smart, subdued surroundings acclaimed Australian chef David Thompson serves up a series of exquisitely constructed, authentically flavoured Thai dishes, offering a gourmet glimpse into this richly varied cuisine.

South-East Asian Food Shops

NORTH

Khoai *LL*

▱ *6 Topsfield Parade, Middle Lane, N8*

☎ *020 8341 2120*

🚌 *Finsbury Park LU/Rail, then the W7 bus*

Simple surroundings, combined with polite, friendly service, make this a pleasantly unpretentious place to sample traditional Vietnamese dishes, including betel leaf-wrapped beef and pho, in flavourful stock.

Lemongrass *LL*

▱ *243 Royal College Street, NW1*

☎ *020 7284 1116*

🚌 *Camden Town LU*

This charming, intimate restaurant offers a rare chance to try Cambodian-inspired cuisine. The prettily presented dishes are freshly prepared and taste as good as they look.

O's Thai Café *LL*

▱ *10 Topsfield Parade, N8*

☎ *020 8348 6898*

🚌 *Finsbury Park LU/Rail, then the W7 bus*

Bright, light and funky, O's attracts a stream of Crouch End diners drawn by the chance to try tasty Thai dishes (such as green chicken curry) at very reasonable prices.

Singapore Garden *LLL*

▱ *83-83a Fairfax Road, NW6*

☎ *020 7328 5314*

🚌 *Swiss Cottage LU*

A loyal multi-cultural clientele testifies to this smart restaurant's commitment to admirably authentic Singaporean food. The menu offers predominantly Chinese food, but includes a selection of South-East Asian delicacies such as mouth-watering and gloriously messy chilli crab, excellent satay and oyster omelette, and the best cendol (a coconut milk drink) in town.

WEST

Blue Elephant *££££*
⊡ *4-6 Fulham Broadway, SW6*
☎ *020 7385 6595*
🚌 *Fulham Broadway LU*

A veteran Thai restaurant, the Blue Elephant comes complete with lavish tropical-inspired décor and attentive staff. The cooking is above average, with the set-price Sunday buffet lunch a popular family occasion.

Mawar *£*
⊡ *175A Edgware Road, W2*
☎ *020 2762 1663*
🚌 *Edgware Road LU*

Discreetly hidden in basement premises this unpretentious, friendly eating place serves up tasty Malay food at remarkably reasonable prices. A buffet-style lunch and snacks such as colourful kueh and tasty curry puffs attracts Malay students, while in the evening one can order à la carte.

Nyonya *££-£££*
⊡ *2A Kensington Park Road, W11*
☎ *020 7243 1800*
🚌 *Notting Hill Gate LU*

This elegant Notting Hill restaurant offers dainty portions of Malaysian dishes, with the home-made, pretty Nonya kuih (cakes), flavoured with coconut, palm sugar and pandan leaves, a particular speciality.

Satay House *££*
⊡ *13 Sale Place, W2*
☎ *020 7723 6763*
🚌 *Edgware Road LU, Paddington LU/Rail*

Tucked away in a quiet side street, this is a peaceful place in which to enjoy Malaysian dishes such as murtabak (mince-stuffed flat bread) and tasty char kway teow. Authentic versions of pulot hitam or ice kacang are on offer for dessert.

Southeast W9 *£££-££££*

⌧ *239 Elgin Avenue, W9*

☎ *020 7328 8883*

🚌 *Maida Vale LU*

Thai chef Vatcharin Bhumichtr's elegantly airy restaurant, with its pan-South-East Asian menu, allows diners to sample less familiar dishes such as Laotian laap (minced chicken salad) or Vietnamese Bo Xao Mang (beef with bamboo shoots).

Tawana *££*

⌧ *3 Westbourne Grove, W2*

☎ *020 7229 3785*

🚌 *Bayswater LU*

Run by the owners of Tawana Supermarket, this friendly, unpretentious Thai restaurant has built up a loyal local following.

EAST

Song Que Café *£*

⌧ *134 Kingsland Road E2*

☎ *020 76133 222*

🚌 *Old Street LU/Rail*

Highly recommended by pho-loving friends, this down-to-earth café serves flavourful Vietnamese food, including splendid pho, at rock-bottom prices.

Kaffir Limes

Cookbooks

Modern Thai Food
Martin Boetz
A stylish contemporary cookbook, combining mouth-watering photographs with appetising, well-written recipes.

Thai Cooking
Jennifer Brennan
A classic book on Thai cuisine, lovingly and authoratively written.

South-East Asian Food
Rosemary Brissenden
A mine of delicious recipes from throughout the region.

The Flavours of Vietnam
Meera Freeman
A clearly written, appetising Vietnamese cookbook.

Food and Travels Asia
Alastair Hendy
A spectacular book with evocative photographs.

Far Eastern Cookery
Madhur Jaffrey
An appetising regional journey, with clear, useable recipes.

Indonesian Food and Cookery
Sri Owen
An authoritative and in-depth book by Indonesian food.

New Wave Asian
Sri Owen
A handsome book with cutting edge recipes from South-East Asia.

The Complete Asian Cookbook
Charmaine Solomon
An impressively comprehensive cookbook.

Spanish & Portuguese London

Brindisa

Although a Spanish presence in London can be traced back to the Middle Ages, the real growth in the capital's Spanish and Portuguese communities came in the twentieth century. Following the Spanish Civil War (1936-39), many Spanish refugees and political exiles came to Britain. Republican exiles set up El Hogar Español (The Spanish House) in Bayswater: a cultural, social and political focal point. In addition to political reasons for coming to Britain, economic ones also played their part. During the 1950s and 1960s, millions of working-class Spaniards were forced to leave Spain and look for work abroad because of the lack of opportunities at home. The area around Ladbroke Grove was a focal point for the Spanish community. Many of the Spanish in Britain are from Galicia, the north-west coastal region of Spain which has a seafaring and travelling tradition and which suffered in the post-war depression.

Despite the fact that Portugal is Britain's oldest ally (a tie dating back to the Treaty of Windsor in 1386) the Portuguese community in London is small. It was the decades after the Second World War which saw an influx of Portuguese arriving in London, largely as a result of a lack of economic opportunities in Portugal.

One focal point for the city's Iberian community is the area around Golborne Road and Portobello. On these roads, the community is served by a Spanish school, Spanish and Portuguese delicatessens, and cafés and bars in which to meet other members of the community. Camden Town, Stockwell and Vauxhall, too, are home to a number of Portuguese food shops, cafés and restaurants.

Spanish & Portuguese Cuisine

Both Spanish and Portuguese cookery share many characteristic ingredients: salted cod, paprika sausages, rice, beans, garlic and olive oil. The Moorish occupation of the Iberian Peninsula from AD 711 has left its mark on the sweets of both countries, with ground almonds and egg yolks used in desserts and cakes such as the Portuguese touchino de ceu or Spanish tarta de naranja.

Seafood is important in both cuisines, with an extensive range fished on the countries' long coastlines. Many of the famous regional dishes are seafood-based, such as zarzuela (Catalan seafood stew), marmitako (Basque bonito soup) and Northern-Portuguese caldeirada. There is no squeamishness when it comes to seafood. Lampreys are eaten in Northern Portugal in a famous dish, lapreia a moda do Minho; while Spanish calamares en su tinta, calls for squid to be cooked in its own black ink. Absolute freshness is demanded and one traditional Spanish fish dish is nicknamed mato mulo (mule killer) because the fish used in it had to be rushed by mule from the coast to Madrid.

There are some obvious differences between the cuisines and national dishes. From Portugal's former colonies come spices and flavourings such as spicy piri piri sauce – used in both Brazil and East Africa. Tapas, however, are quintessentially Spanish. The term means 'little lid' and is thought to come from the bar tradition of covering glasses with a saucer of olives or nuts. Bars vie with each other to offer good tapas and the discerning Spanish, who both enjoy their food and take it seriously, hunt out their favourites with a passion.

Both Spain and Portugal retain a strong sense of regionalism, with traditional dishes still cherished. Many recipes feature a place name, such as de salmao a Lisboeta, or fabada Asturiana. As in Italian cuisine, certain areas or towns are known for the quality of their food, with the best Spanish seafood coming from Cadiz or Galicia and the best Portugese caldo verde from the Minho.

Glossary

Aguardiente (orujo): a potent Spanish spirit, distilled from the left-over grapes and pips after wine has been made.

Anchovies (boquerones, biqueiros): tiny cured fish, usually filleted, with a strong, salty flavour.

Anchovies

Capers (alcaparras): the unopened buds of a Mediterranean shrub, sold and used in their pickled form. Spain is the world's largest producer of capers.

Cava: sparkling Spanish wine made using the champagne method, with Cordoniu and Frexenet among the best producers.

Charcuterie: *butifarra*, a white Spanish sausage, spiced with cinnamon, cloves and nutmeg; *chorizo* or *chourico*, paprika sausages, used in cooked dishes, to which they add a distinctive colour and flavour, or eaten as a salami; *jamon de Serrano*, a highly prized, salt-cured Spanish ham, the best of which is made from the acorn-fed pigs of the Estremadura region; *lomo,* cured pork loin from Spain; *presunto*, a fine salt-cured ham from Portugal, traditionally made from acorn-fed pigs from Tras-os-Montes.

Cheese: *azeitaio*, small Portuguese sheep's milk cream cheeses; *cabrales*, a famous Spanish blue-veined cheese, made from cow's milk but sometimes with sheep's or goat's milk added; *evora*, a creamy, strong, salty sheep's milk cheese from Portugal; *idiazabal*, a much-prized, semi-soft cheese with a dark rind made from sheep's milk in the Basque region of Spain; *ilha*, a Portuguese Cheddar-like cheese made from cow's milk; *mahon*, a flavourful Spanish semi-soft cow's milk cheese; *manchego*, one of Spain's best-known cheeses, made with sheep's milk and sold in three grades depending on age; *roncal*, a hard, Spanish, sheep's milk cheese; *serra*, a soft, Portuguese, sheep's milk cheese.

Chickpeas (garbanzos, grado): hazelnut-shaped, yellow peas.

Coriander (coentros): a sharp-flavoured green herb, similar in appearance to continental parsley, widely used in Portuguese cookery.

265

Madeira: a famous Portuguese fortified wine, from the island of Madeira.

Madelenas: small, sweet, golden-brown cakes, eaten for breakfast in Spain.

Muscatel raisins: dried muscatel grapes, with a distinctive flavour.

Olive oil: olive oil is produced in both Spain and Portugal and is the main cooking oil in both countries. Carbonell, with its elegant Art Nouveau labels, is one of Spain's famous brands.

Muscatel raisins

Olives: green olives stuffed with anchovies are particularly popular in Spain.

Paprika: a bright red powder, made from ground sweet or spicy peppers and used as a spice.

Pimenton

Pimenton: Spanish paprika, made from ground Spanish paprika peppers, has a sweetness of flavour and is available smoked or unsmoked. It is a popular Spanish spice, adding, for example, flavour and colour to chorizo sausages.

Pimientos de padron: slightly piquant, small peppers, delicious pan-fried and sprinkled with sea salt.

Pine kernels (pinon, pinhao): small, ivory-coloured stone pine kernels, used in both sweet and savoury dishes.

Piri piri: a hot Portuguese sauce made from chillies, a culinary legacy from Portugal's colonial past.

Port: a fortified wine from the Douro valley in North-West Portugal. Its creation can be traced back to the early seventeenth century when, due to Anglo-French hostilities, Portuguese wine rather than French claret was exported to England.

Piri piri

Quince paste (membrillo, marmelo): a thick, golden, jelly-like paste made from quinces, eaten as a sweetmeat or as a classic accompaniment to cheese.

Rice: introduced by the Moors to Spain and Portugal in AD 711. Short-grain rice is used for Spanish paella.

Saffron: a costly spice made from the stigmas of a type of crocus, sold in either thread or powdered form.

Salt cod (bacalao, bacalhau): dried, salted cod traditionally eaten on Fridays for religious reasons. In Portugal it is regarded as a national delicacy and there is said to be a different bacalhau recipe for every day of the year. It should be soaked for 24–36 hours before cooking to remove excess salt.

Saffron

Sherry: a classic Spanish wine named after the town of Jerez and imported by the British since the fifteenth century.

Tiger nut (chufa): a small, wrinkled rhizome from which horchata, a refreshing almond-flavoured drink thought to have been introduced by the Moors, is made.

Turron: Spanish nougat, available in two forms: *alicante*, crisp and textured with chopped nuts, or *jijona*, soft and crumbly, made from ground nuts. Traditionally this is a Christmas treat but it is now available all the year round.

Vinho verde: delicate effervescent wines, both white and red, which form around a quarter of Portugal's wine production.

Food Shops

As with London's Italian food stores, many of these shops began as corner shops, selling everyday ingredients to their community.

Lisboa

CENTRAL

Brindisa

- 32 Exmouth Market, EC1
- 020 7713 1666
- Farringdon LU/Rail or King's Cross LU/Rail
- Tue-Fri 10am-6pm, Sat 9am-5pm

This small, stylish shop is a showcase for some of Spain's finest foodstuffs. Here one can find hand-carved Iberico and Serrano hams, fine chorizo, salchicon and cheeses and sweet treats including Enric Rovira's stylish chocolates. The emphasis is firmly on flavourful, top quality Spanish foods, from superb extra virgin olive oils and wine vinegars to dangerously moreish almonds.

Also at Borough Market on Friday and Saturday (p.56)

Delicias de Portugal

⌨ *43 Warwick Way, SW1*

☎ *020 7630 5597*

🚇 *Pimlico LU, Victoria LU/Rail*

🕐 *Mon-Sat 8am-8pm, Sun 9am-2pm*

This pretty delicatessen caters to hungry office workers, offering pasteis de bacalhau and a selection of Portuguese cakes and pastries as well as sandwiches. There is a large range of deli goods, including huge slabs of bacalhau (cut on demand), packets of 'flan' and a choice of goat's cheeses.

Madeira Patisserie

⌨ *46A-C Albert Embankment, SE1*

☎ *020 7820 1117*

🚇 *Vauxhall LU/Rail*

🕐 *020 7820 1117*

Under the railway arches at Vauxhall, Madeira Patisserie (a wholesale Portuguese bakery) runs a down-to-earth café where one can sit and sample their tarts and cakes. Their delicatessen is next door, a Portuguese grocer's offering a large range of foodstuffs, from tinned seafood and pulses to sweets and biscuits.

NORTH

Delicias de Portugal

⌨ *1008 Harrow Road, NW10*

☎ *020 8960 7933*

🚇 *Kensal Green LU*

🕐 *Mon-Sat 8.30am-7.30pm, Sun 9am-2pm*

A pleasant, well-stocked Portuguese food shop.

Ferreira

⌨ *40 Delancey Street, NW1*

☎ *020 7485 2351*

🚇 *Camden Town LU*

🕐 *Mon-Sat 8am-9pm, Sun 8am-8pm*

A friendly Portuguese corner store which has something for everybody. On the counter is a selection of cakes such as pasteis de nata, inside are Portuguese cheeses and sausages, while behind are shelves of Portuguese breakfast cereals. In addition, there is a selection of tinned and bottled groceries, wines and slabs of bacalhau.

Lisboa

⌨ *4 Plender Street, NW1*

☎ *020 7387 1782*

🚌 *Camden Town LU*

🕐 *Tue-Fri 9.30am-6.30pm, Sat 9am-7pm, Sun 10am-2pm*

A branch of the established Portuguese delicatessen (see p.273 West London for further details).

Villa Franca

⌨ *3 Plender Street, NW1*

☎ *020 7387 8236*

🚌 *Camden Town LU*

🕐 *Mon-Sat 7am-8pm, Sun 9am-7pm*

A small down-to-earth shop-cum-café selling a mixture of Portuguese and English patisserie plus a range of foodstuffs: bacalhau (stored beneath the counter), cured meats, soft drinks and cheeses such as queijo Evora. Downstairs is a smoking room from which blares the sound of Portuguese satellite TV.

The Wine Cellar

⌨ *193 Kentish Town Road, NW5*

☎ *020 7267 9501*

🚌 *Kentish Town LU/Rail*

🕐 *Mon-Fri 8am-8pm, Sat 9am-8pm*

This long, narrow, homely Portuguese food shop-cum-café stocks basic foodstuffs including cheeses, pancetta, pig's trotters, chourico, plus tinned seafood, pulses and packets of 'pudim'. Downstairs, the reason for the shop's name becomes clear: the entire basement is stocked with a wide variety of Portuguese wines plus port and Madeira.

Rias Altas

⌨ *97 Frampton Street, NW8*

☎ *020 7262 4340*

🚌 *Edgware Road LU*

🕐 *Mon-Sat 9am-7.30pm*

A long, narrow Spanish delicatessen, well-stocked with foodstuffs such as Spanish cheeses, cured meats, bacalao and Spanish wines.

WEST

Garcia R. & Sons

⌖ *248 Portobello Road, W11*
☎ *020 7221 6119*
🚇 *Ladbroke Road LU, Notting Hill Gate LU*
🕐 *Tue-Sat 8.30am-6pm*

The Garcia family have had a Spanish food-shop on Portobello Road for over 40 years. Their present shop is London's largest Spanish food shop and retains a pleasantly old-fashioned feel. The deli counter does a roaring trade in Jamon Serrano and costly Jamon Iberico (from acorn-fed black-footed pigs), which are deftly sliced to order. In addition, there are groceries such as chorizo sausages, pimenton, paella rice, tinned seafood, bacalao and olive oil. Turrons are kept throughout the year, with the range expanding at Christmas time.

Lisboa

⌖ *6 World's End Place, SW10*
☎ *020 7376 3639*
🚇 *Fulham Broadway LU*
🚇 *Mon-Sat 8am-6pm*

A branch of the well-established Golborne Road emporium.

Lisboa Delicatessen

⌖ *54 Golborne Road, W10*
☎ *020 8969 1052*
🚇 *Westbourne Park LU*
🕐 *Mon-Sat 9.30am-7.30pm, Sun 10am-1pm*

When Carlos Gomes opened this shop over 20 years ago, it was the first Portuguese delicatessen in London and he and his partners 'imported' their own stock in suitcases from Portugal. All the essential ingredients for Portuguese cooking can be found in this characterful shop: pungent bacalhau, pulses including Brazilian black beans, sausages and trayfuls of pickled and salted pig's trotters, snouts, tails and ears. A back room contains a selection of Portuguese wines and spirits, including port.

Lisboa Patisserie

🏠 *57 Golborne Road, W10*

☎ *020 8968 5242*

🚇 *Westbourne Park LU*

🕐 *Daily 8am-8pm*

Across the road from the delicatessen, this small, popular patisserie supplies a constant stream of customers with delicious Portuguese pastries freshly baked on the premises such as pasteis de nata (custard tarts) and bolo arroz (rice cakes).

P. de la Fuente

🏠 *288 Portobello Road, W10*

☎ *020 8960 5687*

🚇 *Ladbroke Road LU, Notting Hill Gate LU*

🕐 *Mon-Sat 9am-6pm*

Just down the road from the large Spanish College, is this small, friendly, down-to-earth Spanish food shop, offering an excellent stock of essentials.

SOUTH-WEST

A & C. Continental Groceries

🏠 *3 Atlantic Road, SW9*

☎ *020 7733 3766*

🚇 *Brixton LU/Rail*

🕐 *Mon-Sat 8am-8pm*

Under the arches, this friendly neighbourhood shop has an excellent range of basics, from fresh fruit and vegetables and bunches of herbs outside, to loaves of bread inside. Portuguese chourico, morcela (black pudding) and cheeses can be found at the deli counter, plus daily delivered pasties de nata and baccalau rissoles.

Delicias de Portugal

🏠 *280 Wandsworth Road, SW8*

☎ *020 7622 9811*

🚇 *Wandsworth Road Rail*

🕐 *Mon-Fri 9am-8pm; Sat 9am-7pm; Sun 10am-7pm*

A down-to-earth, friendly food shop, filled with a good selection of Portuguese staples.

Sintra Delicatessen

⌨ *146-48 Stockwell Road, SW9*

☎ *020 7733 9402*

🚌 *Stockwell LU*

🕐 *Daily 9am-8pm*

The scent of bacalhau and the hum of conversation evoke Portugal as you enter this homely shop, which is attached to a down-to-earth café and restaurant. There is a good selection of foodstuffs: chourico, presunto and morcela and Portuguese cakes and bread. The shelves are lined with Portuguese groceries: cereals, olive oil, Portuguese wines and boxes of Ancora crochet yarn

Eating Places

CENTRAL

Fino *£££*

⌨ *33 Charlotte Street, W1*

☎ *020 7813 8010*

🚌 *Goodge Street LU, Tottenham Court Road LU*

A stylish Fitzrovia basement eaterie, serving creative, contemporary tapas plus an excellent range of sherries and wines.

Meson Don Felipe *££*

⌨ *53 The Cut, SE1*

☎ *020 7928 3237*

🚌 *Waterloo LU/Rail*

A large, attractive tapas bar, with a central counter piled high with appetising morsels.

Moro *££££*

⌨ *34-36 Exmouth Market, EC1*

☎ *020 7833 8336*

🚌 *Farringdon LU/Rail*

Much critical acclaim has greeted this convivial restaurant, which draws on both Spanish and North African cuisines to create an inventive and richly flavourful menu.

Navarros   *£££*

⌨ *67 Charlotte Street, W1*

☎ *020 7637 7713*

🚌 *Goodge Street LU*

A prettily decorated, traditional tapas bar, with a loyal following, serving consistently tasty classic tapas, from tortilla to prawns in garlic.

Tapas Brindisa   *£££*

⌨ *Borough Market, 8-20 Southwark Street, SE1*

☎ *020 7357 8880*

🚌 *London Bridge LU/Rail*

On the corner of Borough Market, this pleasantly informal, contemporary tapas bar, housed in an old potato warehouse, was set up by Brindisa, the noted Spanish food importers, to showcase their ingredients. A jamoneria (ham counter) serves prime Iberian ham, while diners can start their day with hot chocolate and breakfast dishes, moving on via lunch to evening tapas such as Iberian ham croquetas or butterflied prawns with pimenton, washed down with a glass of fine sherry, cava or delicious Spanish wine.

NORTH

La Bota   *££*

⌨ *31 Broadway Parade, Tottenham Lane, N8*

☎ *020 8340 3082*

🚌 *Finsbury Park LU/Rail, then the W7 bus*

A straightforward tapas bar which attracts a lively crowd.

El Parador   *££*

⌨ *245 Eversholt Street, NW1*

☎ *020 7387 3789*

🚌 *Camden Town LU*

This tapas bar comes into its own in the summer, when you can sit in the garden at the back and sample a variety of tapas washed down with Spanish wines and beers.

WEST

Café Garcia £-££
⊞ *246 Portobello Road, W11*
☎ *020 7221 6119*
🚇 *Ladbroke Road LU, Notting Hill Gate LU*

Owned by the Spanish food shop next door, this contemporary café serves up "proper" Spanish hot chocolate with churros, own-made horchata (the almond-flavoured drink made from tigers nuts), and assorted tapas.

Galicia ££
⊞ *323 Portobello Road, SW10*
☎ *020 8969 3539*
🚇 *Ladbroke Grove LU, Notting Hill Gate LU*

This atmospheric tapas bar-cum-restaurant, popular with the local Spanish community, specialises in food from Galicia, hence the large number of fish and seafood dishes.

Lisboa Patisserie £
⊞ *57 Golborne Road, W10*
☎ *020 8968 5242*
🚇 *Ladbroke Grove LU, Notting Hill Gate LU*

This delightful Portuguese patisserie, with its excellent cakes (including delectable pasteis de nata custard tarts), is usually full of regulars sampling coffee and pastries.

SOUTH-WEST

The Gallery ££
⊞ *256A Brixton Hill, SW2*
☎ *020 8671 8311*
🚇 *Brixton LU/Rail*

Stockwell's Portuguese community are well served by this friendly, down-to-earth restaurant offering large portions of tasty, authentic food.

Rebatos ££
⊞ *169 South Lambeth Road, SW8*
☎ *020 7735 6388*
🚇 *Stockwell LU*

An atmospheric and popular well-established tapas bar, with above-average tapas served at the front bar and a large restaurant area at the back.

Cookbooks

Portuguese Cookery
Ursula Bourne
A basic introduction to Portuguese cuisine.

The Spanish Kitchen
Nicholas Butcher
A knowledgeable book conveying the regional diversity of Spanish cooking.

The Foods and Wines of Spain
Penelope Casas
A comprehensive and appetising survey of Spanish cuisine.

Casa Moro
Sam & Sam Clark
Guaranteed to make you want to cook, with gutsy flavourful Spanish and Arabic-inspired recipes, ranging from tapas dishes such as clams with white beans and saffron to partridge with oloroso sherry.

Moro: the Cookbook
Sam & Sam Clark
A wonderful resource from the chef-owners of Moro restaurant, filled with simple, flavourful recipes, drawing on Spanish and Arabic cuisine.

The Food of Spain and Portugal
Elizabeth Lambert Ortiz
An authoratitive look at Iberian cooking, with accessible recipes.

The Food of Spain & Portugal
Elizabeth Luard
An attractive, written guide to Iberian cuisine, with accessible recipes.

The Taste of Portugal
Edite Vieira
A wonderfully evocative and appetising cookbook, offering a considerable insight into Portuguese cuisine.

Miscellaneous

Afghan

Afghan Kitchen *£-££*

⌨ *35 Islington Green, N1*

☏ *020 7359 8019*

🚌 *Angel LU*

This tiny, minimalist restaurant offers simple, tasty home-style Afghani food at very reasonable prices and with friendly service.

American

Hummingbird Bakery

⌨ *133 Portobello Road, W11*

☏ *020 7229 6446*

🚌 *Notting Hill Gate LU*

A small American-style bakery selling treats such as eye-catching, brightly frosted cupcakes, pecan pie and lemon meringue pie, pulling in Notting Hill locals and market visitors alike.

Panzer's

⌨ *13-19 Circus Road, NW8*

☏ *020 7722 8596*

🚌 *St John's Wood LU*

🕐 *Mon-Fri 8am-7pm, Sat 8am-6pm, Sun 8am-2pm*

St John's Wood affluent American ex-pat community is shrewdly catered for by this large Jewish delicatessen which makes a point of stocking foodstuffs such as grape jelly, Karo syrup, Mr and Mrs T. Bloody Mary mix, flour tortillas and mini-marshmallows.

Rosslyn Delicatessen

⌨ *56 Rosslyn Hill, NW3*

☎ *020 7794 9210*

🚌 *Hampstead LU*

🕐 *Mon-Sat 8.30an-9.30pm, Sun 8.30am-8pm*

This well-established delicatessen offers North London's American community an entire section devoted to American foodstuffs imported from the USA, including cereals, confectionery, dressings and baking products. Expect classics like Betty Crocker cake mixes, Froot Loops cereal and Aunt Jemima's pancake mix.

Belgian

Belgo Noord *££*

⌨ *72 Chalk Farm Road, NW1*

☎ *020 7267 0718*

🚌 *Chalk Farm LU*

Mussels and frites washed down with flavourful Belgian beers are the house speciality at this popular restaurant, with its minimalist décor and bustling atmosphere.

Brazilian

Armadillo *£££*

⌨ *41 Broadway Market, E8*

☎ *020 7249 3633*

🚌 *London Fields Rail*

Pleasantly funky restaurant where chef Rogerio David cooks up creative Brazilian fare.

Burmese

Mandalay *££-£££*

⌨ *444 Edgware Road, W2*

☎ *020 7258 3696*

🚌 *Edgware Road LU*

This relaxed, friendly restaurant offers a rare chance to sample Burmese cuisine, a fascinating blend of Asian, Chinese and Thai ingredients and cooking techniques. Dwight Ally, who runs the restaurant with his brother, is happy to offer menu advice and guidance.

Colombian

Brixton Market

⊞ *Brixton Station Road, Pope's Road,*
  Atlantic Road, Electric Road and Electric Avenue, SW9

🚌 *Brixton LU/Rail*

🕐 *Mon, Tue & Thur-Sat 8am-5.30pm, Wed 8am-1pm*

These days Brixton Market houses a number of Colombian businesses, ranging from cafés and bars to several food shops, including butchers and fishmongers.

German

Backhaus

⊞ *175 Ashburnham Road, TW10*

🚌 *Richmond LU/Rail, then bus 371*

🕐 *Mon-Fri 8am-6pm, Sat 8am-4pm*

This neatly arranged delicatessen stocks a wide range of products imported from Germany, including frozen ready-meals and a huge choice of hams and sausages, such as bratwurst and leberwurst. Just down the road is the shop's bakery which produces an impressive array of German baked goods, including rye breads, pretzel and caraway sticks and, at Christmas, lovingly prepared stollen, made in September and matured for eight weeks.

German Wurst Delicatessen

⊞ *127 Central Street, EC1*

☎ *020 7250 1322*

✎ *germanwurstdelicatessen@btinternet.com*

🚌 *Old Street LU/Rail*

As the name of this small, neat shop makes clear this is indeed a German sausage specialist, with around 30 different types of sausages made on the premises. These are seriously meaty sausages, ranging from 'proper' frankfurters and bratwurst to slicing sausages and brawn, which is proving very popular with English OAPs. Though sausages are the shop's forte, they also stock rye bread, pretzels and a wide range of German mustards.

Hungarian

The Gay Hussar   £££-££££
⌨ *2 Greek Street, W1*
☎ *020 7437 0973*
🚇 *Leicester Square LU, Tottenham Court Road LU*

A venerable Soho restaurant, noted for its literary and political clientele as well as its generous portions of authentic Hungarian food, such as chilled cherry soup and Transylvanian stuffed cabbage.

Louis Patisserie   £
⌨ *32 Heath Street, NW3*
☎ *020 7435 9908*
🚇 *Hampstead LU*
🕐 *Daily 9.30am-6pm*

Set up by Mr Louis over 30 years ago, this charmingly old-fashioned patisserie sells Hungarian cakes and pastries such as dobos (caramel cake) and makos (poppyseed slice), all of which can be enjoyed with a cup of coffee in the tearoom.

Korean

Centre Point Food Store
⌨ *20-21 St Giles High Street, WC2*
☎ *020 7836 9860*
🚇 *Tottenham Court Road LU*
🕐 *Mon-Sat 10am-10.30pm, Sun 12noon-8pm*

In the shadow of Centre Point's looming tower, the Centre Point Food Store is a large, well-stocked food shop, with around half the shop given over to a neatly displayed, comprehensive selection of Korean foodstuffs.

Hanna
⌨ *41 Store Street, WC1*
☎ *020 7636 4118*
🚇 *Goodge St LU*
🕐 *Mon-Sat 10am-6pm*

Hidden down a peaceful Bloomsbury side-street, this tidy shop stocks a good range of Korean foodstuffs, from rice to pickles.

Song's Supermarket

⊞ *76-78 Burlington Road, New Malden, Surrey, KT3*

☎ *020 8942 8471*

🚌 *New Malden Rail*

🕐 *Daily 9am-8.30pm*

New Malden's substantial Korean community is served by a number of restaurants and shops. Song's is next to Jie's Café, an informal Korean café from which the most appetising, savoury aromas waft out. Neatly arranged, Song's has an impressive range of stock: fresh meat and fish counters, fresh fruit, vegetables and herbs and a huge array of groceries. Particularly tempting is the extensive range of chilled, ready-made dishes such as spinach with garlic and chilli.

Mauritian

Chez Liline   *££-££*

⊞ *101 Stroud Green Road, N4*

☎ *020 7263 6550*

🚌 *Finsbury Park LU/Rail*

Laid-back and unpretentious, this is a place to enjoy large portions of Mauritian seafood, combining both tropical and French flavours.

Mexican

Cool Chile Company

⊞ *P.O. Box 5702, London, W11 2GS*

☎ *0870 902 1145*

✐ *www.coolchile.co.uk*

(Also at Portobello Market, on a stall on Portobello Road, near the junction with Blenheim Crescent on Saturdays 10.30am-5.30pm and at Borough Market on Saturdays 10am-5pm).

An impressive range of Mexican chillies plus certain key ingredients are available from the Cool Chile Company. Dodie is a genuine enthusiast and happy to offer advice and recipes. For a taste of real Mexican street food (rather than the Tex-Mex stuff normally on offer) visit Dodie's stall at Portobello or Borough Markets.

New Zealand

Kiwifruits

⌷ *6-7 Royal Opera Arcade, Pall Mall, SW1*
☎ *020 7930 4587*
🚇 *Piccadilly Circus LU*

In the heart of a smart West End shopping arcade, this shop caters to ex-pat Kiwis with stock including books, music, clothing, jewellery and a large range of foodstuffs from several types of manuka honey and avocado oil to a generous selection of N.Z. confectionery.

Russian

Dacha

⌷ *34 Aylmer Parade, Aylmer Road, N2*
☎ *020 8341 2475*
🚇 *East Finchley LU, Highgate LU*
🕙 *Mon-Sat 10am-7pm, Sun 10am-5pm*

Specialising in Russian and Ukranian cuisine, Alexander Andreyev's neat, shop stocks a large range of East European foodstuffs, from pouring yoghurt and sour cream to own-made pirozhki (cabbage, meat or mushroom) and dried, salted fish "to eat with beer". Wooden shelves are lined with jarred and canned fish, meat, fruits, vegetables and pickles. Pride of place is given to the competitively priced oscetra, beluga and sevruga caviar

Kalinka

⌷ *35 Queensway, W2*
☎ *020 7243 6125*
🚇 *Bayswater LU, Queensway LU*
🕙 *Mon-Sat 11am-8pm, Sun 12noon-6.30pm*

Behind its window proudly decorated with a Moscow scene, this long narrow shop is well-stocked with Russian and Ukranian foodstuffs, catering to the nearby Russian and Ukranian embassies. Stock ranges from basics such as savoury salted fish and sausages to condiments, biscuits, cakes and a colourful display of confectionery.

South African

St Marcus

⌗ *1 Rockingham Close, Priory Lane,*
Roehampton, SW15
☎ *020 8878 1898*
🚎 *Barnes Rail*
🕐 *Daily 9am-6pm*

Lovers of biltong and braai can satisfy their cravings at this 'mini-market', run with zest by South African master butcher Emory St Marcus.

South Africa Shop

⌗ *15 Henrietta Street, WC2*
☎ *020 7836 2292*
🚎 *Covent Garden LU*
🕐 *Mon-Fri 10.30am-6.30pm,*
Sat 11am-6.30pm, Sun 11am-5.30pm

This cheery shop, which also stocks Australian and New Zealand goods, offers a small selection of South African edibles, including the inevitable biltong, plus droewors and confectionery.

Scandinavian

Glas   *££-£££*

⌗ *3 Park Street, SE1*
☎ *020-7357 6060*
🚎 *London Bridge LU/ Rail*

Restaurateur Anna Mossesson's pretty new eaterie offers a chance to sample traditional Swedish dishes, such as Jansson's temptation, pickled herring and classic gravadlax.

Ikea

⌗ *2 Drury Way*
North Circular Road, NW10
☎ *020 8451 5611*
🕐 *Mon-Fri 10am-8pm, Sat 9am-6pm, Sun 11am-5pm*

Situated on the North Circular, this popular Swedish furniture store has a small food outlet selling essentials such as huge circular crispbreads, gravadlax, lingonberries and frozen Swedish meatballs.

Lundum's *£££*

⌨ *119 Old Brompton Road, SW7*
☎ *020 7373 7774*
🚌 *South Kensington LU*

Warmly recommended by Danish friends, this smart restaurant serves excellent Danish food with the Sunday buffet particularly popular.

Skandium

⌨ *86 Marylebone High Street, W1*
☎ *020 7935 2077*
🚌 *Baker Street LU*
🕐 *Mon-Wed, Fri-Sat 10am-6.30pm, Thur 11am-5pm, Sun 11am-5pm*

This stylish, spacious shop offers Nordic design classics such as furniture, glassware and fabrics, plus a select stock of Scandinavian edibles.

A Swedish Affair

⌨ *32 Crawford Street, W1*
☎ *020 7224 9300*
🚌 *Baker Street LU*
🕐 *Mon-Fri 10am-6pm, Sat 10am-5pm*

Patriotically painted in yellow and blue (the colours of the Swedish flag) this pretty shop carries a whole range of Swedish edibles, from crispbreads and pickled herrings to treats such as liquorice sweets. Akvavit (an aromatic spirit) and snuff – is kept behind the counter.

In the winter months look out for the following Christmas fairs which offer a chance to sample a host of Finnish, Norwegian and Swedish seasonal treats:

Swedish Christmas Fair

Swedish Church at 6 Harcourt Street, W1
(www.swedish-church.org.uk)

Finnish Church Christmas Bazaar

Finnish Church at 33 Albion Street, SE16
www.finnishchurch.org.uk

Norwegian Christmas Fair

St Olav's Church, 1 St Olav's Square, Albion Street, SE16

Scandinavian

Kitchenware

CENTRAL

Divertimenti

- 33-34 Marylebone High Street, W1
- 020 7935 0689
- Baker Street LU
- Mon-Wed & Fri 9.30am-6pm, Thur 9.30am-7pm,
  Sat 10am-6pm, Sun 10am-5.30pm

This attractive, airy kitchenware store (complete with a café area) offers a discerning mixture of ceramic tableware, from classic white French porcelain to colourful rustic ware, alongside pots, pans and Magimix and Kitchen Aid gadgets. The downstairs Cookery Theatre hosts a range of cookery classes by well-known food writers and chefs.

Habitat

- 196 Tottenham Court Road, W1
- 020 7631 3880
- Goodge Street LU
- Mon-Wed 10am-6pm; Thur 10am-8pm; Fri & Sat 10am-6.30pm;
  Sun 12noon-6pm

Stacks of saucepans, plates and mugs lend a bazaar-like quality to the kitchen section here. Useful for colourful, reasonably priced tableware, Habitat also stocks basic pots and pans.

Heal's

- 196 Tottenham Court Road, W1
- 020 7636 1666
- Goodge Street LU
- Mon-Wed 10am-6pm, Thur 10am-8pm, Fri 10am-6.30pm,
  Sat 9.30am-6.30pm

The elegant kitchen section is strong on design classics such as Alessi blue bird kettles, Dualit toasters and Waring blenders. It also has a select range of cookware and a well chosen display of elegant and stylish tableware.

John Lewis

⌨ *Oxford Street, W1*
☎ *020 7629 7711*
🚌 *Oxford Circus LU*
🕐 *Mon-Wed & Fri 9.30am-6pm, Thur 10am-8pm, Sat 9am-6pm*

This large, neatly arranged kitchenware department has an excellent range of cookware, including Circulon, Prestige and Le Creuset. It also stocks microwave ware, assorted storage jars, knives and baking paraphenalia, as well as gadgets including strawberry hullers, lemon wedge covers and garni bags. Prices are competitive and staff are helpful.

Leon Jaeggi

⌨ *77 Shaftesbury Avenue, W1*
☎ *020 7580 1974 or 020 7434 4545*
🚌 *Leicester Square LU, Piccadilly Circus LU*
🕐 *Mon-Sat 9am-5.30pm*

Trading since 1919, Jaeggi specialises in professional catering equipment and utensils. Highlights include top-notch cook's knives, from brands such as Global and Gustav, and French stainless steel pots and pans. Stock is extensive and the staff are helpful and knowledgeable. Note that prices do not include VAT.

David Mellor

⌨ *4 Sloane Square, SW1*
☎ *020 7730 4259*
🚌 *Sloane Square LU*
🕐 *Mon-Sat 9.30am-6pm*

An elegant shop with tasteful stock including a good selection of wooden salad bowls and Mellor's trademark own-designed cutlery.

Pages

⌨ *121 Shaftesbury Avenue, W1*
☎ *020-7240 4259*
🚌 *Leicester Square LU, Tottenham Court Road LU*
🕐 *Mon-Fri 9am-6pm, Sat 9am-5pm*

Aimed primarily at the catering trade, this large well-stocked shop offers professional kitchen equipment, from ice cream makers to ice sculpture moulds. Useful items for home cooks include superior knives, white ceramic tableware and a range of blenders and processors.

NORTH

Gill Wing Cookshop
⌗ *190 Upper Street, N1*
☎ *020 7226 5392*
🚌 *Highbury & Islington LU/Rail*
🕐 *Mon-Sat 9.30am-6pm, Sun 10am-6pm*

A friendly, well-stocked kitchen shop with goods ranging from stainless steel saucepans to decorative tableware.
Branch: 45 Park Road, N8 (020 8348 3451)

Richard Dare
⌗ *93 Regent's Park Road, NW1*
☎ *020 7722 9428*
🚌 *Chalk Farm LU*
🕐 *Mon-Fri 9.30am-6pm, Sat 10am-4pm*

This well-established, attractive kitchenware shop offers a tempting mix of stock, including richly-coloured ceramic tableware, elegant wine glasses and top-notch cake tins.

The Scullery
⌗ *123 Muswell Hill Broadway, N10*
☎ *020 8444 5236*
🚌 *Bus 134*
🕐 *Mon-Sat 9.30am-6pm*

A neat, cheery shop with a wide range of tableware including Portmerion china and hand-painted dishes, plus kitchen utensils and cookware.

SOUTH-WEST

La Cuisiniere
⌗ *81-83 Northcote Road, SW11*
☎ *020 7223 4487*
🚌 *Clapham Junction Rail*
🕐 *Mon-Sat 9.30am-6pm*

The thinking behind this Aladdin's cave of a shop is that 'life goes on in the kitchen'. As a result, stock ranges from kitchen and tableware to specialist gadgets, with friendly staff on hand to proffer advice.

The Kitchenware Company

⌷ *36 Hill Street, TW9*
☎ *020 8948 7785*
🚇 *Richmond LU/Rail*
🕐 *Mon-Sat 10am-6pm, Sat 10am-5pm*

This well-stocked shop offers a mail order service. Stock runs the gamut from everyday basics and gadgets to more specialist equipment.

Kooks Unlimited

⌷ *2-4 Eton Street, TW10*
☎ *020 8332 3030*
🚇 *Richmond LU/Rail*
🕐 *Mon-Sat 9.30am-5.30pm*

This friendly shop is crammed to the gills with stock, ranging from reputable cookware to gastro-gizmos. Unusual items include crème brûlée blowtorches and coffee frothers.

WEST

The Conran Shop

⌷ *Michelin House, 81 Fulham Road, SW3*
☎ *020 7589 7401*
🚇 *South Kensington LU*
🕐 *Mon, Wed-Sat 9.30am-6pm; Tue 10am-6pm; Sun 12noon-5pm*

This stylish store has an alluring kitchen and tableware section. Stock ranges from wacky glass tumblers to exclusive Quaglino china, from wooden-handled tin openers to elegant espresso-makers.

Divertimenti

⌷ *227-229 Brompton Road, SW3*
☎ *020 7581 8065*
🚇 *Knightsbridge LU, South Kensington LU*
🕐 *Mon-Tue & Thur-Fri 9.30am-6pm, Wed 9.30am-7pm,*
   Sat 10am-6pm, Sun 12noon-5.30pm

A spacious new branch of the kitchenware shop, offering the hallmark mixture of desirable ceramics, an impressive range of cookware and a café area for relaxation and refreshment. The store has recently installed a demonstration kitchen for cookery classes and wine tastings.

Kitchenware

Kitchen Ideas

- *70 Westbourne Grove, W2*
- *020 7229 3388*
- *Notting Hill Gate LU*
- *Mon-Sat 9.30am-6pm*

A down-to-earth shop with stock aimed at the catering trade.
Branch: 23 New Broadway, W5 (020 8566 5620)

MAIL ORDER

Lakeland Ltd

- *Alexandra Buildings,*
  Windermere, Cumbria LA 23 1BQ
- *05394 88100*
- *www.lakelandlimited.co.uk*

This well-established, efficient Cumbria-based mail order kitchenware
company inspires a loyal following across the U.K. The range of stock
is impressive, from essentials such as baking and icing equipment to
specialized gadgets such as strawberry hullers and cherry and olive
stoners.

GILL WING COOKSHOP

The finest kitchenware including Global Knives,
Salter, Anolon, Chasseur, Le Creuset, Dualit,
De Longhi, Seamens Porsche and much more.
Come in for a browse.

190 Upper Street,
Islington, N1
020 7226 5392
Mon-Sat 9.30am-6pm,
Sun 10am-6pm

45 Park Road,
Crouch End, N8
020 8348 3451
Mon-Sat 9.30am-6.30pm,
Sun 11am-5pm

Bookshops

Books For Cooks

⌨ *4 Blenheim Crescent, W11*

☎ *020 7221 1992*

✎ *www.booksforcooks.com*

🚇 *Ladbroke Grove LU*

🕐 *Tue-Sat 9.30am-6pm*

This Notting Hill bookshop, crammed with cookbooks from floor to ceiling, is a mecca for anyone interested in food and cookery. The stock is extensive, covering cuisines across the world, and usefully includes American publications. Staff are knowledgeable and helpful. Appetising cooking smells waft out from the small back kitchen, where recipes from books stocked in the shop are tested out and which can be sampled in the back-room café area.

Cooking The Books

⌨ *The Glen, St Brides Netherwent,*
Caldicot, NP26 3AT

☎ *01633 400150*

✎ *cooking_the_books@msn.com*

Run with genial enthusiasm and depth of knowledge by Brian and Gill Cashman, Cooking the Books is a mail order business specialising in second-hand and out-of-print cookery books. Their humorously written monthly catalogues offer a huge range of books, from classics to obscure gems, and if you're trying to track down a particular out-of-print title it's well worth approaching them.

Japan Centre

⌨ *212 Piccadilly, W1*

☎ *020 7434 4218*

🚇 *Piccadilly Circus LU*

🕐 *Mon-Fri 10am-7pm, Sat 10.30am-8pm, Sun 11am-7pm*

In addition to its basement food shop, the Japan Centre offers a good selection of Japanese cookbooks.

Mail Order & Websites

Mail order can be an effective way of sourcing specialist ingredients and an increasing number of small producers and specialist importers now offer mail order facilities. The growth of the internet has also seen a rise of gastro e-commerce, with many specialist food producers and suppliers running websites and offering delivery service.

Bacon & Ham

Emmett's Stores

- *Peasenhall, Saxmundham, Suffolk, IP17 2HJ*
- *01728 660250*
- *www.emmettsham.co.uk*

This remarkable village store is noted for its own-made, sweet, traditional Suffolk cured bacon and ham, for which it received a Royal Warrant from the late Queen Mother.

British Foods

Forman & Field

- *30a Marshgate Lane, London, E15 2NH*
- *020 8221 3939*
- *www.formanandfield.com*

Top quality British foods are on offer from this mail order business, (established by Forman's, producers of smoked salmon). The emphasis is on fine foods, so luxuries such as caviar, game and goose are very much to the fore, with seasonal specialities also a feature.

Cakes

Bettys by Post

- *1 Parliament Street, Harrogate, North Yorkshire, HG1 2QU*
- *0845 345 3636*
- *www.bettysbypost.co.uk*

Established in 1919, Bettys Tea Room has been a much-loved Yorkshire institution ever since. Its mail order service offers a chance to try Bettys' own-baked cakes and baked goods, including Yorkshire fat rascals, Simnel cakes, hot cross buns and parkin.

Chillies

Cool Chile Company

- *P.O. Box 5702, London, W11 2GS*
- *0870 902 1145*
- *www.coolchile.co.uk*

A must for chilli connoisseurs, Dodie Miller's mail order company sells an extensive range of dried Central American chillies from mild guajillo to intensely hot habaneros, plus Mexican ingredients such as blue Masa Harina.

Mail Order & Websites

Peppers by Post

⊡ *Sea Spring Farm,*
West Bexington, Dorchester,
Dorset, DT2 9DD

☎ *01308 897892*

✐ *www.peppersbypost.biz*

Chilli-enthusiasts Michael and Joy Michaud run a mail order service selling fresh chillies and tomatillos grown on their own Dorset farm, freshly picked then delivered the following day. On offer are a range of chillies, including Jalapeno, Hungarian Hot Wax and Serrano.

Coffee

Union Coffee Roasters

See page 63

Geese

Seldom Seen Farm

⊡ *Billesdon,*
Leicestershire, LE7 9FA

☎ *0116 259 6742*

Claire and Robert Symington specialise in free-range geese, carefully reared on their own Leicestershire farm, which are then slaughtered humanely, dry-plucked and hung for at least 10 days. Very much a seasonal treat, the geese are available in November and December.

Italian Ingredients

Esperya

✐ *www.esperya.com*

Widely acclaimed for the quality and range of artisanal Italian ingredients it offers, this well-designed website features regional Italian foodstuffs such as prime mozzarella, vintage balsamic vinegar, superb olive oils. Well worth investigating.

Savoria

☎ *0870 2421823*

✍ *www.savoria.com*

This reputable company, noted for the quality of its products, doesn't disappoint with its website, which offers artisinal foods from around Italy.

Meat and Game

Fletchers of Auchtermuchty

🖃 *Reediehill Farm, Auchtermuchty, Fife, Scotland, KY14 7HS*

☎ *01337 828369*

✍ *www.fletcherscotland.co.uk*

Nicola and John Fletcher sell prime Scottish venison from deer raised on their own farm in Fife. Their mail order business offers numerous cuts of venison from medallions and carpaccio to osso buco or boned and rolled haunch of venison. If you're uncertain how to cook venison, Nicola is only too happy to share her considerable expertise in game cookery.

Graig Farm Organics

🖃 *Dolau, Llandrindod Wells, Powys, LD1 5TL*

☎ *01597 851 655*

✍ *www.graigfarm.co.uk*

This pioneering organic meat company is noted for the quality of its organic meat, ranging from beef and pork to game and goat.

Heal Farm

🖃 *Kings Nympton, Devon, EX37 9TB*

☎ *01769 574 341*

Anne Petch's passionate commitment to creating a market for rare breeds has resulted in a flourishing mail order business, offering traditionally reared beef, lamb, pork and poultry.

Mail Order & Website

Higher Hacknell Farm

*Burrington, Umberleigh,
Devon, EX37 9LX*

☎ *01769 560909*

This organic meat, mail-order
business gets all produce from its
home farm in North Devon.
Higher Hacknell offers prime,
organically-reared beef, lamb,
pork and chicken, with a
comprehensive range of cuts
from which to choose and the
facility to have meat cut to
requirement.

Sheepdrove Organic Farm

*Lambourn,
Berkshire, RG17 7UU*

✍ *www.sheepdrove.co.uk*

Excellent organically reared meat,
including lamb, mutton, pork,
beef, chicken and turkey from
Peter and Juliet Kindersley's
lovingly run, mixed organic farm.

Swaddles Green Farm

*Swaddles Green, Hare Lane,
Buckland St Mary, Chard,
Somerset, TA20 3JR*

☎ *0845 456 1768*

✍ *www.swaddles.co.uk*

✍ *orders@swaddle.co.uk*

Own-produced organic meat is
on offer here, with customers
able to specify not only the cuts,
but the weight and thickness
required.

Mediterranean Foods

Belazu

✍ *www.belazu.com*

✍ *info@belazu.com*

George Bennell's and Adam Wells
offer a discriminatingly chosen,
upmarket range of Mediterranean
specialities, including argan oil,
rose harissa, good olives and fine
olive oils.

Organic Produce

Abel & Cole

⌨ *08452 626262*
✎ *www.abel-cole.co.uk*

An impressively efficient organic box company, supplying boxes of fresh organic produce and organic staples around the capital.

Smoked Salmon

H. Forman & Son

⌨ *6 Queen's Yard, Whitepost Lane, E9*
☎ *020 8985 9977*
✎ *www.formans.co.uk*

Established in 1905 this veteran London-based smokery is noted for the quality of its smoked salmon (using a mild 'London cure'), in particular its smoked wild salmon, which has a notable depth of flavour and distinctive drier texture.

Spices

Gramma's Pepper Sauce

See page 81

Seasoned Pioneers

See page 64

Simply Spice

See page 64

Thai

Thai4uk.com

✎ *www.thai4uk.com*

A web-based shop offering an extensive range of Thai ingredients, including sauces, curry pastes and (Tue–Thur) fresh Thai vegetables and herbs.

Mail Order & Websites · Kitchenware

Soho Area Map

Shops

1) Algerian Coffee Store p.61
2) Angelucci p.164
3) Arigato p.189
4) I Camisa & Son p.164
5) Far East p.120
6) Fresh & Wild p.47
7) Golden Gate Hong Supermarket p.120
8) Good Harvest Fish & Meat p.120
9) The Grocer on Warwick p.29
10) Lina Stores p.165
11) Loon Fung Supermarket p.121
12) Maison Bertaux p.139
13) New Loon Moon Supermarket p.121
14) See Woo p.121
15) Wonderful Patisserie p.122

Eateries

a) Abeno Too p.194
b) Bar Italia p.176
c) C & R p.257
d) Café de HK p.124
e) Carluccio's Caffe p.176
f) Ecapital p.124
g) Fung Shing p.125
h) The Gay Hussar p.281
i) Golden Dragon p.125
j) Hakkasan p.125
k) Imperial China p.125
l) Joy King Lau p.124
m) Kulu Kulu p.195
n) New World p.126
o) Poons p.126
p) Satsuma p.195
q) Spiga p.178
r) Ten Ten Tei p.195
s) Yauatcha p.127
t) Yming p.127

Soho

Marylebone Area Map

Shops

1) Biggles p.13
2) De Gustibus p.5
3) Divertimenti p.286
4) Fishworks p.40
5) The Ginger Pig p.13
6) La Fromagerie p.21, 138
7) Le Pain Quotidien p.6
8) Paul p.6
9) Selfridges p.46
10) Skandium p.285
11)) Speck p.166
12) Total Organics p.49
13) Marylebone Farmers' Market p.299

Eateries

a) Fishworks p.40
b) Golden Hind p.69
c) La Galette p.143
d) La Spighetta p.178
e) Le Pain Quotidien p.6
f) Rococo p.25
g) Royal China p.126

Notting Hill Area Map

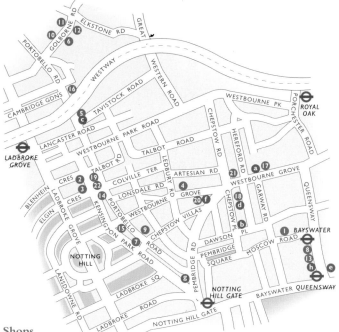

Shops

1) Athenian Grocery p.154
2) Books for Cooks p.292
3) Felicitous p.31
4) Fresh & Wild p.51
5) Garcia R. & Sons p.271
6) Golborne Fisheries p.44
7) Hummingbird Bakery p.278
8) Kalinka p.283
9) Kingsland Edwardian Butchersp.16
10) Le Marrakech p.223
11) Lisboa Delicatessen p.271
12) Lisboa Patisserie p.272
13) Masagana Filipino Groceries p.253
14) Mr Christians p.32
15) Negozio Classica p.172
16) P. de la Fuente p.272

17) Planet Organic p.51
18) Sara Super Market p.224
19) Spice Shop p.64
20) Tavola p.32, 173
21) Tawana p.254
22) The Grocer on Elgin p.31

Eateries

a) Alounak p.229
b) Assaggi p.179
c) Café Garcia p.276
d) Hafez p.229
e) Mandarin Kitchen p.127
f) Mandola p.84
g) Nyonya p.259
h) Royal China p.128

Chiswick/Turnham Green Area Map

Shops

1) Adamou p.154
2) Covent Garden Fishmonger p.43
3) Fishworks p.44
4) Indigo p.31
5) Macken Bros p.17
6) Mortimer & Bennett p.32
7) Theobroma Cacao p.26

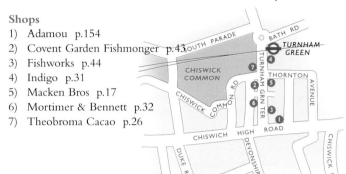

Northcote Road Area Map

Shops

1) A. Dove & Son p.18
2) Fresh & Wild p.52
3) Hamish Johnston p.23
4) Kelly's Organic Foods p.52
5) La Cuisiniere p.288
6) Lighthouse Bakery p.10

7) Mise-en-Place p.34
8) Salumeria Napoli p.174
9) I Sapori p.174
━━━ Northcote Road Market

BIBLIOGRAPHY

The books used for my research include all the cookbooks I've recommended in each section of the book; those listed below are additional sources.

Across Seven Seas *Caroline Adams* (Tharp Books, 1987)
The Best of Thai Cooking *Chalie Amatyakul*
(Travel Publishing Asia, 1988)
The British Museum Cookbook *Michelle Berriedale-Johnson*
(British Museum Publications, 1987)
Just Like It Was *Harry Blacker* (Vallentine, Mitchell & Co., 1974)
Fruits and Vegetables of the Caribbean
M.J. Bourne, G.W. Lennox, S.A. Seddon (Macmillan, 1988)
South-East Asian Food *Rosemary Brissenden* (Penguin, 1970)
The Club *Stephen Brook* (Constable, 1989)
Polish Cookbook *Zofia Czerny*
(Panstowowe Wydawnictwo Ekonomiczne, 1975)
The Oxford Companion to Food *Alan Davidson*
(Oxford University Press)
Galing Galing *Nora and Mariles Daza* (Daza, 1974)
The Fine Art of Japanese Cooking *Hideo Dekura* (Bay Books, n.d.)
Inside Soho *Mark Edmonds* (Robert Nicholson, 1988)
The Streets of East London *William Fishman* (Duckworth, 1979)
Staying Power *Peter Fryer* (Pluto Press, 1984)
Jewish Cookbook *Florence Greenberg* (Hamlyn, 1980).
Jane Grigson's Vegetable Book *Jane Grigson* (Penguin, 1980)
Exotic Fruits & Vegetables *Jane Grigson & Charlotte Knox*
(Jonathan Cape, 1986)
Singapore Food *Wendy Hutton* (Times Books International, 1989)
Filipino Cooking Here and Abroad
Eleanor Laquian and Irene Sobrevinas (National Book Store Inc., 1977)
Old Polish Traditions in the Kitchen and at the Table
Maria Lemnis and Henryk Vitry (Interpress Publishers, n.d.)
East End Story *A.B. Levy* (Vallentine, Mitchell & Co., 1950)
Guide to Ethnic London *Ian McAuley* (Michael Haag, 1987)

The Peopling of London *Nick Merriman* (Museum of London, 1993)

Flavours of Korea *Marc and Kim Millon* (Andre Deutsch, 1991)

A Popular Guide to Chinese Vegetables
Karen Philipps and Martha Dahlen (Frederick Muller, 1983)

Fruits of South-East Asia *Jacqueline M. Piper*
(Oxford University Press, 1989)

Living London *George Sims* (Cassell, 1904–1906)

The Best of Singapore Cooking *Mrs Leong Yee Soo*
(Times Books International, 1988)

Penang Nonya Cooking *Cecilia Tan* (Times Books International 1983)

Sushi Made Easy *Nobuko Tsuda* (John Weatherhill Inc, 1982)

The London Encyclopaedia *Ben Weinreb & Christopher Hibbert*
(Papermac, 1987)

Cooking the Polish-Jewish Way *Eugeniusz Wirkowski*
(Interpress Publishers, 1988)

Jewish London *Linda Zoff* (Piatkus, 1986)

Index

Index

Index of Ingredients

Index

Index of Ingredients

Index

Order our other Metro Titles

The following titles are also available from Metro Publications. Please send your order along with a cheque made payable to Metro Publications to the address below. **Postage and packaging is free**.

Alternatively call our customer order line on **020 8533 7777** (Visa/Mastercard/Switch), Open Mon-Fri 9am-6pm

Metro Publications
PO Box 6336, London N1 6PY
metro@dircon.co.uk
www.metropublications.com

London Architecture
Author: Marianne Butler
£8.99 ISBN1-902910-18-4

London Theatre Guide
Author: Richard Andrews
ISBN 1-902910-08-7 **£7.99**

Museums & Galleries of London
3rd ed Author: Abigail Willis
£8.99 ISBN 1-902910-20-6

Bargain Hunters' London
3rd ed Author: Andrew Kershman
£6.99 ISBN 1-902910-15-X

Veggie & Organic London
Author: Russell Rose
ISBN 1-902910-21-4 £6.99

London Market Guide 3rd ed
Author: Andrew Kershman
£6.99 ISBN 1-902910-14-1

Book Lovers' London 2nd ed
Author: Lesley Reader
ISBN 1-902910-13-3 £8.99

Guide to Cookery Course
3rd ed Author: Eric Treuille
£7.99 ISBN 1-902910-17-6

Gastro-Soho Tours

Aimed at anyone interested in food, Jenny Linford's **Gastro-Soho Tours** are guided tours around Soho's diverse and fascinating food shops. The tours start in Chinatown, exploring the wealth of unusual ingredients and exotic fruit and vegetables found in Chinese supermarkets, pauses for refreshment, then goes on to explore Soho's European food heritage, including classic Italian delis and historic coffee shops. Throughout the tour, food writer Jenny Linford offers ingredient information and recommendations, plus recipe suggestions

For details of **Gastro-Soho Tours** ring *020 8440 0794*

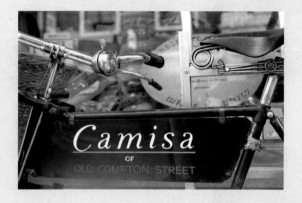